A SONG OF FAREWELL

Charles Frederick Proctor

April 5 1906 - November 26 1996

A catalogue record of this book is available from the British Library

First Edition: July 2006

ISBN: 1-84375-261-1

To order additional copies of this book please visit:
http://www.upso.co.uk/janespurr

Published by: UPSO Ltd
5 Stirling Road, Castleham Business Park,
St Leonards-on-Sea, East Sussex TN38 9NW United Kingdom
Tel: 01424 853349 Fax: 0870 191 3991
Email: info@upso.co.uk   Web: http://www.upso.co.uk

A SONG OF FAREWELL

Charles Frederick Proctor

April 5 1906 - November 26 1996

Jane Spurr

UPSO

For my husband, Howard

Acknowledgements

I am deeply indebted to the following for help in the preparation of this book: Jennifer Bate, Valerie Cardnell, Geoffrey Hanson, Canon Eric James, Geoffrey Morgan, Eric Wayman; also to those who responded to my plea for memories and impressions of Charles Proctor. My most grateful thanks go to my husband, Howard, for not only reading my script, (and its many revisions), and for all his constructive comments, but above all, for supporting me in what has been a labour of love.

CONTENTS

IN THE BEGINNING

"Every man must die but the world is permanently changed by each man's existence." *The Old Pattern and the New*: Colin Murray Parkes

This book requires a certain amount of explanation so the reader can understand its construction and its background. It is neither a biography nor an autobiography. It is something of both. My meeting with Charles Proctor and my part in his life is the purpose of this Introduction.

Life in 1963

It is important to understand what life was like in the 1960s. Things were very different from now in so many areas of life. There were no computers, no mobile phones, the Internet had not been invented, and Concorde had come into being only recently - seemingly telescoping distances and time. Eurostar and Space Shuttles were the stuff of science fiction. As a result, the pace of life was much slower. Values were very different. Respect for other people was also different.

I first met Charles Proctor when I went to Trinity College of Music as a very raw 'up-from-the-country' student in

September 1963. The older students told me that 'Mr. Proctor' was a formidable man but one who was held in high regard. Being a stranger to London, everything to do with my new and unfamiliar surroundings was impressive. Travelling to College (which was then in Mandeville Place in the West End of London) on the 159 bus from Kennington, I stared at the famous landmarks, previously only names to me and only seen in pictures or on TV - the Houses of Parliament, Westminster Abbey, Whitehall, Trafalgar Square. In 1963, young people were not seasoned travellers as they are now. There was no 'gap year' in which we might have had the opportunity to travel to different parts of the country - let alone 'abroad'. Even if these opportunities had existed, I would never have been able to take them as my family had no spare money. Holidays were rare - and much saved for - events. I had rarely left Aldridge, the village in the Midlands where I was born and which was my home until I went to College. When I arrived at Trinity College of Music, I learned that Charles Proctor conducted the College Choir so I went along to the first rehearsal with a feeling of anxiety, which was not misplaced. He seemed to 'put the fear of God' into us, whilst, at the same time, making us give of our best. It was felt by us all that if anyone made a mistake, 'Mr Proctor' knew who it was and we dreaded his gaze falling on us. It made us rather nervous.

Then an extraordinary thing happened. During this very first rehearsal and what was to be my first encounter with Charles Proctor, I found that I was drawn, very powerfully, towards him, and I knew straight away that I wanted to get to know him - and to know him well. (I also knew this was out of the question, as he was a very important person within the College and, compared to me, he existed in the stratosphere, while I remained with my musical feet firmly planted on planet earth! Apart from his teaching and lecturing, he was also an Examiner and a member of the Corporation, the governing body of the

College at that time. I was merely a very green student.) I have never forgotten that feeling, and even now, when I bring it to mind, I can recapture how I felt that afternoon. Needless to say, I could not explain it - and cannot explain it now. All I can say is that, from that very moment and for the remaining thirty-three years of his life, this feeling never changed. As you will read, my unspoken but longed-for wish was granted, and I had the enormous privilege of getting to know him (and his wife, Rosemary) very well indeed. I can say with certainty that I have never met anyone else who has had such a powerful and lasting effect on me, or from whom I have learned so much about music - and life. I consider it to be one of the greatest gifts I have been given. George Bernard Shaw had a close friendship with the boxer Gene Tunney. George Bernard Shaw said that he saw something in him 'that touched his soul'. That same statement could be applied to my friendship with Charles Proctor.

While it is important to understand something of what life was like in the 1960s, so that things can be considered in the perspective of the time, it is equally important to understand something of the generation *before* my own - and what life was like then, for it is from that generation that Charles Proctor came. I am clear that if you read this book 'wearing twenty-first century spectacles', you will find it a difficult, and unrewarding, task. I beg you, therefore, to read it from the perspective of someone born in 1906 and who lived until 1996, whose upbringing, values and way of looking at life were fashioned in what, to us now, is a 'bygone age'. Charles was also a deeply spiritual man, a devout Christian, with an unswerving faith in God; a man of immense self-discipline, who 'felt things very deeply' but who would speak about them only very rarely - if at all - to anyone except his beloved Rosemary. Both of them were extremely private people - their desire for privacy extending to what might be considered extraordinary lengths.

It is not difficult to understand, therefore, that Charles Proctor sometimes found life in the latter part of the twentieth century very much an uphill struggle. The reader is not asked to pass judgment on this - merely to accept it, because 'that was the man', and these factors underlay all he thought, wrote and said.

My part in his life

At this point, I must explain how and why I became involved in Charles Proctor's life and how my 'longed-for wish' came to fulfilment, so that, hopefully, the reader will understand why I have undertaken this work.

I graduated from Trinity College of Music in July 1966 and went to work for Wilfrid Van Wyck - at that time a notable concert agent - whose offices were in Wigmore Street, just around the corner from Trinity. In the four years I worked there, I learned the 'ins and outs' of concert management and artists' representation (an 'eye-opener' to me!). On his extensive Artists' List were luminaries like Victoria de los Angeles, Artur Rubinstein, Tamas Vásáry, Julius Katchen - to name but a few. I mention that only to demonstrate the kind of people with whom the agency was involved - but from my vantage point, on the 'lowest level of existence' in the office, I was able to learn the nuts and bolts of concert management. During those four years, I joined the Alexandra Choir, which Charles Proctor had founded in 1940 and of which he was still the conductor. In 1970, I returned to Trinity College of Music as Secretary to the Registrar. Here I came into almost daily contact with Charles Proctor, as he was still a member of the professorial staff whilst continuing all his other musical activities. Our paths crossed in matters of administration as a result of the work I had to do in the Registrar's office. In 1973, on the resignation of Vic Carter from the post of Secretary of the Alexandra Choir, Charles asked me if I would take on this role. He made the request at the end of a week, asking me to think about it over the weekend and to give him my reply on the following Monday. He also asked me not to discuss the matter with anyone! This meant I could not share my thoughts with anyone and had to make the decision entirely on my own. This request did not surprise me, knowing Charles, even then, as I thought I did. I knew that the Secretaryship of the Choir was a huge job and that it would demand many hours of my 'spare' time. The following Monday, I accepted the position, and that, really, was the start of our long and fruitful friendship. There was an enormous amount of 'admin' involved in the Secretaryship and we established a mutually beneficial way of working which involved my writing him a long letter once a week, with points which needed discussion. We would meet for a meal (at the Boulevard restaurant in Wigmore Street) on a Wednesday evening immediately prior to the rehearsal and go through all the outstanding matters. Since we both worked at Trinity College, there was opportunity for daily contact about minor choir matters - something which made life much easier than it otherwise might have been.

Charles retired from the conductorship of the Alexandra Choir in 1978 and, at the same time, I resigned as Secretary. He had retired from Trinity College of Music in July 1975 and had moved to Winchelsea, where he and his wife lived until their deaths. When he left Trinity, I had offered to continue my secretarial work, should he so wish, and to do anything that I could to help him in his musical endeavours, especially anything he needed in London, thereby sparing him the necessity of having to go there, something he no longer enjoyed. This offer he accepted with alacrity and my relationship with both him and Rosemary was to become much closer from this time. A unique feature of this deepening relationship was the letters we continued to exchange. They were no longer about matters concerning the Choir but became almost a diary of our respective lives. I have kept them all, carefully filed in date order, and I have drawn on them very much in the preparation of this book. (I kept a carbon copy of my letters to him so that I knew to what he was referring when his reply came. His letters were a great joy to me but they were often written 'as he thought' and so his train of thought would not necessarily follow the order of the matters raised in my letter to him!) I was in a full-time job during this time and had many other 'outside activities', so it was relatively difficult for me to write more than once a week. (The letters were very long.) If my letter had not arrived by the anticipated date, I would get a 'phone call checking that all was well and mentioning 'we don't seem to have heard from you this week...' On more than one occasion they told me that they so looked forward to my letters dropping through their letter-box, that, as soon as they arrived, everything would stop while one of them read out the letter to the other! Letter-writing seems to be a 'dying art' in this age of computers, e-mails, text messages etc. - of none of which am I a fan - so in addition to the pleasure I got from *writing* them, it was very gratifying to think that the Proctors derived so much pleasure from *receiving* them.

I continued my secretarial help when needed. Typing Charles' lectures was a frequent activity. He was called upon by many organisations to give talks - usually on musical subjects. He would type the initial version, but spelling and grammar, by his own admission, were not his strong points. (In a letter to me dated May 30 1973, he wrote: "My typing is BAD my SPELLING is TERRIBLE but as you know the family call me L'Immpossible anyway....." The capitals and the misspelling are his.) I would prepare a more acceptable version of his text. My major work was yet to come. Charles became involved with the publisher Oecumuse (a fledging organisation at that time) and its Director, Barry Brunton, but it was necessary for Charles' work to be copied from his original manuscript and a score prepared which would be suitable for publication. I quote from the Oecumuse Newsletter which appeared shortly after his death in 1996:

"Charles never had need of an amanuensis as such, of course, putting his hundreds of scores boldly, if a little untidily, down on paper until the very last. But it was Jane who acted as proof-reader, correspondent, secretary and general 'woman Friday'. When it became plain (in the period before computer-setting was predominant at Oecumuse) that a hand-copyist would need to undertake a herculean task if Charles' huge output was to be got safely into print, Jane herself stepped bravely and unhesitatingly into the breach. Within weeks, she had turned herself into an accomplished performer with pen and manuscript paper. You may witness the fruits of her labours in the hundreds of handcopied pages which make up *Resurgam, Passacaglia on a Given Theme, Seven Chorale Preludes* and *Ten Occasional Pieces*, reissued in digitally remastered form this month. Without Jane's unflagging determination and tenacity these splendid and hugely approachable organ works would almost certainly not have appeared in the Oecumuse catalogue at all. Now, greatly esteemed by players and listeners alike, they will in due course be candidates for full-blown computer-setting."

I include that paragraph as it explains very clearly what was involved in that part of my work with Charles. It meant starting work at 5. am so that I could work in natural light (seasons permitting) and in silence. It was very demanding work (all stems were measured and drawn with a ruler, each bar was measured exactly as required etc.), quite a strain on my eyesight, which has never been 'of the best', and very tiring, especially as I had a full day's work ahead of me after my first three hours of copying. I was very glad to do it for Charles as I realised what a lot it meant to him to be able to get his compositions into print.

In later years, and to my astonishment, he took to sending me his compositions 'for comment'. He made it clear that he did not want me merely to return his manuscript with a note saying 'Wonderful'. He wanted detailed examination and comment. I would fill two or three typed A4 sheets with this, and, in most cases, he would accept my suggested changes, additions, deletions. Let me say straight away that they were comments only on the musical grammar, harmonic accuracy, working out of canons, fugues and similar details - not suggestions of how he should write it differently! It is so easy to include 'grammatical errors' when writing music, just as when writing prose. I found it a rather interesting situation, in that, many years before, when I was preparing to take a diploma in The Theory and Practice of Composition, it was *he* who took his red pen to *my* work - and now, here was I doing the same thing to his! Life had come full circle!

All these activities continued right till the day of his death. He had telephoned me the day before he died to say that he had his latest composition ready to send me and he would take it to the post the next morning. The envelope remained, unposted, on his grand piano, on the morning he died.

Charles Proctor - the man

And so to the reason for this book. Charles Proctor is not a name that is 'on everyone's lips' - nor has it ever been. However, his life, his example, his wisdom, his musicianship, his profound faith, have all contributed in so many ways to the lives of so many people - especially those who were fortunate enough to have learned their art from him. The reason for the book, therefore, is to put on record my personal gratitude to this outstanding man - gratitude which is shared by many with whom he came into contact during a long life. Tributes from others, later in this volume, will bear witness to this. "Every man must die but the world is permanently changed by each man's existence." Many people's 'worlds' have been changed because of the existence of Charles Proctor.

This is not intended to be a work of great scholarship, containing lists of dates, places, concerts, compositions. That is something which can provide material for a thesis by a music student of the future - should anyone wish to undertake it.

This book is both a record of Charles Proctor's life and a tribute to him. I feel that this is something eminently worth recording, and, as long as a copy of it can be found in Trinity College of Music archives, I shall feel my task has been completed. If others wish to read about the life of an extraordinary man, then that is pleasing. For some, it may make fascinating reading as an account of what it is like to be so dedicated to your art that you will spend eight hours a day totally immersed in it - practising. That can be a glib thing to say - but I suggest the reader thinks how many different things he or she has done in the last eight hours and compare that with what it must be like to work single-mindedly at one thing for that period of time - with nothing *tangible* to show for it at the end. In these materialistic times, things being so transient, it is difficult to appreciate the concept of someone devoting their whole life to something which might be considered to be rather esoteric, with no obvious financial reward, or even any recognition. But without people like Charles Proctor, the music which has been written would remain on pieces of manuscript paper, and would never be 'brought to life' in sound so that the world can know it.

As will be seen, when the goal which Charles had set himself - to become a concert pianist - seemingly drew nearer and nearer, he realised he was never going to be able to achieve his dream. By now, he had expended so much effort, both mental and physical, only to discover, for reasons entirely beyond his control, that 'it was not to be'. Most people would find it very hard, if not impossible, to cope with that stark circumstance - and the ensuing circumstances which prevailed when he had to decide "what next?". That is something Charles had to face. (One of his maxims in life, inherited from his father-in-law, was 'Never give up.....do your best things in the worst times....!') He went on to have a career as a professional musician which, with the benefit of hindsight, may well have given infinitely more to the world than if he had pursued his chosen path of becoming a concert pianist. The reader may discover that, as a result of learning of the struggles of one man in his particular sphere of activity, he finds in it something that will inform his own life. If this should be so, it may be that Charles' influence on others continues, even after his death.

Underpinning Charles' whole life was his desire "To do the will of God, unquestioningly, no matter what the cost". In some writings of his which I found in his desk, three sentences stand out:

> "Schweitzer's book on St Paul has only underlined all my own experiences of the faith of being with Christ to do his willl, no matter what the cost - to live in Him and do His work must suffice."

> "I will do what the Lord asks and be content."

> "I wait on the Lord and try to have constant faith."

I believe he did not 'do music' for the glory it brought to him.

He did it because his whole being could not help but 'be in music' in the same way that the rest of us cannot help but breathe in air. Three letters he wrote come to mind:

One dated April 18 1986 read: "I am convinced that to create for its own sake - or *Ad Maiorem Dei Gloriam* (to the greater glory of God) - is the only thing worth living for."

In another letter, written in reply to a letter from me thanking him for what had been a never-to-be-forgotten concert performance of the *Hiawatha* Trilogy: "I am glad you of the 'new generation' can show appreciation of the real worth of music and poetic feeling once it has been presented to you. That is one of my missions in life....I feel, from your letter, my mission has in small part been successful. This is my reward - I ask no other."

Yet another letter: "Often the musician, the composer, has to make his own work to the greater glory of God (AMDG) as it is revealed to him personally and sometimes outside the confines of the church to which he is attached. There is a secret life in these composers which is not revealed to the average man or woman, only to those musicians who can read between the lines. We can comfort ourselves in the thought that 'God moves in a mysterious way' and we don't yet know the half of it."

In an interview on an American radio programme, he said: "I have a strong faith - the only thing that is of any value at all. I have come to the conclusion that the most *tangible* thing in life is the *intangible*, therefore it is that which cannot be seen, which cannot be spoken about, the eternal, and that I find is my consolation and that is in my music, because it is something one doesn't speak about. I would say if you want to know the sort of person I am, it's in the music......"

Charles was a deeply spiritual man. He was steeped in the Anglo-Catholic tradition, so modern practices were anathema to him - clergy not suitably attired for taking a service, a lack of reverence in church, the church becoming a 'coffee shop' the minute the service was over - and, of course, the language of the ASB and greeting fellow worshippers at the Peace. He was a man who seemed quite out of place in the late twentieth century. His way of life, his way of thinking, were from a different age, and he never really felt at home in the era in which he found himself. The modern 'way of the world' was very alien to him - not only in national and international affairs but in the day-to-day things that 'needed to be coped with' - as he was often wont to say. Answering machines, microwaves, plastic cards, computers - all these were things he found hard - if not impossible - to comprehend. (I remember trying to explain to him how to put things on a computer disc. I felt I might as well have been talking to him in Russian - such was his total non-comprehension of the subject.) His faith and the love and devotion of his wife, Rosemary, were the things that 'kept him going' when he was not absorbed in his music.

In a lecture on Church Music, he said "What comfort can I offer the next generation? My only possible suggestion would be to remind them of St. Paul's words:

'Whatsoever things are true, whatsoever things are honest, whatsoever things are just, whatsoever things are pure, whatsoever things are lovely, whatsoever things are of good report, if there be any virtue and if there be any praise, think on these things.'

The rest will be added unto you."

Sorrow is hard to bear, and doubt is slow to clear,
Each sufferer says his say, his scheme of the weal and woe:

A Song of Farewell

But God has a few of us whom he whispers in the ear;
The rest may reason and welcome; 'Tis we musicians know.
(Robert Browning)

Chapter 1

A Note About the Autobiographical Section

The first eight sections of this book are autobiographical. In a diary which Charles wrote between May 1980 and July 1992, there is an entry for February 26 1981 reading: "Have begun my autobiography *Dear Ralphie*. In the form of a long letter to Ralph [Millais]. 4 pages day 1. A good title for the book could well be *My dear Ralphie*." On February 28 1981, he wrote "Have done 12 pages of the above. I intend to do 3/4 pages a day so as not to get too involved." By March 1 of the same year: "The book progresses promisingly. I have decided to revert to the original title I had planned....*There is always something....*" No more mention of this project was made until January 1986. "I think you did offer to type my autobiography....in a weak moment. Does that offer still stand? I have done about 15 pages for Chapter 1 which takes me from DAY 1 to entering the RAM." I replied in the affirmative - but no pages ever arrived!

When clearing his house after his death, I found the material which is reproduced here. It required some editing, but I have kept that to a minimum as I am anxious not to 'interrupt' his style. There is some repetition in the text. Had he shown it to anyone, this would have been picked up and could have been amended. However, there are so few examples that I have left them as they stand, as they do not impair the text at all. Like the Letters which appear later in the book, the grammar, capital letters and some spellings, which may seem odd or wrong, are his, and again I have left them as he wrote them.

The last section - Royal Concerts - stops rather suddenly and appears incomplete, but I found no more material.

My sadness is that he never completed his task but I include what he *did* leave as a very important contribution to the picture of his life.

1 - THE GOOD OLD DAYS

In the process of time, one is inclined to bore people by repeating the phrase that 'things are now not what they were....' and deprecate the present conditions in contrast to what the older members of our population thought were 'the good old days....'

A good deal of this I have come to believe is the result of looking to the past with a more romantic and rosy-coloured hue than is warranted. In short, the contrast of what was good with what was bad in past years was far greater than one can possibly realise in the present days.

Having been born in London at the turn of the century, I have vivid pictures in my mind which, on reflection, can only be recalled as nothing short of nightmarish situations.

My own childhood was clouded with poverty and darkness. The poverty we experienced was not that of the 'lower order of people', as my mother called them, as we were always fairly well-dressed and had enough to eat. But this was the result of the fact that my father had to work overtime to make enough money to keep us 'respectable' and this meant that he had to catch the train into the City at 7.20 am and often did not get home until 8.pm or 9.pm. Half day Saturdays and all day Sundays were 'off' and these parts of the week were used as relaxation. What was that relaxation? In my eyes, it seemed to be either cutting the grass and hedges of the house, or my father playing the clarinet for which I had to play the accompaniments, or playing pianoforte duets with him. These were part of my musical training for which I am ever grateful but they were a great trial to me. I loathed the gardening 'helping' and, as for playing the duets, my father shouted at me and I had to count the time values very carefully not to excite his anger. I had to sight-read music as a matter of course, for my father was a good musician without any real formal training. He knew absolutely nothing about the fundamental aspects of harmony and counterpoint. However, I recall composing a piece (I forget what) which he harmonised, writing in the harmony as he felt it to be - and I was astonished at the fine musical sounds he had discovered for it. One of the revelations in our musical world was when I went in for the North London Music Festival competitions and we heard for the first time Dunhill's *Cloths of Heaven* song, with its beautiful harmony of fifths in the right hand. This enchanted us both and became, in our minds, the modern idiom which was the natural thought after Beethoven. My father encouraged me to compose as it was our estimation of the qualities of a musician that he should be able to do 'anything' in the musical world - not merely be able to play an instrument and music learned for the occasion of a performance.

The First World War years were a great part of my childhood, being eight years old when war broke out in 1914. The atmosphere in London was gloomy in the extreme. Fogs abounded and they were not the misty airs we now know. Air pollution was accepted as the natural outcome of civilisation. When fogs did come in London in November, the atmosphere was so dense that one came home with one's breathing impaired and, on using a handkerchief, the result was a black smear. Although no blackout as such was thought of at the beginning of the war, it was not long before the Zeppelin raids made it essential. One of my earliest recollections was seeing the Zeppelin being shot down in flames near Potters Bar. My mother was concerned with the fate of the men. I was pleased that the enemy had been vanquished in this instance and recall most vividly the scene of the falling burning airship. In fact, although this was vivid, earlier events made an impression as I found that my mother and all ladies, including my aunts, were suddenly going about with red-eyed tearful faces and choosing black dresses. I later conjectured that it was the death of Edward VII, for the following year I recall the Coronation. I had a paper Admiral's hat, with a lot of golden printing on it and the top opened to reveal a golden paper expanding crown. I had no idea what a Coronation was. I had no childish friends as my companions and, being an only child, it was often 'taken for granted' that I knew things - whereas I was often quite ignorant of simple things that were known to my parents. I never really understood the rules and aims of any games. When we were out on one of our 'walks' and saw a football match being played in the fields near our home, my father, who was a footballer of considerable prowess and renown in Lincolnshire, would shout "Pass" with much vehemence to the players. I never understood what that meant and he never explained why, or for what purpose, for when I had to play football at school, I always found the greatest bullies in the team 'kept the ball' for themselves as much as possible. I, who loathed the game, spent most of my time trying to 'keep out of the way' - and once, on returning home, I had the muddy mark on my face of a full impact with the football. I expected this to be greeted by my father as an identification of my prowess in playing the game. The result was a fierce reprimand for being so silly as to be in the way of the ball. This remark only made my loathing of the game more intense, a loathing which has lasted to this day.

The fogs of London were so real that my mother, when at the top of our road, had to enlist a passing stranger to help her to find the road where we lived, although she was within yards of it. Gas light was the order of the day, both for houses and streets. A more dismal form of lighting has never been invented. My parents were very economical, perforce, so that the lighting of the living rooms was the gas mantle of fragile texture that had to be guarded from untoward contact. The rest of the house had the gas 'fishtail' jets which were depressing in the extreme.

On reflection, my whole life in London was one of gloom and misery and loneliness. This was made bearable by the prospects of holidays in Spalding with my grandmother and we went there as a family trio. The rather well-to-do living pleased me and the air of the country and the sea connection with the Wash made for happiness I found nowhere else. I find the recollections of Betjeman, as recorded on TV and in his poems, almost a replay of my own childhood. His delight of Cornwall as my delight in Lincolnshire, his distaste of school and games, and the 'other world' of the imagination that he lived in were all akin to my own experience. One hears from musicians of long experience that 'things are not as they were in my day'. How true. I must say at once that the standard of performance is immeasurably higher today than it has ever been. The youth orchestras of today are better than most professional orchestras of my youth. I have attended concerts of the Royal Philharmonic Society which would horrify most students of today. Bowing of the violins was 'anyhow', the French horn playing was so frequently faulty that it was a 'hit or miss' event if a phrase could be played without a splutter. I know that Borsdorf and Brain were wonderful players, but these two were exceptional and the ordinary rank and file players were anything but first class. Outstanding players like Murchie, Draper and Solomon were exceptionally fine - and almost household names among musicians. But this alone strengthens my point. One could count the best players on the fingers of one's hands.

2 - CHILDHOOD AND SCHOOL

I was born on April 5th 1906 in a flat in London (so I am told) known as Struen Villas, East Finchley, after which my parents moved to the house opposite, 8 Park Lodge Villas - the number was later altered to 15. Park Lodge Villas was a small group of houses built in the estate of Park Lodge, a large place nearby. 'Market Place' was the correct address but mother insisted that Park Lodge Villas was more appropriate. 'Market Place' was always omitted from our address. My parents were Lincolnshire people. My father, born in Spalding, Lincolnshire, lost his father at the age of fourteen. The Proctor grandfather (a rather moody man so I am led to believe), was a great devotee of music and built a music room at the back of their house in the London Road. My grandmother, whom I loved, survived him until about 1917. Hearsay tells me that the Proctors, being very musical, had music meetings at least once a week, if not more often, and a London firm of music publishers sent down music on hire from their library, which supplemented my grandfather's already extensive music library. The whole of one wall of the music room was lined with shelves and, on them, the folios that contained band parts of symphonies, masses, opera and dance music of that time. I recall the stack of music when my grandmother died and the library was dispersed. Some of the folios and band parts survived to the present day. (It may interest you to know that I am, at this moment, wearing my grandfather's paisley dressing gown and, as he was a collector of violins, he kept them in a cupboard, hanging on pegs, as there were no shelves at that time.)

There exist accounts of the Proctor Band which, after my grandfather died, flourished even more under the management of my grandmother. Apparently this Band used to play at functions in South Lincolnshire, such as Flower Festivals and similar occasions. The Band, then known as Mrs Proctor's Band, comprised (according to extant photographs) Mrs Tonge (my great-grandmother) who played the harp, Ridlington - a first-class trumpet player, two further members of that family, one playing the *three*-stringed double bass, my grandmother the piano, my father the clarinet, my uncle Charles Cooke Proctor, the violin - and others, making a total of about eleven players. I understand that Sunday evening was one of the occasions in the week when the Band was joined by some local singers. These performed masses by Mozart, Haydn, Hummel and others. Band parts and vocal scores existed up to my own time. All this was about the 1890 period.

My father left home at an early age and went to work in Scotland as an engineer but kept up his love and prowess as a clarinet player until he was in his eightieth year. He was a very fine player, a good reader and had an excellent tone, but was unversed in the grammar of music beyond quite elementary standards. A fine ear and sense of good phrasing were his greatest attributes, together with accuracy in pitch and rhythm. My mother came from some twelve miles from Spalding where my father had lived as a boy - at Gedney Broadgate. Her mother had died and left a family of some eight children in the care of her eldest daughter. My mother was second in age of the family. Grandfather was a farmer and later went into the building business and was able to survive the hardships of the bad weather which had destroyed so many families in the latter part of the nineteenth century. Mother was a good scholar, as far as it went, and became a teacher in the local school in the Spalding outskirts known as Little London. It was at that period that my parents met and then came to London at the beginning of their married life. They lived in London until my father retired, when they went back to Fleet, the next village to Gedney, and settled down to a retired life, once again in their native Lincolnshire.

My mother, although she lived to the ripe age of ninety-seven, was, throughout her life, delicate, and some time after my own arrival here, she was unable to go about much, so that my christening was somewhat delayed. We all went to Spalding to stay with my grandmother and there, on a Sunday afternoon, the Congregational Minister came and the ceremony of christening took place in the drawing room, the water held in the best tea service 'slop bowl', as it used to be called. Both my parents' families were Lincolnshire people and, to this day, I find myself sometimes uttering Lincolnshire phrases which are unfamiliar to a great number of my non-Lincolnshire friends.

Lincolnshire has been described as the flattest and wettest place on earth. This may have been so until the fens were drained and the marshes cultivated into the most fertile growing land in England. But even in my own childhood times, my grandmother's house in Spalding was often flooded by the Welland river running across the road, so that duckboards were a feature of the underground kitchen and 'gig' house, where various machines of transport were housed, including a penny-farthing bicycle and a large hooded bath chair or invalid carriage. Those familiar with the map of England know of the part of the sea called the Wash. This is, in fact, the basin into which flowed the rivers Welland, Nene and Ouse. But this I could never understand - for me the Wash was that hinterland between Spalding and Peterborough. This hinterland was flooded every winter for miles so that there was, in fact, an inland sea, where wild fowl were in abundance. In icy weather this was iced over and the great Lincolnshire Fen Skating races were held. Hundreds of people came for the great event, which lasted some days and even weeks. The draining of these fens in recent years has completely altered the aspect of this part of the country. (It is no small wonder that, in discovering Romney Marsh, I found vistas and aspects so reminiscent of my native fens and marshes that I at once felt I had returned home.)

Dorset and Thomas Hardy are well-known to most who value the stories of country life of bygone days. I assure you that Lincolnshire fens were even more primitive and isolated than Hardy's description of Dorset. The skimmity ride, as described in one of Hardy's novels, has a parallel in my own time. My mother, by chance, heard the word 'Maukin' when I described a folk song I had come across when giving recitals with a singer who specialised in Norfolk folk songs. My mother uttered a sound I can only describe as a cry of suppressed horror, for she explained to me that, in her childhood, when a villager had been thought guilty of maltreating his wife, some villagers had made a doll, stuck pins in it and left it by his house door. She hadn't heard that word for seventy years. The isolated village people always ran indoors if a stranger happened to pass and children were herded into the safety of the house if any unknown occurrence happened to disturb the known ways of the village.

As I have mentioned, my parents returned to Lincolnshire (after my father retired from London) to a village called Fleet, but five miles from the village where my mother was born. My grandparents owned a farm in Fleet run by distant cousins who were real village people. In our own time, one such was the village carpenter who kept no account of the work he did about the villages but in his shed he had bits of wood, cut-offs of the job he had performed. This recalled for him the job he had done and he claimed payment from the farmer who had employed him. He was the local undertaker as well and in his living room was an empty coffin he had made ready to receive him when his time came. He was known as CHARLIE Proctor.

Thomas Hardy describes the Church and the Church band who played at services in the village church. This again was enacted at Fleet and I have the clarinet used in Fleet Church and the part-books written by some of the Proctor family. I may have inherited some of the Proctor musical gifts but assuredly no gift of beautiful handwriting has come my way.

The farm remains in the family still at Fleet and, when it was handed over to that branch of the family and we came to live here, we called this house Bay Tree House, as the farm is known as Bay Tree Farm.

As a small boy, I used to cycle along the lonely roads, often singing and waving my arms as I conducted large choirs and orchestras in my mind. The children ran into the houses calling out that a mad man was riding my - only soothed by women who said "Oh, it's only Miss Bateman's young nephew. He is quite harmless."

But I return to my narrative. The centre of my childhood life was round the personality of my grandmother Proctor and later my grandfather Bateman, in a village some twelve miles distant from Spalding, where my mother was born.

My own life in London as a child was spent in somewhat gloomy conditions, owing to the rather meagre earnings of my father at Cassells and later Spottiswoode printing works. When he left there later on, to go to the Evening Standard and Daily Sketch offices, we enjoyed a fair degree of comfort. The early years seemed either very dark and gloomy or bright with wonderful sunshine. The holidays when we went to Spalding were a great joy, especially at Christmas time. My grandmother had, by that time, adopted a niece, Gertie Tonge, who acted as housekeeper and they had a resident maid.

My grandmother was an excellent pianist and was a wonderful reader who could play almost anything at sight. Gertie was made to learn the harp, which she loathed - and she was not really musical. My grandmother played the piano every day for her own pleasure and was a little proud of her own accomplishments in that line. Her whole life was immersed in music and she attended, in the earlier days, many Festivals held in Sheffield and Leeds and Peterborough. She always had a vocal score of the oratorios and pencilled in the names of the soloists and comments on the items that she enjoyed. 'Beautiful'..... 'Very beautiful' was written in a clear hand. In the early days, she took my father to Peterborough and heard the choirboys singing there, all of which was a great delight to my father who enquired if the little choirboys were in fact 'angels'. Hearing Schubert's *Unfinished Symphony* in the Cathedral, he heard for the first time the sound of the clarinet and, shortly after this, took lessons on the clarinet from a near neighbour in Spalding.

Many years later, I conducted a Festival in Peterborough Cathedral with massed choirs from that district, my own Alexandra Choir from London and the orchestra gathered together from the Peterborough area - my father among them. Dr Hopkins, organist of the Cathedral, and I each composed a piece for the occasion. Mine was the setting of the *Veni Creator*. At the close of this piece, I had contrived that the last phrase should be played by the clarinet alone. My father played this. It was rather moving to know he had heard the sound of the clarinet in that place for the first time some sixty years earlier and played his son's own composition, solo, in the same Cathedral.

The tradition of music in the Proctor family was strong, only weakened by the fact that my father's elder brother went to South Africa, keeping up the family tradition in that country and, in his own family, still keeping up with music - his grandson being a professional musician in Venice.

My mother's family, although farmers, were, I believe, from Yorkshire in the earlier days. All the Bateman family (including cousins who lived in Wisbech and Sutton Bridge) were extremely clever. All could have made a real mark in any profession they had taken up, but, alas, in those days it was not possible. They were for business and farming. They were all bound by the conventions of the time and the whole lot of them were class conscious and proud to a high degree. "What *they* would think" was the standard that guarded all their thinking. They, like my father's family, were staunch nonconformists. But this by no means meant they would not conform to the right and proper behaviour as they imagined it to be. They therefore became Church of England, were confirmed and eventually buried in the churchyard, to prove their allegiance to the conventional and established Church of the Realm.

My father's family were also nonconformists and that meant they were *not* conformists. My grandmother had friends among the Church, Roman Catholics, Salvation Army and, in fact, anyone who she thought to be interested in anything at all in which she had some interest herself. There was therefore a somewhat divided atmosphere in which I was brought up. Father's nonconformity as against the more rigid outlook of a distinctly Low Church of England of my mother. In a word, mother was a 'square' and father a more open-minded, liberal person. As a child, I recall that I would go to the Congregational church on a Sunday morning while mother cooked the dinner. Sometimes we would all go together, but mother hated the chitchat after the service and disliked the 'familiar' approach of the congregation towards her. The hand shaking and gossiping after service irritated her considerably.

When I was old enough, it was my father's ambition that I become a choirboy. This I did at St James', Muswell Hill while G D Cunningham was the organist and rather explosive choirmaster. I did not make much headway. I was young and shy and my happiness was quite satisfied to 'lead in' the choir with another boy while the top boys came last. My devotion to Cunningham was complete as far as music was concerned. He was a musician of the first degree - but his behaviour surprised and even shocked me.

Cunningham was, at this time, the resident organist at the local Alexandra Palace, with its vast concert hall and gigantic organ - one of the finest and largest in Europe. I recall going there with my father on a Sunday afternoon to hear Cunningham play. At this time, I had learned to play my very first piano solo, called *Raindrops*. I whispered to my father that I thought *Raindrops* would sound very fine on that organ. I couldn't understand why he laughed to himself.

My early schools were in Finchley and the first one I recall with any clarity was run by two sisters, known as Miss Good. The nice one was, I believe, the Head; the nasty one, the second. Her name was Kate - an angular woman who played the piano at Assembly. Music has always been something of a Sacrament as far as I personally am concerned. As a small child, I recall vividly my distaste of Kate who was offered a hymn book by a senior pupil from which to play the Assembly hymn. The fact that Kate could and did play from memory, which filled me with pleasure, was dispelled by the fact that she rudely declined the use of the book. Music has always been something I have held in awesome respect - something that one had to serve - and anything that put music in disrespect was painful to me. This rather unusual aspect I have always had and I took it for granted that music was a sacred thing, not to be trifled with or disregarded - a thing of religion and, as I have said, a Sacrament. This is no pose, nor is it something acquired. It has always been there and anything or anyone who had not this inborn respect for music was looked upon by me as being a savage - or worse. I knew nothing of Shakespeare and his views about 'the man who hath no music', but this was my own view and I was gratified that, in Shakespeare, I found someone of like views.

(Music as a background to conversation is to this day a great trial. Quite recently, someone asked to hear a record played and two people in the room engaged in conversation the whole time. My distaste of these two people dates from that moment and however they may try to ingratiate themselves into my good offices, they will never know that they are barred forever from my serious regard.)

It was at this Miss Good's School that I learned the twenty-third Psalm. Although I had no knowledge of the religious significance of the words, as I had to learn the words by heart, I devised a plan of imagining the scene and thus recalled the words in my memory. Sheep I knew about, and a shepherd, from my holidays in Lincolnshire. 'Lie down', 'green pastures' and like images became quite clear and helped fix the sequence of the words in my mind.

I did not enjoy school. In time, I had to go to a more grown-up school known as the East Finchley Grammar School. This was in the High Road and was a private school run by a very dark-haired Headmaster called Elliot Button. This is a name to be met in Chant books but I have no knowledge that he had any connection with music and, as I did not much care for him, I would think it rather unlikely. The War came and he left and was followed by a man called Dickinson. He was a very thin man with a violent temper and unpredictable behaviour. I recall some of his behaviour in caning boys on their hands for what I often thought small and innocuous behaviour. His passionate temperament intrigued me. He made us all go to All Saints' Church for an Ash Wednesday service. Here I heard the hymn 'Forty days and forty nights', which thrilled me. A great minor tune of great dignity, played on the organ by the second master whom I admired as being a musician. This really 'opened my ears' in a real way. I had accepted so much already but here was an experience that seemed to enter my musical soul. The sadistic Headmaster became a clergyman later and followed the High Church practices, which no doubt befitted his sense of the theatrical and cruel sense of justice. He was followed by another beastly man called Mr Burke, who was too old to go to the War as Dickinson had done.

At home my musical development was being fashioned by my father. Next door but one was a family known as the Pennys. Miss Penny played the piano quite well and was invoked to teach me music. My father, being at work all day and on Saturdays up to lunch time, was not able to supervise me much. I had agreeable lessons with Miss Penny and I recall that the money for my lessons was left on the piano each week for her to collect at the time of my lesson which, of course, was given in our own house. One day my father made me play for him what I had learned. He then asked me questions about the note values and other items of simple music grammar. I was unable to satisfy him with my answers and was reduced to tears. It was made clear to me that I was not in disgrace for not knowing what I had not been taught. By next lesson, there was a note on the piano for Miss Penny to the effect that her services would no longer be required as 'I do not want my son just to be able to play pieces, but to become a musician.' It was Miss Penny's turn to weep, which she did. We were not on speaking terms with our neighbours. As a result of this, my father found an establishment known as the Muswell Hill Conservatoire of Music. This was a private school run by Madam Edith Hands, a singer of some local renown - a formidable lady whose photograph adorned the largest room in the Conservatoire; long dress, great hat, many furs - a typical flamboyant Edwardian lady who, in those days, sang at concerts and festivals so dressed. The Conservatoire was part of a building known as the Atheneum. It had a concert hall (later turned into a cinema), several rooms that were suitable as studios, and shops beneath. This Atheneum lasted until the Second World War and the Hall was used for the congregation when St James' Church opposite was burned out during an air raid. The Conservatoire was later taken over by a music company who used it for tuition.

In my time, they had a rather remarkable man, Egerton Lowe, as Director of Studies. He was a man of much erudition and wrote many books on musical education. He was an Examiner for Trinity College of Music, London and went on many overseas tours for that College. He brought in to the Conservatoire a wonderful teacher named Helen Ellison. She was an Australian whose father was a doctor. They all came over after his death, Helen earning money to help educate her brother who became a medical practitioner. Helen was a born teacher and she taught me from the beginning in the Curwen Method, whereby one's whole musical education was complete and cultivated as far as it is possible for a child. I went on to the Royal Academy of Music at a later date, but it shows how good Miss Ellison was as a teacher and how thorough her work that, after one attendance at the Academy Rudiments Class, I was told I need not attend any further but go on to 'Harmony' - which I did.

At the end of the first year at the Academy, all students had to pass the Rudiments Examination. I passed, but several of my friends failed, among them one or two who did very well for themselves in the profession later. The point I wish to make is that by the time I entered the Academy, I could read at sight very well, take music from dictation, answer all Rudiments questions and transpose and read in Tenor and Alto clefs. This was all due to Miss Ellison who had been trained at Trinity College.

While still at the Conservatoire and the Grammar School, my father constantly kept watch on my musical progress so that he could have a really musical boy - not just a player of a musical instrument. I had to play all the clarinet solo accompaniments that were within my musical grasp - and many that were too difficult - but, by that means, my sight reading and general musicianship were assured. Moreover, my father could play the piano well - well enough to make me play piano duets with him every day, in addition to his clarinet accompaniments. By the time I went to the Academy, I had played as piano duets most of the symphonies of Beethoven, Mozart and Haydn, overtures and similar orchestral works. It was all taken for granted - so I was appalled by the ignorance in these matters of my fellow students at the Academy when I arrived there. I had to enter all the Associated Board examinations for Piano and Trinity College of Music examinations for Theory. Trinity College of Music Theory examinations were founded on text books that I followed throughout so that my theory and practical knowledge were kept hand in hand. As a choirboy with Cunningham, I had been used to hearing him extemporise on the organ and, again, took it as normal that I should do likewise. My own extemporising was fluent but rather like 'playing a choir in' than any formal set style - which I learned much later was the *desideratum* in such matters. Again, I could do what few Academy students could do. Stringing together yards and yards of harmonic material and expression on the piano was so normal to me that it was only secondary to speech. All this was so natural that I could not understand it was in any way difficult or impossible for anyone who called himself a musician. It had drawbacks, as I was to learn later, as I found it difficult to learn from the printed page with any degree of accuracy and concentration, preferring to 'do my own thing in my own way'. My teachers and my father insisted that the printed page was to be adhered to - and this was all right so long as one had the facility I possessed to call upon if required.

Formal composition on paper was encouraged and I was often trying to compose pieces and songs to words that interested me. I recall several such pieces - Preludes and Tone Poems. Chamber music was not neglected. My father had several friends whom he cultivated if they were really musical. The Sellars family at Muswell Hill were such people. The husband, Frank, was a violinist of great enthusiasm. He was really a very bad player indeed but his enthusiasm, knowledge and real musical interest were immense. His wife, Kate played the viola. They, together with more friends, collected enough to have regular meetings playing quartets and this included my father who played the Mozart and Brahms Clarinet Quintets frequently, so I knew these works by ear, as it were from my own beginning. Later these dear people, Frank and Kate, whom I greatly loved, included me in their circle to play the Schumann and Dvořák Quintets and like pieces. I did not always play the notes as written but 'got by' (as they say) because I had been taught to 'keep up' with the others and my own musicianship provided me with the means of making my own version of some of the more difficult passages. My father also arranged for clarinet some violin parts of Mendelssohn pieces - for instance the slow movement of the Violin Concerto - and, again, I had to play the orchestral part. Likewise Mendelssohn Trios were arranged so that we needed only the services of a 'cello player and we could play the Trios....or such parts as were within my grasp. My father belonged to several orchestral societies in the North London area. I could go with him to these rehearsals. On looking back, the Sellars proved a rather interesting link with events and tastes that developed within me in later life. Their house in Muswell Hill was more than a mere place for us to meet and play chamber music, for Frank was a keen astronomer and had some telescopes in the top attic. Kate was an artist, chiefly in pastels. Their music room, which was two large rooms thrown into one, had many large and interesting oils and pastels on the wall, done (I believe) by her father, Runciman. So they were known as Mr and Mrs Runciman Sellars, which impressed my mother considerably. Her brother was John Runciman, the critic and advocate of Wagner, and later her uncle became Lord Runciman. This again made capital for my mother. Kate and Frank knew no snobbery. This endeared them to me. Anyone who was musical became their friends. Edric Cundell was an intimate in this circle. His original name was Griefenhagen but this was changed to Cundell during the First World War as anything sounding foreign was suspect. Edric was a composer, had studied at Trinity College of Music and later became head of the Guildhall School of Music in London after Sir Landon Ronald. He was an excellent musician and encouraged me in composition, always asking if I had "done anything lately". I was rather intrigued that a little piece of Grieg was looked upon by a musician I respect as being 'genius'. I therefore set out to write a masterpiece in like manner. It was in G minor, very simple, 3/4 in the right hand, like a slow dignified waltz. The left hand I wrote in 2/4, which gave it a rather unusual flavour. I thought nothing of it. At his request, I played for Cundell my latest Chromatic Prelude of which I was very proud, as I had just found the vocabulary for chromatic thinking. He was impressed, but not as much as I had hoped. I then went on to play my little 3/4 2/4 Waltz trifle. He was thrilled and asked for a repeat. From that moment, my opinion of Cundell sank to its lowest ebb. The little Waltz had cost me so little and my Chromatic Prelude so much - and he couldn't tell the difference! It was years later that I learned that the 'effort' is not necessarily the hallmark of genius.

My parents had a way of rather 'playing down' my accomplishments, though I now believe they were somewhat proud of my childish efforts. I do recall that my mother said "I do not want Charles to astonish people at the age of fifteen but at fifty". I don't know if her wishes were fulfilled but they nevertheless were a pointer to her own way of thinking which is, of course, absolutely right.

Kate did a pastel portrait of me in Eton collar. I don't know what happened to it but it was a rather soulless face with no character at all to be seen. She also started one of my mother in a blue velvet dress but this was not finished as mother had a 'few words' with Kate about a sitting she went to not wearing the blue dress. Kate was displeased, mother likewise, so the portrait was never finished.

The chief event about this time was that I left my local Grammar School and went to a school in Muswell Hill - a good school known as Tollington, run by a father and later his son, called Brown. A girls' school was half a mile away and the boys' school was in Tetherdown, Muswell Hill. Here I learned the basic necessities of school learning but did not care for it much. Then I was sent to Highgate School, going straight into the Upper School on arrival. I stayed at Highgate until I left to go to the Royal Academy of Music.

At Highgate, my cousin Owen Strong and his elder brother, Edward, were pupils. Owen was clever and in a higher class, although we were the same age. Eddie was killed in the War. The Public School was regarded by my mother as the *desideratum* for anyone aspiring to any degree of respectability. My aunt, Owen's mother, was a musically minded woman who played the viola excruciatingly, the piano quite well, and was a member of the Alexandra Palace Choral Society and, later, the Bach Choir, which she pronounced with a vehement "ch" followed by an imperceptible pause, before she went on to the mundane word "Choir".

My aunt had been consulted and had spoken to the music master who was the noted F Cunningham Woods. Woods was an MA Mus Bac Oxon, therefore the height of respectability, an FRCO who had been assistant to Stainer at St Paul's and also organist to the Duke of Marlborough at Blenheim Palace. He was a real character, cultured, and a real gentleman, of course. Mother and I had met him *en passant* as he had adjudicated at a Festival in North London which I had entered and we were both struck by his sense of humour, culture and erudition.

It was the practice at Highgate that, on the first day, after morning service in Chapel, all new boys would go before Woods for an audition to see if they could be persuaded to become members of the School Chapel. Woods at once saw that I was very musical and discovered for himself (and to my surprise) that I had a promising voice. I was quite unaware of this, but had great ambitions to join the choir. The first choir practice I attended promised well. I was admitted and, very shortly, was to sing solos in Chapel and at the Annual School Concert. I was asked to join the school orchestra and played the piano with them, to fill in the missing parts in the orchestral score, Woods continually calling upon me to "play the interior harmonies". This I could do with my inborn sense of musicianship, rather than 'just playing the printed notes'.

One event at a School Concert was somewhat dramatic. There was a stage upon which were ranked the choir and orchestra but at the back of the stage was the most primitive illumination one can imagine. I had only seen the like in markets. It consisted of between fifty and sixty fishtail burners in one long row, burning gas. There were no mantles or shades, but naked flames. These had been lit at the beginning of the evening and, when the summer evening grew dark, were controlled by a tap at the side of the hall - the tap being regulated by a spanner. The school porter was ordered, at the appropriate moment, to turn on the fishtail burners to give added light. Alas, he turned the tap the wrong way, when it was too late, and half the fishtails were without gas. He elected to reprieve his mistake by turning up the tap in the opposite direction. The resulting gas smell and flickering burners caused near panic as well as amusement and the Headmaster directed him to turn off the burners completely. The result was that the concert had to be brought to a rather inconclusive finish. I was allowed to play my solo, which was Palmgren's *Evening Whispers*, but after that, the programme was brought to an ignoble close. One irate mother was very displeased as I believe my solo was brought forward and took the place of another boy's contribution. I heard Woods mutter to another member of staff "What I suffered at the tongue of *that* woman....".

Academic subjects had no attention from me. I was inattentive and listless as all I wanted to do was take part in such musical activities in school as I was permitted to do. Woods allowed me to play at the Chapel Day Service on occasions and I was complimented by the Headmaster as he passed by - an unheard-of compliment as it was well known he had little time for music.

Woods was my teacher and I was brought up on a strict basis though I have to admit that the musical standard in school was really very low indeed by modern standards. However there were for me some very revealing moments that I have treasured to this day.

Woods told us once that, as he had been educated in Frankfurt, he had to play for Assembly. He was chosen to do this because he had the one required attribute - "I could improvise *between the lines of the Chorale*". This stuck in my mind, but it was a long time before I could link this with the Chorale settings of Bach and Buxtehude and could see the significance of Wagner's setting of the Chorale at the opening scene of *Die Meistersinger*. I long to hear a performance of the Bach Passions done in this way, with the organist improvising between each line of the Chorales - although, for modern ears, it might prolong the performance beyond the prescribed conditions required by the Musicians' Union.

I left school as soon as it could be conveniently managed as my own ambition was to go to an Academy or College of Music. Woods was of the opinion that the Royal College of Music should be my next venture - to pursue the organist's path that would lead me to holding some dignified position, with the organist's post as the pivot or centre for my further musical prowess.

Then a most unexpected thing happened. I was taken to a pianoforte recital at the Aeolian Hall of English (old) and Russian music given by Mark Hambourg. This was a revelation to me - and a most disturbing one. I had never dreamed that a piano could be played to sound in such a way. I also, at the other extreme, was taken to hear Pachmann at the Royal Albert Hall. I was so shattered by this and the previous experience that I was completely 'put off my balance'. Chopin and piano playing was all I could think of - even a visit to Queen's Hall, to a Promenade concert which I heard from the top gallery, was insignificant for me, except for the piano concerto.

During a holiday, I discovered a girl cousin of mine in Wisbech who was a pupil at the Royal Academy. She entertained us by playing a whole programme from memory. She was a pupil of Claude Pollard who was a professor at the Academy - a highly sought-after professor of high renown. It was thought that I might gain a Scholarship at the Academy and I had prepared the first movement of the Rheinberger Organ Sonata in D minor with that end in view. GD Cunningham was, by then, a professor at the Academy and his opinion was sought by my father, much to Woods' annoyance. Cunningham was of the opinion that Rheinberger would be a very unwise choice and suggested the Bach *St Anne Fugue* as a substitute. Then he played for me and I was enchanted and bent my ways to his suggestion.

I did not obtain the Scholarship I coveted. It went to someone else. So the path was clear for me to enter the Academy as a student with piano as first study and an introduction to Pollard was arranged. All was set for a pianistic career, as befitted my ambitions.

I clearly recall my Entrance Examination. The Principal was Sir Alexander Mackenzie, the Curator, Frederick Corder. Mackenzie was a terrifying old man even then. He heard me play after which he muttered words to the effect that "the piece wasn't difficult anyway". My father attended this interview and sat in the corner watching carefully what was said and done as we had had no connection with such august people or institutions before. I had taken in with me, at my father's behest, my compositions - songs and piano pieces. Mackenzie looked through them in a desultory way and even showed them to Corder, more as a gesture than anything. He asked me to play. I played the first bar, which began on a whimsical chord high on the keyboard, representing I am not sure what, at which Mackenzie flew into a rage and thumped the piano, where there was room, playing my whimsical chord over and over again - *fortissimo* - to my horror. I had never in all my life seen such a demented human being nor one who treated the piano with so little respect. He screamed at me in a high-pitched voice "Call that *music?*", which reduced me to terror, not unmixed with real hate at that fiend of a man. Corder made no movement whatsoever. My father, however, showed a side I had not dreamed of. In the utmost quiet and respectful way, he said "No, Sir Alexander. He does not. He hopes to come to the Academy to learn." At this, Sir Alexander turned to my father and said, in the most friendly fashion imaginable "Yes, Mr. Proctor. Your son is a very talented little boy and he will be admitted to the Academy." I learned my first lesson on how to treat a bully and how unpredictable the future of a musician's life could be.

And thus was taken the first step on the career on which I had set my heart - to become a Concert Pianist.

3 - ROYAL ACADEMY OF MUSIC UNTIL SAUER

Before relating something of the life and times of the Academy during my student days, I must relate some of the incidents and personalities of my time.

Frederick Corder became my Harmony professor, following an introduction to him by Pollard, with whom I studied Piano. Corder was unknown to me by name or reputation before I met him. I was told he was the greatest professor of Harmony and Composition in the Academy - as Stanford was (similarly) the greatest at the Royal College of Music. At my Entrance Examination, he crouched over a table, a dark satanic-looking man, swarthy complexion, brown bald head, (not shiny and pink like Mackenzie), a doleful drooping moustache, large ears, black eyebrows, black eyes - and rounded - rounded throughout. I mean he was not angular, tall or thin - as a satanic being is usually depicted - but round and crouching. When I met him in his room for my first lesson, his glowing black eyes were not unfriendly and I found him quite kind and often silent. I always had to make the first move. He sat like a large bald black cat. His answers were monosyllabic. He seldom spoke unless spoken to, so his silence was heavy and full of gloom. His methods of teaching, however, were a revelation and I was a devoted pupil, but maybe not an exceedingly clever one.

I had been given the elements of Harmony from Woods at school and had, as a text book, Bridge and Sawyer. This was dull and, although I worked the exercises, I could not understand their significance - if any. My method was to do what I was told and then go over the exercises with a small tooth comb, searching for consecutive fifths and octaves, doubled major thirds, false relation and tritones. For what purpose I had no idea. All the work was done at the desk and Woods felt that it was bad form to play on the keyboard. Not so Corder. I was told to get the text books of Stewart Macpherson and these proved to be something of a revelation. A further revelation was to be asked to listen to my efforts being played by Corder. He made grimaces when things sounded unmusical and looked in my direction to see if I agreed with his opinion of the offending passages. I recall that I was not convinced on one occasion and told him that, when I played my exercises, they sounded quite nice, especially if I played them quickly. This drew from him a laugh - and I had learned my lesson.

He always brought forth his critical faculties when talking about the great composers. He showed me their 'faults' - how Beethoven had not written a passage as *he* would have done it because Beethoven had not as many notes on his piano. Later, he showed that obviously Beethoven had got 'stuck' at a point in a composition so 'took off' in another direction. All this made music a living thing and even the great masters were shown to be human as well as divine. Corder's books on composition and like subjects are out of print now - and considered 'old-fashioned' - more's the pity.

Anything in my exercise that was 'awkward' from a musical point of view was shown to me by his hands becoming knotted up and his arms and shoulders almost out of joint. My own essays at composition were treated with equal disrespect and when I wrote a *Lullaby* out of the range of a soprano voice, he didn't blame the possible singer for having limited ability so much as blame *me* for composing a *Lullaby* through which no baby could possibly be expected to go to sleep and would probably scream in horror if it heard the song.

I went through Harmony and Counterpoint in all the species possible. A great friend of mine played a composition in my presence when some three or four students were together. I remonstrated that there were some consecutive fifths to which he replied "Oh, you are a disciple of Corder" and expected me to be vanquished.

One of the most interesting aspects of my time with Corder was that the lessons had no beginning and no end. Often I had to 'take myself off' when I could stand no more. Sometimes he would be giving a lesson to a gifted student and I came in and sat at the back of the room out of his view. I would wait perhaps more than half an hour for him to finish or for the student to leave.

Corder and his brother had translated Wagner's operas from the German and he told me that the *Parsifal* piano score arrived scene by scene from the publisher. When he got the music of the beginning of Act III, he was horrified at what Wagner had done and thought he had gone quite mad. But he went on to say "what a revelation when he heard the music on the orchestra at that point in the opera". So my childish aspirations were made in the light and shadow of such a person as Corder, for which I am eternally grateful.

My piano studies were well directed by Pollard who had a real pianist's 'touch' and I began to feel that I could play more like a real pianist that hitherto.

My second study was violin as we had several instruments in

the family and my teacher was James Lockyer, who was in several London orchestras. He was a good teacher but I disliked the violin and only practised when I had to. I took a first examination which I passed but, on reflection, it was achieved by sheer willpower rather than any inspired gift of the instrument. However, in later times, it was to provide me with knowledge of the basic principles of bowing and double stopping which was very useful when my compositions or arrangements were performed.

Aural Training was taught by Ernest Read. Luckily there was a stringent series of examinations within the Academy which consequently insisted on a real attention to all steps in one's studies. These annual examinations were treated with much respect by professors and students alike. Diplomas were, of course, extra-curricular examinations. I obtained the highest award of the Academy in two subjects by the end of my third year.

The orchestra rehearsals were directed by Mackenzie and nothing more dreary could be imagined. Later, when Mackenzie had retired and had been replaced by Sir John McEwen, a revolution took place overnight as Sir Henry Wood was engaged twice a week for this purpose.

Modern outlooks towards music and the profession have undergone great changes during my own lifetime. The conductor today is a person to be reckoned with as a man of integrity and independence. Earlier on in the present century, it may be recalled that a 'good musician', be he a composer or administrator, was regarded as competent to act as a conductor. Often these excellent people had no training in the art of conducting *per se* and scanty - if any - experience of playing in an orchestra under a professional conductor such as one associates with the names of Nikisch or Richter. If, as a composer or administrator, they had achieved a Doctorate or Knighthood, they were *ipso facto* able to conduct, whereas nothing could be further from the truth. Cathedral organists were supposed to be completely equipped to deal with an orchestra. Yet, to my certain knowledge, a Doctor and Knight found it impossible to change the tempo in a Mendelssohn aria in an oratorio in a way that could be entrusted to a student at any of our academies today.

Sir Henry Wood was the great exception because, by his very efficiency and knowledge, he was able to deal with all the problems of an orchestra and did so in no uncertain manner. From the time he took his first rehearsal in Duke's Hall, the standard was set for the young orchestral player. Matthay was, of course, one of the most celebrated of the pianoforte teachers, on account of his organised teaching in practice and theory. Hans Wesley, a prototype of Kreisler, was head of the violin staff and with Stewart Macpherson, with the more modern and liberal outlook among teachers of theory, the Academy had a formidable set of professors.

Among fellow students that brought me much pleasure were Jean Pougnet - violin, Harry Burley - the finest viola player I have ever heard, Clifford Curzon - piano, Roy Henderson - baritone and, later, Arthur Fear.

After Corder had retired, I was sent to Julius Harrison, whose musicianship I rank as second to none. He was chiefly concerned with the Opera Class and brought the operatic performances to a high standard. The Academy hired the Scala Theatre for a week and there were fine performances of high professional standard. I recall *Falstaff* and *Meistersinger* as being outstanding.

Harrison for composition was a wonderful inspiration. His

methods were unique. By that time, I had obtained the Bronze Medal for Harmony so could bring my compositions to his notice with a degree of confidence. He looked at my work and quietly put the whole lot aside. He then wrote some contrapuntal exercise and sketched in how I was to proceed.

I soon found him and his teaching much to my liking and gave myself wholeheartedly to doing as he told me in the way he desired. I was flabbergasted when my end of year report came through to the effect that I wrote 'good counterpoint'. The fact is that I was completely unaware that my work was good or that it was 'counterpoint'. I just found it fascinating to think along the lines he suggested.

I suddenly had a great desire to write a Sonata for Viola. Burley's wonderful tone and technique had inspired me. Although I never at any time spoke to Burley (as I was too shy to do so), nevertheless I just reacted to that wonderful viola tone I had never heard before or since. The instrument was gigantic - more like a 'cello that he lifted to his shoulder - and it required all his own great size and power to get round the thing. I can scarce think of the time even now without lamenting the passing of this sound from earth, for he met his end at a very early age. Harrison was keen to help me with my Sonata, which began very promisingly but, alas, by the time of my next lesson, I had got stuck and could in no wise find a way of continuing. Now was shown to me the genius of Harrison. He asked me time and time again to play the opening. Then I suggested a 'going on'. He silenced me at once and brooded. Then he pushed me away from the piano and 'carried on', improvising the next page or so. He showed me that the 'mood' was to be felt and to be carried on, with such 'different' contrasts in rhythm and tonality that was required. For a moment he 'became me'. He suggested means of contrast and development of material that were an inspiration. He accepted me and my work and went on from there. The result, as far as I was concerned, was that I made great headway. My Sonata was finished and I heard Harrison say to me "Take it to Tertis". Truly I could have had no greater reward than had he said, as an Old Testament prophet, "Offer it to God".

I found out what day of the week Tertis would be at the Academy and calculated what path he would take. I lay in wait with my Sonata duly copied out in my best handwriting and packed in a parcel worthy of the occasion and, I hoped, worthy of the attention of Tertis. He passed as I had thought he would. Waylaying him, with the utmost respect and reverence, I told him my Composition professor had suggested he might be kind enough to look at this Sonata. Very politely he told me he was going on holiday and could not examine the work then - and returned the parcel to my hands, unopened. That spot in the Academy is to me the place where the betrayal took place - unhallowed to this day.

It was during the latter part of my period at the Academy that I heard the great pianist Emil Sauer at the Wigmore Hall. My professor was a personal friend of Sauer and his best pupil, Isabel Gray, went to Dresden for lessons with this great virtuoso. Pollard suggested that I might go and have, say, three or four months with him. This prospect overjoyed me. I had long dreamed of learning from what, to my mind, was a great pianist of the very first dimension.

What had struck me about Sauer was his immense power, his sense of poetry and, at the same time, his dignity in presenting the great piano works. The Schumann *Toccata* was a point to note. Here was playing on the grand scale as I had dreamed about. It was agreed by my father that I should go to Dresden (where Sauer lived) in August for a few months. As luck would have it, another pupil of Pollard had like intentions so we set out together.

But before I venture into this aspect of my life, I include some further recollections of life at the Academy.

Corder was quite one of the most extraordinary people I have ever met. He had the ability to make people quote him and have recollections of him which seemed to make him immortal in his own time. He spoke of the great masters of music - Bach, Beethoven and Wagner - as though he knew them intimately as friends. He did have the astonishingly new approach to music and musicians which is the exact opposite of the usual and accepted respectful veneration in which the great masters are held. To hear him say that Beethoven 'couldn't do this or that' was unusual in a professor at such an institution as the Royal Academy. The astonishing thing was that these pronounce-ments were accepted *in toto* by his students and we, the disciples of Corder, would not countenance any other views to be expressed in our presence. To us, what Corder said was true - 'and that's the end on't'. His personal appearance was quite distasteful to most people. In a word, he was dirty. I don't mean untidy for he was not. At a distance, one could see him sitting or walking in Regent's Park, hard by the Academy, and one got the impression that here was and must be a most distinguished professor of some subject or other - maybe music, as the Academy was just round the corner. I always took care not to see him or cross his path - my fear of him was the result of such respect that I was rather like a terrified rabbit, hoping not to be noticed by a stoat. As Curator, he was second in command at the Academy and when the Principal, Mackenzie, was away, which only happened about three times to my certain knowledge, it was Corder who conducted the orchestra in his stead. Mackenzie always sat to conduct. Corder stood. I always knew when Corder was to take the orchestra as my lessons took place during the morning on the same day, in the afternoon of which the orchestral rehearsal took place. As I entered Corder's room, two things would 'give the show away' as far as I was concerned. His hair, which stood out somewhat as a fringe round his bald head and was mostly black with a tinge of grey, had been plastered down to adhere to his bald head by the application of what I would think might be guessed at as water. But I doubt if he ever used water for any other purpose as his face, ears and neck were caked in dirt and grime. No self-respecting lady would want to share a seat with him in the park and I couldn't help but wonder how his female pupils reacted to such a distressing person so close. He had a fascination for young ladies and, should a girl student be in his good books, he would beam and his face would light up so it was as though the sun had come forth from behind black lowering clouds. To my mind, the more forthright of the young girls could 'manage' him in a rather pathetic way. During the First World War, before I knew him, history relates that he grew a beard - it was said in order to economise on soap, which was in short supply. The other 'giveaway' regarding the fact that he was going to take the orchestral rehearsal was that there was a rather faded morning coat hanging on the hat stand, limp and sad, like a rabbit skin that had been discarded by its owner. He would be somewhat 'tetchy' in nervous anticipation of his afternoon's work. The orchestral rehearsals were dull and boring under Mackenzie. There were equally - and even more so - under Corder.

I think my distaste and even loathing of Mozart might be attributed to these orchestral rehearsals I attended - not because I was obliged to do so but out of my wish to try and learn as much as possible from every occasion that might be open to me. The Mozart *Symphony in G Minor* is a case in point. This work I cannot hear without a feeling of *ennui* and nausea which is accountable to the experience of hearing this work rehearsed at the Academy by Mackenzie. The second part of the rehearsal was always devoted to a run-through of any concerto movement or aria submitted by a student for rehearsal, if the professor recommended it. I played the Beethoven G major concerto on such an occasion.

Mackenzie indulged his prowess for bullying on such occasions but I did not come in for censure. By something of a miracle, I was permitted to play the cadenza. This was something rather novel and I heard that another piano professor scolded my professor for allowing me to play such a 'rubbishy' cadenza. My own professor scored in this instance by revealing it was Beethoven's own cadenza that I played. It reveals that not much love was lost, especially was this so between teachers of the two schools of pianism - Matthay and his followers and the more 'conventional' school to which I belonged. Matthay's pupils were noted for their swaying and swimming antics as they played. They talked endlessly about relaxation and forearm rotation and such things.

The summer of the year that I went to the Academy was about the year of its centenary. I took no part in this, of course, but there were notices in the daily papers of the day and I recall that, among some of the events, there was notice of some chamber music played by the students of one J B McEwen. He was patronised by one of the papers as a student who showed some promise. The critics were unaware of the fact that McEwen was at that time one the senior professors of composition and that very shortly he was to succeed Mackenzie as Principal. (There was a bit of a row about that - I can tell you!)

Cunningham was one of the organ professors and later, after leaving St James' Muswell Hill, where I had been a choirboy in his time, he went to St Alban's Holborn, where very high church practices and music were part of that establishment. Cunningham had already done something in this line at Stroud Green and performed masses with orchestra. I recall with great pleasure hearing Schubert's *Mass in B flat* there. My father played in this *ad hoc* orchestra, both at Stroud Green and St Alban's.

Cunningham later went to Birmingham and became Town Hall organist. It is interesting to note the weight and talent of the two rivals in London - the Royal Academy and the later founded Royal College of Music. The history of these two Colleges of Music has been written by inmates of each institution but I venture to think that both will be a result of a somewhat jaundiced viewpoint. Each institute thinks of itself as superior to the other and, in fact, each institution *knows* that it is superior to its rival. But the fact is that, in my time, both institutions had completely different views about the profession and even the Art of Music.

The fact must be stated that the Profession of Music is one thing and the Art of Music another. One wishes it were other. The Academy was all for public performance. The Royal College was centred more around the closed confines of the universities' and cathedral organists' activities.

Woods, at Highgate School, was all for me going to the College. I, for myself, favoured the Academy as it had more of the performing and concert world within its ambit and, as I have said, I was much taken with the pianists that I had heard and my ambitions lay in that direction. The organ world was intensified for me through Cunningham, who was a public performer of considerable renown. Moreover I was not inclined towards the scholastic side of music. Degrees in music meant nothing to me. So many musicians I knew I despised and found frequently that they were possessors of university degrees. My heroes were not of that kidney. So I elected to go to the Academy, especially as it seemed providential that my cousin was already there and so I got an *entrée* to that establishment, whereas the College was more distant from home in the uncharted waters of South Kensington. True, the Albert Hall, where I had heard Paderewski, Pachmann and the like perform, was in South Kensington, but that only emphasised for me the remoteness the College had for me as being so far from my pianistic ambitions.

Trinity College of Music was not to be thought of. It had to be a Royal institution or nothing.

It was not to be wondered at that I would go to Dresden and study with Sauer, (pupil of Liszt and Nicholas Rubinstein), a virtuoso who was touring the world, playing recitals in all the capitals of Europe and playing with great orchestras and conductors of the world. He had been awarded the great Philharmonic Gold Medal by the Society, which was reckoned to be the foremost Society in Music in the kingdom - the one which had sent money to Beethoven in his distress and whose bust stood staring at the audience from the platform at all its concerts. All this was grist to my mill.

Dark, dank cathedral organ lofts, choirs singing psalms endlessly without apparent reason or understanding, lots of unaccompanied anthems, frequently in Latin or, even worse, frightful Victorian church music of such sentimentality to make one squirm; could this be the same *music* that I worshipped with Beethoven and Schumann? No. I would go forth into the land of great music and would not be contaminated with the trivia of local and restricted viewpoints one associates with one's own environment.

How this was met and how one returned to one's native heath

and had to be reconciled to one's limitations is the real subject of this exercise. That painful path had to be trodden and trodden alone and of that we shall learn as it took place.

Author's note: The Royal Academy of Music Student Record for Charles Proctor indicates that he went there at the start of the Michaelmas Term 1922 and left at the end of the Midsummer Term 1926. He received a Bronze Medal for Piano and Sight Singing in 1923, Silver for Piano and Sight Singing in 1924 and Certificate for Piano and Sight Singing in 1925. In 1926, as well as satisfying the examiners with his continued progress in piano, there being no higher award to receive, he received a bronze medal for Harmony. Diplomas: LRAM Piano Performers in 1930, ARAM on March 17 1932 and FRAM on March 29 1945.

4 - STUDYING WITH SAUER IN DRESDEN AND VIENNA

Emil von Sauer (1862-1942) was sixty-four and I about twenty when I went to Dresden. Sauer lived in a lovely villa. Dresden at that time was, indeed, a beautiful city and the part where he lived, and near where I had my room, was a refined suburb.

Sauer's home was very comfortable and roomy and he lived in good style. His wife and family were about the house and his music room was large, with space to walk about. The piano, a Bechstein Concert Grand, was placed with the keyboard behind which one could walk, but the other end was against folding doors leading to the dining room. It was disconcerting to play knowing he could see you playing and yet you couldn't see him. Above the piano was a large portrait of himself in oils, giving the appearance that he had just at that moment finished a recital and was facing the audience. It was quite frightening. On the side wall was another painting, by the same artist, of a lady in evening dress. This, too, was startling and he told us that the lady 'fainted away' when she saw the finished picture, it was so lifelike. To the left, a bay window in which were music cabinets with roll-down fronts and many shelves. Sofas and chairs and a desk completed the room.

As I arrived, he came forward to meet me for the first time, enquired about my Academy professor and asked me what I was to play for him. It was Beethoven's *Appassionata Sonata*. I knew it well and played it, as I thought, to a very creditable standard. He heard most of it, then said "Technique good, interpretation weak". This was the surprise of my life. I had imagined that my interpretation was good and musical and that my technique, by his standards, was most inadequate. I had told myself that, if I could acquire his technique, the rest of my musical equipment would tell me how to play. His verdict was the exact opposite of my estimation of my gifts. We began again, from the beginning. "No pedal" was the first instruction. Fingering was given and the position of the hands was insisted upon. However, the most difficult thing was to play the triplet as he wanted it. He was never insistent and never got angry, but a clicking of his tongue on this teeth was enough to make one feel his exasperation. (We students would compare the number of 'clicks' we got in the hour's lesson.) He played for me. Where was the passion I had heard in London, the fire and the sense of power? Never to be seen or heard. But I knew I was at close quarters with a great musical experience. It was like being close to a great railway engine, sitting in a station, not moving, gentle purring noises coming only from its own strength. The fires in Sauer were there, but the cinders were alarmingly cold. I was somewhat bewildered.

Then and there I resolved that I would do exactly as he told me, imitating his actions and very musical thought. I knew it was not my place to question anything at all. For as he sat and played, I knew I was listening to things only heard and thought of in another world. He played little, but when I sat at the piano afterwards playing such a simple few bars as the opening of the slow movement, my playing was like the finger painting of a kindergarten child compared with the stroke of an artist's brush. I was conscious of only one thing - how far I had to go.

I came out of the room in a state of near collapse, not from my efforts but from my inadequacy.

Some ten months afterwards, my mother came with me for my lesson in Vienna. She heard me play - I don't remember what - and then Sauer played the same piece. She told me that the difference was as between my playing and that of a little girl pupil I taught in London aged about ten. My mother, no musician except by instinct, saw the position and heard it in a flash. I could only agree - and that was after I had spent some ten months with Sauer, having gone to him after four years at the Academy where I was 'well-thought-of'. No wonder I was dejected on my return to my rooms after my first lesson. But this only made my resolve the stronger.

Sauer used to spend his holiday time at Baden-Baden. From there he went to Dresden for a month or so and then to Vienna, where he made his headquarters from which he went on tour. These tours lasted between four and seven weeks, according to his engagements. During this time, his pupils had time to prepare their work for him to be ready for his return when they would resume their twice-weekly lessons of an hour each. After the first month at Dresden, I went to Vienna where lodgings had been found for me. Several students had as their headquarters a flat run by Frau von Wassilko. Frau Wassilko had arranged separate rooms around Vienna, close to the headquarters, where we had a room and breakfast. All other meals we had together - midday dinner and supper. My own room was some twelve minutes' walk away and was a single room, clean and bright with a washbasin with a bucket below to catch the used water. A jug of cold water, a stove for the winter months, a table, bed, small carpet and a sort of day sofa - this and a small cupboard for all my belongings constituted my work/living room. Hot water was delivered by my Haus Frau as was my breakfast of one roll and butter and a cup of coffee.

That is all I saw of my Haus Frau - a pleasant enough woman. The room was cleaned each day during the lunch hour. I hired a grand piano.

I had evolved a system of study worked out by the clock. I allotted myself seven hours piano practice with one half hour each morning and afternoon for composition - to be a respite from my piano study. Breakfast was counted as half an hour during which I read German. Lunch at midday gave me the walk I needed to and from the dinner table (which was unhurried) and again timed so that no time was lost. Evening supper was timed again and, after supper, a walk or visit to a café or cinema with friends. We elected to be in bed by 10. pm.

The rigours of this were extreme. I found it unwise to allow myself any deviation from the set self-made timetable or time would be lost and frittered away with nothing done. Sunday afternoons and evenings were free when we went to such places outside Vienna as took our fancy. Calenberg, Conenzal, Heiligenstadt were our favourite haunts, walking up the hills of the Danube from these suburban heights.

My lesson with Sauer was usually during a morning for which I had to allow half an hour to get there and, after the lesson, I would go to a café to drink coffee and go over the work of the lesson, recalling all the points made. I made a resolve and told myself over and over again "I have only limited time here. I must not waste a minute or be deviated from my purpose which is to study the piano under Sauer."

We did go to the opera but preferred to do this on a Sunday if possible as our afternoon/evening off. We looked upon the opera not as a diversion but part of our musical experience. We had to *stand* through performances of *The Ring, Rosenkavalier, Parsifal* and the like, there being a space at the back of the stalls reserved for 'standing only' and, as we could not afford seats, we had to take our places there. I recall having to spend the intervals leaning over a rail to get my back curving properly, as the ache in having to stand for three or four hours without support is trying, to say the least. *Tristan* was particularly trying in this respect. *Rosenkavalier* I heard several times and loved this work more than any other. On one occasion, Strauss conducted and I found this to be the most disappointing performance of my experience. It went with such little meaning or dramatic effect. Later, in London, I attended Kleiber's performance and found this more satisfying than others. I had the advantage of hearing Elisabeth Schumann as Sophie, Lotte Lehmann as the Marschalin and Mayr as the Baron. What a trio that was. The magic of the Rose presentation was unbelievable and the orchestration at that point enchanted me with its genius. We attended symphony concerts and piano recitals where we heard Dohnányi, Friedman, Muntz and others. Sauer gave his recital during the season and enchanted us all. The Chopin *B Minor Sonata* was a *tour de force*. His own trivia as encores were delightful in their way, especially a *Valse de Vienna*, which he played with tremendous élan - likewise the *Hungarian Rhapsody* of Liszt where, halfway through, the scale passage runs down the keyboard and then an upward arpeggio made their effect. Such was Sauer's playing of this that the whole audience clapped. One could not think of such a thing being possible in London. After the recital, those who could pushed their way to the platform and stood in reverent awe by the piano as he played encore after encore, including the arrangement of the *Blue Danube* which brought the audience to the point of ecstasy.

I refused to attend any church service on a Sunday morning as it would break into my schedule of practice. Nor would I go to the cemetery to pay my respects to the masters buried therein. I would only serve living music they had written for their memorial.

There is nothing more indicative of the change in the musical style of the profession than the queer chances and quirks of fashion and invention that govern life. When I met Sauer, about 1926, he had been the victim of the 1918 War inasmuch as, for some years after the war, his appearances in this country were not welcome. He was a German musician and the anti-German feeling was not only rife during the war but lasted some years afterwards. Moreover, Sauer had an almost pathological dislike of sea travel and that was, at that time, shared by a great number of Europeans. As air travel had not been invented, there was no other choice if you wanted to visit the British Isles. Moreover, in England, Sauer was not a popular pianist (as Paderewski *was*) but had a following among 'high society' rather than popular acclaim. However, the connoisseurs of pianism would not miss a performance by this artist. His prowess was of such a refined and intellectual quality that only the most discerning would want to attend a recital. Nevertheless there was a most interesting contradiction here as his performances, in spite of this aloofness in style, did reach a 'playing to the gallery' kind of performance which was at the other extreme. His own compositions are a case in point.

It is a painful aspect one has to admit to oneself, (even if one tries to conceal it from one's friends), that his compositions were often cheap 'claptrap', barren of musical discretion. For example, his *Piano Concerto* was so banal and 'silly' that no self-respecting musician would dream of playing it. Sauer did play it, though I never heard a performance but I understand the finale had to be repeated in performance, so great was its immediate appeal. I knew the piece, as a great friend of mine had to learn it at Sauer's behest. The technique was pianistic and effective to a degree and the sensationalism of its performance, to an uncritical audience, was assured. His piano *Etudes* were masterly written for the keyboard and I spent many hours in learning these to acquire something of the style and piano technique of the Master. This I believe I did but, when I came back to London, the musical climate was such that I never dared to play them in public. Also, it is interesting to note that my mother, who was not versed in musical matters in any way, liked me to play these pieces for her delight, whereas my father, who was a good musician of taste and experience, could not bear to hear their trivialities. I relate this to show the difficulty to which one had to reconcile oneself.

Nothing could have been more noble than Sauer's playing of Beethoven. Yet this curious streak (his compositions) was evident and most distressing to some of us. This was all the more distressing as we knew he had a very high regard for his own compositions. All of which, I am safe in saying, found publishers and good sales.

Apart from his prowess as a player, he had done most notable work in bringing out, at the insistence of publishers, all the Brahms piano works for Peters, all Schumann's piano works for Peters, likewise all Chopin's piano works for Schott. I think he did not edit Beethoven as there were the Bülow, d'Albert and other editions. We students had to use the Singer edition for Beethoven, of which Sauer approved. These huge tasks were monumental in the extreme and certainly not to be undertaken lightly. Each work was fingered and phrased as he himself indicated and used.

In England his reputation had not kept up with the advent of pianists with a more modern outlook. It is noteworthy to find the exact times in musical history in which Sauer's reputation was at its zenith. One must remember that he was born in 1862, which made him two years younger than Paderewski.

Rachmaninoff was born ten years later than Sauer and Backhaus twenty-two years after Sauer. He therefore belongs to a bygone age, quite out of touch with the 'modern' style of playing by Rachmaninoff and later Horowitz. And although there was but ten years difference, that ten years was an epoch as far as musical culture was concerned.

Weingartner was one year younger than Sauer, but again he seemed to be of a more modern era.

In 1913, when Sauer was fifty one, a book appeared called *Modern Musicians* by Cuthbert Hadden. A quote from the first paragraph on Emil Sauer reads: 'There is no greater pianist at the present time than Emil Sauer. His individuality is almost as well defined and fascinating as that of Paderewski or Pachmann and his technique is as marvellously perfect as their's or Busoni's. Pugno says he is the greatest of the four great - the others being Busoni, D'Albert and Siloti. His characteristics are so heroic that it is even permissible to evoke the shades of Liszt and Rubinstein if we desire to multiply our comparisons.' The article goes on in that style for several pages.

It was at the age of sixty-four that he first appeared to me as my Master, while I was about twenty years of age. When I returned to London, I was met on all sides by friends who were stunned by the appearance of Schnabel. Schnabel had played a Brahms Concerto at the Royal Philharmonic Society's concert at Queen's Hall and it had been a sensation. He had come over from Berlin where, of course, he had an immense reputation and, at one blow at this concert, conquered London and the musical followers.

There was a reaction from the anti-German hostility and now appeared the German who looked like a German, played like one and behaved like one. He played on a German piano and only played German music. (In this I include Schubert as I would Mozart.) Beethoven was his forte. He played in a clear precise style without in any way yielding to the public audience, either by way of playing encores or acknowledging his applause. His hair was short and bushy and was cut high above his ears. He wore a bowler hat and in every respect was the opposite in every way to the old Romantic conception of what a musician ought to be. He recorded pretty well all Beethoven and it was noticeable that the repetition of a musical phrase was executed in exactly and precisely the same way both by tone phrase and musical content so that, for instance, a piece like Beethoven's *Für Elise* was as precise in its reproductions of one of the phrases like the repetition one can see on a wallpaper. He had an immense following and took many pupils back to Berlin with him. There he held classes for his pupils in a most orderly and organised way. His reputation in this country was enhanced by the devoted and ecstatic critiques of W H Turner, who had just completed his book on Beethoven for the Beethoven Centenary of 1927.

The significance of Schnabel was not only due to his first class piano playing, his performance of Beethoven and Schubert, but his whole attitude to a piano recital was quite relentless and unique. He played complete solo concerts of composers with no regard for the audience at all. At one fell swoop, the programmes we were accustomed to, from Paderewski and the like, were suddenly regarded as old-fashioned and 'playing to the gallery'. At the time of Paderewski, the format of nearly all the great virtuosi was to a strict pattern that could be predicted before one entered the hall. The programme began with a classical piece - eg Haydn *Variations* or Scarlatti sonatas. After a time the second group would appear as great sonatas by Beethoven, Liszt, Brahms, Chopin or the like - maybe Mendelssohn *Variations* or some serious work by one of the lesser 'classics'. Then the interval. After the interval, the audience had been led to expect the real enjoyment of the music could be counted upon - Chopin *Waltzes*, *Mazurkas*, *Nocturnes*. Then a group of real 'delights' of virtuoso type of music - Liszt, Rubinstein, Mussorgsky - and most probably pieces written by the pianist himself, ending up with a Liszt *Rhapsody*, Balakiref *Islamey* or some real virtuoso piece - maybe Liszt *Mephisto Waltz*, *Venusberg Music* from *Tannhäuser* arranged by Mussorgsky and the like. Then a real 'hair standing on end' bravura piece would finish the concert. Then came the encores - often compositions of the pianist himself - or well known pieces which amateurs could play - ending up with a show piece like the more glamorous *Etudes* of Chopin. The fame of the player depended on the number of encores he could get the audience to demand. It was in this world of 'delights' that Sauer had lived and into which I had been trained to think by him.

Small wonder that my attitude was 'out of date' with a London audience and the critics. Moreover, Sauer had told my father that the one thing lacking in my playing was the 'Latin' outlook and style. Liszt had all this and Sauer was the greatest exponent of this style. Small wonder then that the contemporary thinking of the time found Liszt an 'empty characterless composer'. The charm of Sauer's playing was that he, a German, so wholly interpreted the Latin way of playing and musical thought. This, of course, was shown in his own compositions which were of very poor quality indeed - but the two characteristics were that they were pianistic and of the Latin way of thinking. Like all great pianists, he made the very trivialities sound quite wonderful and certainly inspiring. We got this attitude from Paderewski as well, as he played Mendelssohn pieces (only fit for young ladies to play after dinner in a Victorian drawing room) as really great pieces.

So it was that I found myself returning to a London which could not be further from the style and outlook of one whose first consideration in music is that it was never to be considered that the repetition of a single phrase must be a replica, but either an echo or confirmation. So Sauer, by this time, 'cut no ice' in London as far as critics and outlook were concerned. He belonged to another world.....I felt equally ill at ease.

But we should not forget that the Royal Philharmonic Society gave its Gold Medal to all the great musicians in their own time and amongst these we find such names as Paderewski, Rachmaninoff, Elgar, Vaughan Williams, Ferrier and Barbirolli.

There was the 'art of the Salon', where the aristocratic society, fringed with royalty, would hold receptions - 'At Homes', soirées and similar gatherings. Political figures could be found amongst the great artists of the day - ambassadors, consuls and churchmen.

So it was that a Sauer recital was attended by not so much the students or dilettantes, but the intellectual and high society figures. His pianoforte in Dresden was covered by silver photograph frames of royalty, duly signed by the donors. The Queen of Rumania obtained a new Bechstein pianoforte and this was 'inaugurated' by Sauer, who was given, in return, a signed photograph of the Queen. He was the last pianist I saw wear a frock coat at a recital. One felt one was in the presence of a great pianist who belonged to the great 'upper crust' of performers - a race in their own right.

I am not going into the musical creeds held or the musical axioms enjoined by the Master. These are the precious possessions hard won by study and application over the years. But they have held and guided my own thinking in all walks and spheres of musical life.

There is an aspect of 'public performance' which seems sadly to be lost these days. I can only call it the sense of 'delight'. I recall Alfred Clements, the founder of the Society of the South Place Concerts for over fifty years, telling me he would not go to hear Paderewski play at Queen's Hall as it was not advertised what his programme would contain until one got to the hall. This applied to several pianists in my youth. For myself, I didn't care *what* Paderewski played - or Pachmann, or Sauer, or any others. These great ones could, as far as I was concerned, play *anything* and it was worth going to hear. Today one is inclined to think that all play alike and it seldom matters who plays the music; likewise performances by conductors, I would go anywhere to hear Mengelberg or Toscanini, knowing that I would have a unique musical experience. As one orchestral player said recently: "Nowadays one can hardly tell one orchestra from another" and I would go further and say "even one conductor from another".

The experience of 'delight' I mentioned is somewhat borne out these days by the fact that one seldom feels a sense of delight at a performance. Liberace and Carlo Curley are two people in mind. Both delight, but are frowned on by the intelligentsia. We must not forget that in Beethoven's time it was not unusual for an audience to show its delight in a composition by loud applause after the first movement of a symphony and this existed right down to the first performance of Elgar's *First Symphony* in 1908. His wife wrote 'After 3rd movement, E. had to go up on platform & whole Orch. and nos. of audience stood up - wonderful scene. Also at end." (*Edward Elgar. A Creative Life.* Jerrold Northrop Moore p.545.) Now we sit in gloomy apprehensive silence until the end of the new work and wait until we see if it befitting that our personal enthusiam might declare itself. We no longer 'speak our mind', except in political atmospheres of protestation.

From a personal point of view, I would like it to be known that my own distaste and distrust I feel for the tampering with the 1662 Prayer Book makes me say that at my own funeral, if the whole of the Prayer Book Funeral Epistle of St Paul to the Corinthians is tampered with or not said, I shall 'get up and walk out' as protest.

My first few months with Sauer brought from him the suggestion that I should, if possible, stay with him until the summer and this agreed with my own desires. By the good fortune of having sensible and generous parents and the fact that I had inherited some money on the death of an uncle, I was able to do this and even return for the second session again in Vienna.

My routine was exactly as heretofore, except that my ambitions and devotion to my aspirations were intensified even further. I still felt it was my duty to compose and had, from the outset of my studies in Vienna, spent one hour a day in composition, as a relaxation from my piano studies. My *Viola Sonata* I brought with me and played it with a near neighbour in Dresden who was in the Dresden Opera Orchestra. He played it well and, after some time in rehearsal, we gave a studio performance to my friends who showed both enthusiasm and pleasure. Hearing it thus performed by a good player made me convinced I had calculated correctly for my desired results. The music was somewhat Brahmsian, but I consoled myself that, after all, it had to be 'somebody's', so it might as well be Brahms who I greatly admire. The slow movement had a melody of which I was inordinately proud. I only told my friends that it 'stinks of Brahms' partly in self-defence and as something of an excuse to put myself in the Elgarian condemnation of *Gerontius*, that it 'stinks of incense'; my argument being that if Elgar can stink of incense, there should be no reason why I shouldn't stink of Brahms. One somewhat un-Brahmsian point in that movement was that the melody went in triple canon in the recapitulation, which pleased me no end. I learned that the happy gift of accident was not to be dismissed. The Canon, and indeed the Ground Bass and Passacaglia structures in composition have always attracted me and do to this day.

My second 'season' was not different from my first, except it coincided with the Beethoven Centenary in 1927. I heard the *Ninth Symphony* conducted by Weingartner; also the *Mass in C* sung in St Stephen's Cathedral at High Mass. I was fortunate to attend a song recital accompanied by Richard Strauss, whose personality was by no means as exciting as his music - and this always annoyed me.

My father had visited Vienna during my first season there and my mother came the second year. Both met Sauer and my father was able to hear him play his recital in Vienna. It was thought I might give some recitals in the following year but again I was so bewildered by my own inadequacies that I returned to London and gave myself yet another year's work, living with my parents, and yet keeping to such a rigid schedule of work as seems impossible to grasp.

Author's note: I have a photograph of Sauer which he gave to Charles Proctor. The inscription on it reads: "To my dear and excellent pupil Charles Proctor with my best wishes for a brilliant career according to his high gifts. In kind remembrance from his affectionate Emil v. Sauer Vienna, May 28 1928."

5 - BACK IN LONDON

I had a small room at the back of the house, with a grand piano, and I insisted that the local dealer should either weight the action or do something to make a greater resistance to the rather light touch, which I felt would make life too easy for my fingers. I gave myself up to the study of as much Liszt and Chopin as I found I had not already covered. During my stay in Vienna, I had studied most the of great works of Chopin, Schumann, Beethoven and Brahms. This season of study at home was extremely hard to sustain.

My mother had a servant girl living in who was given instructions how I was to have my work declared of the utmost importance. I left my bed at an early hour and made a walk of about two miles in a circuit of the district, exactly at the certain hour and met various people going about their work or on their way to work each morning. On return home, I went to my room and began my work - always scales and exercises. At a given hour, the maid would knock on the door and deliver to me a cup of cocoa, brown bread and butter and a banana. It was forbidden for anyone to see me or speak for fear that my concentration might be broken and trivia engage my attention. This went on for weeks. It was one of the coldest winters on record. (The Danube was iced over, I was told.) In London the cold, damp atmosphere made life almost intolerable for me. I had my back to the window, on account of the light, but had to have a screen up at my back to keep off the draught. There was a very economical gas heater which I had to have on all day in winter, but as I told my friends, it was so economical it used no gas and gave no heat.

I took some engagements in London as they presented themselves and I prepared for the coming winter season for recitals. This was engineered in such a way that I went to Vienna, then to Berlin, then London in that order. About a month afterwards, the scheme was repeated as it was thought that no impact would be made by just one recital unconnected with another appearance. My programmes consisted of the *Appassionata Sonata* of Beethoven, the Brahms *Paganini Variations*, Chopin *Polonaise in F sharp minor* and included the *Mazeppa* of Liszt.

I made friends at this time with one who became my greatest musical friend in London, William Busch. I cannot think of two people who could be found anywhere of such contrasting personalities and viewpoints as Willy (as I called him) and me. He was a pianist, somewhat my senior in years, of German parents. Both spoke with a German accent. His father was a diamond merchant of some wealth and Willy lived with his parents in almost similar conditions as me. His German parents and the fact that his aunt was a very good artist and was related to Knaus, the German engraver, made the whole ménage very dear to me. The contrast between us was quite laughable. Willy was as pro-English as can be imagined and read and respected *The Times* and all the usual English characteristics of our race, while I was so in love with all that was German that we had endless arguments, he defending England and I defending Germany. He had studied the piano with Lander who was a very good teacher among whose pupils would be counted the then little princesses Elizabeth and Margaret. Lander had a studio in Baker Street. Willy was a composer of very good music. He was a pupil of John Ireland and his workmanship was as firm and correct as could be imagined. Personally I did not care much for his music.

After my debut, I found that the difficulties of pursuing a pianistic career were such that I could not count on success. In retrospect, the fact was that neither my family nor I myself knew how to organise this situation. I only knew that, although I had obtained a degree of pianistic ability, I would have to employ myself by other means if I was to make a way in the profession at all. Strange as it may seem, I recall I made two resolves. One that I should be independent of my parents' patronage and two, that even as Bacon had declared "all knowledge is my province" - or was it Goethe? I do not mind - I resolved "All music will be my province". I cast around to see in what way I could make some headway. I was not dismayed at taking a different direction in my musical life. I argued with myself - and always won my arguments of course - that I had done, according to the light of my ambition and self-denial and concentrated action, what I had set out to achieve - a virtuoso technique by studying with one of the greatest pianists of my time. I had done what I had set out to do and if, as I felt, I was not to achieve my ambitions as a solo pianist, then Fate, or what you will, decreed otherwise. This is easy to write about and in retrospect one can see the wisdom of any change of course that would lead to some success even elsewhere than in the direction one had envisaged. These resolves were made secretly and not a soul shared in my resolution or determination to find what I would best be employed in doing. Willy was persuaded that I was a 'born pianist'. He little knew that I thought quite otherwise and had achieved my pianism by sheer willpower, rather than any heaven-sent gifts or from my early training, which should have been geared to pianism from the outset, if that had been my main goal.

My resolve was simple and concise. To become financially independent of my parents as soon as possible and to try to fit in with the environment and way of life as I saw it to be.

Curiously enough, this 'about face' was the result of two things. My friend Willy was of the firm opinion that his parents should support him financially, as they were well able to do, to allow him to pursue his musical career. In this I found I could not adopt the philosophy he advocated. I felt it incumbent upon me to think that my parents should do all within their power to educate and train me in the career of my choice, but beyond that I felt they were not called upon to exercise themselves. It was my firm belief that I should now, in return for the education they had provided, set about to earn money for my keep and obtain some place for myself in the profession. Of course, these philosophies were immature and naive in the extreme, but they belonged to the time when parents had been brought up to believe that they were obligated to train their children in moral and ethical ways and find the best education provided from various sources to fit them for their adult life. This was before the days of the Welfare State, state education and subsidies, National Health, unemployment benefits and the like. My father was a socialist at heart and believed that the poor lower classes, as they were called, should receive benefits from the state. My mother was an Imperialist and very conscious of class distinction. So my outlook was not at any time cut and dried but came upon me after much speculation in these political and social fields. The other thing that convinced me was a quotation I had often heard but never read, to the effect that, in the Prayer Book, one is exhorted to 'get mine own living and to do my duty in that state of life unto which God calls me'. I therefore clung to this as a *raison d'être* for a sort of complacent state of mind that I was secure in the position in which I found myself and need not be in any way doubtful that my position was in any way other than Fate or

Providence had decreed. This was very lucky for me indeed for it put my mind somewhat at rest and I could get on with the business of improving my status and condition without undue worry. My whole life had been stressful to the extreme in mental anguish and self distrust - but here was a form of salvation that benefitted me and gave me strength such as I needed.

It was something of a shock when, some years afterwards, I found my faith shaken in this respect by someone pointing out, in a public address to the school in which I was a member of staff, that this very phrase in the Catechism was so often misquoted. The speaker went on to say that the quotation made was, in fact, erroneous. What the Catechism *did* say was 'unto which it *shall* please God to call me'. The adage 'look up your references' had some significance. This was later brought home to me when I once misquoted, to a professor of a university, Berlioz' original stroke of genius in writing for flutes and bass trombone in the *Requiem*. Luckily there was a full score to hand so that we could look up the musical example. But for the time being it was perhaps providential that my mistaken reading of the Catechism - or rather the very non-reading and going by hearsay - kept me from the more unnerving and uncertain aspect as to what 'it *shall* please God to call me'.

I found a more contented and happier frame of mind now that my resolve was to become self-supporting, come what may. To this end, I took the post of the local organist and choirmaster of a small parish church for the princely sum of £40 a year. This meant two practices a week and two services on Sundays with extra fees of £1 each for weddings and funerals. These were not very frequent. But I argued to myself that 'one thing might lead to another'. I was not incorrect in my supposition. To be confined to the lonely occupation of just playing the piano at infrequent concerts was not conducive to making friends and taking part in music making with others. After a space, I founded a Festival Choir at the church and produced a performance of Mendelssohn's *Hymn of Praise*. The work attracted me as both my father and I were very sympathetic to the Mendelssohn idiom. As a young schoolboy, I had been taken to hear the work sung by the great Royal Choral Society at the Royal Albert Hall. Sir Frederick Bridge was the conductor but the chief impact on my memory was the superb singing of Agnes Nichols in the *Praise ye the Lord* aria, early on in the oratorio. Also the vocal score had been given to me for a birthday present by the second master at the already mentioned East Finchley Grammar School. He was something of a musician and, as mentioned earlier, played the organ at the memorable Ash Wednesday service. My first encounter with myself as a conductor was in the performance of Mendelssohn's *Hymn of Praise* at East Finchley. I had gathered a few friends to form a small orchestra and, with the organ, we had a performance that was memorable in more ways than one. The work begins with a trombone solo. Unfortunately, my trombone soloist, the local boot mender, had lost some teeth that very week so that his performance at the outset was insecure - in fact it was an unholy mess. I had made dozens of cuts in the score to reduce the long-winded *Symphony* to reasonable length for the occasion and the stress of arranging and conducting all this was somewhat exhausting. At the close of the first movement, there is a clarinet cadenza which my father played, as I knew he would, with confidence and accuracy. After the performance, my father asked me my opinion of how he played the cadenza. I replied "I didn't hear it. I was so confident that it would be all right that I didn't take any notice at all for I knew that, at that moment, I had no anxieties at all." I never knew whether he was flattered or disappointed in my reply. I had had to teach the local singers every note of the music - note by note - as most of them were incapable of reading anything at sight. It was a labour of Hercules, but my willpower brought the performance to a conclusion.

I wanted a tenor soloist for this and earlier found that Dr Nicholson had founded the (now) Royal School of Church Music, then in its early stages at Chislehurst. I had met Nicholson for we had joined the Association as I had been a great admirer of Nicholson and thought that one of the first things to do on becoming the local organist was to get them associated to the School. Moreover, we had attended, at St Sepulchre's, Holborn, some demonstration services at which I met Nicholson, late of Westminster Abbey, seated at a tiny two-manual organ in the nave while the old organ was being rebuilt. I was so impressed with this great man's humility and, at the same time, his musical integrity, that to find a soloist 'cheap', I wrote to him and asked if he knew someone to come and sing for my Festival Choir. He sent along a red-headed young man, Harry Barnes, who later became his assistant at Chislehurst and returned to the Abbey as choirmaster in some capacity or other.

After the Festival performance, we adjourned to the parish hall for coffee and, to my horror, I found Nicholson had attended the performance and was busy chatting to all and sundry. Later, I went down to Chislehurst for lunch at the School and got on well with him. My admiration and devotion to him was absolute, but, of course, later he swam out of my own little ambit. But there are memories of him which I will never forget. A personal one was at a time when I wanted to get another church. Barnet church was within easy reach of my home and I wanted to see if I could get his support in an application for the job, especially as I had read that he himself had, at a very early period of his career, been organist there. When I asked Nicholson if he would support my application, he paused for a bit, during which I had qualms that perhaps I had taken an unwarranted liberty in asking for his support. Then he replied that he had already written to the Vicar on my behalf as he knew of the vacancy and thought it would be a most suitable post for me. My astonishment at this altruistic step was a revelation of his character and I became his devoted disciple from that moment. After a lifetime of professional experience, I can count on the fingers of one hand when I have experienced such altruistic help. This and one other stick in my mind with gratitude and will do so to the end of my days.

6 - ALEXANDRA PALACE

An aunt of mine was a member of the Alexandra Choral and Orchestral Society, which originally gave its concerts in the Alexandra Palace. It might well be that here would be a good opportunity to give something of the history of the Palace and its music as far as I am concerned, as my life has been interwoven with this Society and that of the Alexandra Palace itself.

There had been, from the early days of the Alexandra Palace, a Choral and Orchestral Society of amateurs who gave regular concerts in the Palace. During my lifetime, the conductor was Allen Gill. He was not the first conductor of this musical enterprise but, before the 1914-18 war, he had raised the standard of both the orchestra and choir to a high standard. He gave several first performances and, in fact, his Society was a rival to the more prestigious Royal Choral Society at the Albert Hall. It was said that his choir would 'read anything'. I rather doubt that statement if taken too literally. However, we must bear in mind that in the suburbs of London (and it was so in North London) there were many choirs, both Church of England and Nonconformist, that reached a very high standard of singing indeed. As all the Nonconformist choirs consisted of men and women, the nucleus of a choral society was in being in hundreds of localities round London and, of course, in the provinces. Also, as there were in those days not a quarter of the distractions for entertainment we have today, the advantage of self-made music in the homes and in groups was an easy matter.

I was fortunate in living in that era when the Alexandra Palace supported a choir of some 1,000, likewise the Royal Choral Society at the Albert Hall. Other smaller groups at the People's Palace in the Mile End Road, Kingsway Hall and Central Hall Westminster were able to provide an outlet for singers who liked to sing the great choral works. The Handel Triennial Festival, with its choir of some 3,000, was something to have seen and believed and I recall the occasion when, as a small boy, I was taken to hear this choir and orchestra. The 'Chamber Orchestra' for accompanying the soloists was the London Symphony Orchestra, the Great Choir and Orchestra being held in reserve for the great choruses. In my youth, this was conducted by Sir Frederick Cowen. There were other festivals held in the Crystal Palace and I recall that the Tonic Sol-Fa Association had a children's choir of some 4,000. It is strange that it was the Anglican Royal School of Church Music who could carry on the vast choral tradition, instituted by Nicholson, while the Nonconformist element petered out as their Choral Union became less and less effective. So the Alexandra Palace under Gill was one of the great strongholds of choralism in North London.

The 1914-18 war was, of course, responsible for the dispersal of this wonderful body. But they kept going by giving concerts at the Northern Polytechnic concert hall in the Holloway Road. The choir was large and I believe had to take turns about appearing on the somewhat limited stage. The orchestra still belonged to that body and by chance there was a fine Hill organ in the building, which later found its way up the hill to St Joseph's Retreat Roman Catholic Church. At the time of which I speak, about the year 1930, Gill was almost in his last years as conductor and I was imported as a deputy, *incognito*. I sang in the choir and kept watch in the event of Gill being unable to conduct through any incapacity. He knew of my position and was prepared to take me into his confidence, but the matter was quite private, lest the morale of the Choir was in jeopardy. Their devotion to Gill was almost idolatrous and the Committee thought it wise to have me in reserve but, as I have stated, *incognito*. They were very prudent. As things turned out, Gill was to conduct the first concert of the season somewhere about November and the work chosen was *Judas Maccabaeus*. It is straightforward enough but of course, with Handel's oratorios, the necessity for cuts and omissions is a sore trial and added hazard for any conductor. The orchestra was a good amateur body of loyal and devoted Gillites, stiffened, as always, by some professional players. The concert began and I was told to be in evening dress amongst the audience - 'in case'. The Overture began and, all of a sudden, something went wrong. I do not know if it was the fault of the orchestra or conductor but I felt the whole thing would collapse in the first few bars. Gill's skill and willpower brought the thing to rights and the performance went on without further incident. He told me it required the shock of the first few moments of disarray to pull him together and make him take charge of the situation. The whole thing was tragic and I sensed that all felt that he was 'on his last legs'. The tragedy was heightened by the fact that his wife was dying of cancer at home and, although she had some time to go before her end, it too was a hopeless case. She had been his support in all ways and as a musician in her own right, had been a most steadfast help to him. I was their confidant in all these matters. After the concert, Gill had to be revived with whisky in large quantities and, by the end of the evening, he was almost incapable of being able to walk to the car to take him home. The Committee called upon me to take rehearsals from then on and I recall that Gill did attend but was incapable of conducting or directing the rehearsal. But, as in all such cases, the prudent activities of the Committee in appointing me as deputy was challenged by a group of Gillites who thought that the Committee had designs to kick Gill out. Nothing was further from their wishes, but the business of the Society had to be protected and it was lucky that I was present and available to step in if required. My position was unhappy. Gill I much admired and really loved and both of us accepted the position and the solution to the impasse. I continued to take rehearsals but nothing was done officially until it was self-evident that Gill would not be able to take the next concert. In 1931, I was therefore asked to conduct *The Dream of Gerontius* as my first concert with the Society. When this was made public, I bestirred myself to take every possible step to ensure the performance was a success. It was, I am happy to say, an unqualified success. If my memory serves me correctly, Bruce was the tenor and Frank Phillips the bass. He became better known as a BBC announcer in later years. The contralto's name I forget. The Leader was Charles Woodhouse who was, of course, Wood's Promenade Concert Leader, as it was the custom to have one full orchestral rehearsal in the afternoon of the concert with the imported orchestral principals. Woodhouse led for these concerts for many years both for Gill and myself. Now began in earnest my career with orchestras and choirs and it was one of the most productive periods of my musical life.

The Alexandra Choral Society had a large library both for choir and orchestra, a hangover from the Palace days, so that there was a whole corpus of classical choral music to hand. The season was from about September to May or June with six or eight weeks rehearsals for each concert. I learned to space out the 'old favourites' with new works so that the repertoire presented all the classics and a goodly spread of new works to keep up the interest of the choir and interest the younger recruits. The choir was rather old-fashioned in outlook and there were many grey hairs among them.

During this period I managed to conduct Gounod's *Redemption*, Mendelssohn's *Hymn of Praise* and *Elijah*, Bach's *B Minor Mass*, German's *Merrie England*, Holst's *Choral Symphony*, concert version of scenes from Wagner's *Parsifal*, even Beethoven's *Missa Solemnis* (which was a terrible strain for the 'old dears' to learn), Elgar's *Gerontius* and *The Apostles*.

As time went on, I found it necessary to break away from the Choral Society outlook and introduced the stage performance of Boughton's *Bethlehem* with his daughter playing Gabriel. I got Frederick Woodhouse to produce this fine work and he took one of the chief parts, with Mabel Ritchie as Mary. Mabel later changed her name to Margaret and became a famous singer, with Britten writing a special part for her in *Albert Herring*. She was also engaged to sing the Mozart *C Minor Mass* with Beecham and the Beethoven *Choral Symphony* with Krips. I recall saying to my friends "Of all people, Ritchie is the most unsuitable singer I can possibly imagine for Beethoven IXth...." I proved to myself how wrong one can be - for her performance was superb. I learned that purity of voice would carry much more than sheer weight. She managed to soar above choir, orchestra and other soloists in a superb performance. But, of course, this was some years later. The *Bethlehem* performances were a lesson to me in many respects. The Committee backed me to the hilt over my ambition to stage the work but I nearly wrecked my own ambitions by choosing the Secretary to play Joseph. This is not an exacting role and he showed himself willing, and his wife more so. I knew he had a most reliable teacher, he was just right as regards physical weight and had a lovely mellow, sensitive and sympathetic voice. But, alas, as rehearsals went on, it was evident he had no brain at all for the job. His acting was as naught and he couldn't remember to sing and move. After some time I had to engage another singer of experience to replace him. Great indeed was the enmity between us, more particularly as his wife was exceedingly angry and merciless in her venom towards me. But I couldn't risk the performances which were announced. The other difficulty was that we had to be sure this venture would not lead us into bankruptcy. The Chairman had friends in the Scout movement who were anxious to purchase a Scout Park and we felt it might be a good thing if we could give these performances in aid of the Scout Park. The Commissioners of the local Scout movement were keen on the idea and we counted on their cooperation to provide scouts as ticket agents, stewards etc. These, we felt, would guarantee us an audience - especially as we were doing a series of performances including a matinée on the Saturday afternoon. I had no difficulty now as the Choir enjoyed dressing up and liked the music. The staging was simple but effective and Woodhouse was a good and popular producer. Geoffrey Dunn was Herod and his characterisation was known in London as being both artistic and unique, treating Herod as a long, tall, thin man rather than a sort of Falstaff one had always imagined Herod to be. As time went on, having left all the business arrangements to the Chairman and Committee, horror struck me with a vengeance. The Scout movement had not bestirred themselves one iota. No tickets had been sold and no publicity had been given to the enterprise. We ourselves managed to stave off the catastrophe by giant exertions on our part. But here was a lesson I learned at one blow - never to trust anyone, see to everything myself. This became my motto, but of course I *did* trust people and had to leave things to others, but it never worked. So I became more and more insistent on seeing to everything.

During this period of conducting the choral repertoire with this Society, I found myself also conducting the North London

Orchestral Society. I had previously appeared with them as a soloist in a concerto and, when the conductor retired from the scene, I took over the weekly rehearsals and seasons' concerts. There was a goodly number of amateur players but again I had to learn that all they wanted was to play and little else. Again, the Society had been of long standing and had a fair repertoire of classics. We gave concerts and some of the pieces I can recall as they were played under interesting conditions to say the least. Schumann's B flat Symphony was in the repertoire and we gave a really fine performance of this in one of their regular church halls. I recall I was suffering from a terrible toothache at that concert. The Schumann Symphony is something of a sweet piece anyway, and my teeth did not enjoy it any the more. My friend Willy Busch played the Beethoven C Minor Concerto on one occasion. We rehearsed Mozart, Haydn, Beethoven, Mendelssohn so that I got to know well the symphonies and overtures of these masters. The Saint-Saëns 'Cello Concerto appeared in one of our programmes, played wonderfully by Marie Dare. She was a fine player of the Chamber Concert era of which I was a part and I recall the wonderful scale from bottom C to top C in the treble clef which the soloist is called upon to perform in this work. Freda Townsend was another soloist in the Liszt Lorelei and Wagner songs. Also Kersy, the young lady of immense talent who was, later on, one of our soloists. I learned early on that a violinist or 'cellist was cheaper than a pianist as a piano had to be hired in the latter case. It was great experience to learn how to conduct symphonies, overtures and concerti. A goodly number of light pieces was included - Elgar's Serenade for Strings etc. - but again this is not popular with an amateur group who prefer to be 'at it' all the time - not like the professionals I met later on who preferred not to play. I was not very easy to get on with for I was rather out of patience with the foibles of jealousy that one experienced in the ranks of the amateur world.

My father was employed on late-night work at the newspaper office so that he couldn't play for me very often. I recall one of the trials that beset me was having to put up with bad clarinet players who were *bona fide* members of the orchestra. The first clarinet player was a wealthy man of very impressive mien with the shiniest bald head I have ever seen. He was a diamond merchant, very cultured and most charming. However, his bald head was by way of being a menace to him in draughty school rooms where we had rehearsals so he always wore a black trilby hat while he played. The second clarinet was a man one had to respect as he was the owner and editor of *Musical Opinion*. His tone was excruciating and one couldn't imagine how awful it was after being brought up with my father, whose tone was always musical. Should my father ever come to a rehearsal, he was set upon by the other clarinet players who wanted to know where he got his reeds and the lay of the mouthpiece and other silly matters. I learned how to do without certain instruments in an orchestra - for example that a bassoon would be omitted and replaced by a 'cello who also played in the tenor clef if required. Clarinets in C helped when an oboe was missing and like things became my habit of mind. I also learned that it was unwise to suggest that any players be loaned to any other amateur orchestra. There was a great gulf fixed between my Alexandra Choral Society Orchestra and the North London Orchestra. The nearest I ever got to getting them together was when a concert by the North London took place in the hallowed hall of the Northern Polytechnic in the Holloway Road on one occasion. During this period of activity, I was Organist and Choirmaster at East Finchley Church then moved to Wood Green. Here we had a delightful musical set up, but my vicar, the most unimaginative and sour-faced man I have met, reprimanded me on one occasion for having some boys sit in the men's stalls. Why have we got so many boys? We don't want a cathedral choir! When one knew how difficult it was to enlist boys anyway, I felt suddenly sick. In the holidays I wanted to get new music learned and went over in the summer time for a practice with the boys at 8. 30 in the morning so as not to interfere with their holiday play. One Good Friday, we did a fine performance of Nicholson's cantata *Saviour of the World*. I had a silly little two-manual organ and the pedals sloped away from me and the centre D was not in alignment. I rather enjoyed the limitations of this organ for the tone was sweet and, after all, my salary was advanced from £40 a year to £80 so I was well on the way.

Then I read in the *Daily Telegraph* that T C Fairbairn was about to produce a pageant performance at the Royal Albert Hall and was advertising for choir members to join. I had seen the wonderful Fairbairn production of *Hiawatha* done in costume by the Royal Choral Society. I was so thrilled at remembering that that I thought this producer, with his imaginative production, was just the sort of man with whom I would like to work. By this time, I had something of a reputation in London with the Alexandra Choral Society so when I went along and met him, with his manager Scott Millar, I was welcomed with enthusiasm as they thought I would be able to bring along my Alexandra Choral Society Choir and thus help them with the project. I was naive enough to think this might be so. I was very inexperienced in these matters. My choir was rather askance at the idea of joining in 'dressing up' activities. True the Royal Choral had made a success but they had their reputation and loyalty to their tradition. I did manage to recruit some singers to this and, as our weekly rehearsals did not seem to clash, I was glad to join Fairbairn.

Fairbairn had taken the City Temple Church for rehearsals and, as there was a large hall below the church, the set-up was convenient for rehearsals. The choral rehearsals were taken by a young conductor, Arthur Hammond, who was connected with opera productions. He sat at the piano with the chorus in the pews and went through the music phrase by phrase, almost with one finger. Listening to this for one or two rehearsals, I could stand it no longer and told Fairbairn that was not the way to rehearse a large choir. I had attended several rehearsals run by Henry Wood and felt Wood's way with choirs and orchestras was what was required. I had formed my own style of rehearsal on Wood's methods. Hammond's way, keeping three quarters of the choir waiting doing nothing while he rehearsed endlessly just one vocal line, was not to my taste and I suggested that Hammond do half the choir upstairs and I the other half in the hall below. I took the tenors and basses downstairs while Hammond pounded the piano with one finger for the sopranos and altos. This worked wonders for me and the choir for I set about the men with a will. The choir when I joined was only some fifty or sixty, but each rehearsal brought in more and more recruits so that, before long, we had a choir of some two or three hundred and it didn't stop at that. Nothing was organised in any way, except by the figureheads of Fairbairn and Scott Millar, who managed, with some stewards and book-keeping, to get some order into the registers. All this was in the early Autumn and it was fixed that in the Spring of the next year we should be ready for the first production. I don't know where the money came from, but, Fairbairn had a reputation as a producer and got some charitable organisations to sponsor the idea. The plan was to give fourteen performances in the fortnight with a matinée on the Saturday and only by reading the papers was one able to guess what was really going on behind the scenes. I got little or nothing for my services as a répétiteur but that didn't worry me in the slightest as I knew this was what I wanted to do and the people were those with whom I wanted to be. Gradually it leaked out that he had engaged the foremost singers of the day - Stiles Allen, Frank Titterton, Gladys Ripley and other people who regularly sang at the Albert Hall with the Royal Choral Society. The ballet was mentioned and names like Dolin and Markova bandied about. But my greatest joy was to learn that Albert Coates was to conduct.

I must expand somewhat about Albert Coates. He was one of my heroes at the time. While I was at school at Highgate, Cunningham Woods had attended a concert conducted by Coates, who was unknown to me by name or reputation. Woods was, most obviously, completely captivated by his personality and, at our rather dreary afternoon school singing classes, told us about the Englishman with Russian connections who had spent many years in Russia and had been at Covent Garden, sharing conducting with Nikisch. Woods expounded at great length about Coates and, at the end of the lesson, seeing me doubtless wide-eyed, gave me the programme of the concert he had attended and in which there was a photograph of Coates. This I kept for some years. Later on, I went to the Royal Academy of Music and attended the Royal Philharmonic concerts and, as things turned out, Coates was the conductor for the season. I heard many pieces conducted by him, including *Song of the High Hills* of Delius and music of Scriabin. I was overwhelmed by this personality. I recall Harold Bauer was the soloist in Beethoven's *Fourth Piano Concerto*, which made a memorable impression. But Coates, because of his gigantic size and obvious hold on the orchestra and audience, completely won my devotion. I lost sight of him when I took the piano so seriously and went to Vienna but now that I was back to 'normal' and trying to find my way about music in England, he appeared on my horizon. What impressed me was not only his great size but his handsome face and wonderful clothes. Only the best was good enough. To my eyes, he was the personification of what a great conductor should look like. He did not appear until the rehearsals were well prepared, for the poor choral people had, of course, to sing those complicated and often contrapuntal choruses by heart. Coates arrived and made a great impression on everyone. A large, somewhat lofty, but warm, personality surrounded him. He got Hammond to conduct and, in some instances, I conducted - rather unnerving - while he listened and did nothing but look and size up everything. Sometimes he ventured to direct from the side of the hall, a little bit like the *Chorale* at the end of the third chorus, and his spell on the choir was self evident. He soon tired of the sound of the piano accompaniment and told Fairbairn that he wanted organ accompaniment. As it was known I was an organist, I was bidden to climb up and play the accompaniments on what to me was a completely new instrument. They are not easy, by any manner of means. At this time, I was no organist, in the fully cultured meaning of the word but I had imagination and some facility as my musicianship produced the desired results. I became his orchestra. Later on we had floor rehearsals at the Albert Hall with an upright piano. Again I was bidden to ascend the mountainous heights to the organ loft and play that instrument, again one which I had never played before. The distance from the back of the Hall to the console was immense but nobody took the slightest heed of difficulties and I had to plough my way through all the difficulties imaginable.

Later on, I became in effect Chorus Master of the Choir and his assistant, taking choral rehearsals under his supervision. This was a wonderful experience for me. I recall on one occasion I was suffering from a terrible cold, feeling that the last thing I wanted to do, even in these exciting circumstances, was to take a rehearsal. However, I gave my mind to the task with a will. It was a floor rehearsal so all my wits were employed to cope with the moving chorus, giving them all the cues I could. As luck had it, a friend in the choir, seeing my difficulties and reading that some stimulant might be helpful, gave me some spirits. I am not sure what it was. Could it be white whisky or white brandy? I knew not and cared less - anything to give me some *joie de vivre*. So during the interval, I had a good drink. After the interval, somewhat refreshed, I again directed the rehearsal, in the middle of which Coates stopped the whole affair and reprimanded the chorus for not paying attention to me. He ended "Watch the beat.....Proctor is conducting MAGNIFI-CENTLY". There was a round of applause at this from the naughty choir.

Strange as it may seem, at no time have I had recourse to any stimulant before or during a rehearsal or concert. I felt it was a matter of honour to rely completely upon my own prowess, even against seemingly impossible odds.

At this stage, it may be of interest to recall some impressions of Coates. My sense of hero worship somewhat changed during my time with him and one must remember I knew him very intimately during the three or four years he was connected with the Fairbairn Choir. Unfortunately, his records on 78s have not been transcribed on to LPs. The sound of the orchestra has so immeasurably altered for the better that maybe the experts in this field will find some unwillingness to transfer these 78 sounds. It has been done for Elgar's conducting of his own works, with magnificent results but, of course, we have here a historical record that has value of its own. However, the Wagner records done by Coates are often of equal orchestral worth, but, alas, his reputation is not so high these days. He was at the zenith of his powers when I knew him and had an immense Wagnerian reputation. But there was some misman-agement. I understand he conducted a Wagner series of opera at Golders Green Hippodrome. I recall seeing the poster advertising this. I did not attend, for two reasons. I could not afford good seats and I felt the queuing up for the gallery seats was too much. Having heard all Wagner in Vienna, I did not think this discomfort was called for. Moreover the advertise-ments gave the impression that it was sold out. Only years afterwards did I learn that these performances were something of a 'flop'.

Coates was an enigma. It was said he had a Russian mother but he denied this in my hearing, for his mother's name was Gibson, or some such incongruous English name. Having been brought up in Russia, he was Russian in his ways and affected a 'foreign' accent which was engaging as well as quite unnecessary. His beat was wonderful and had a lovely swinging arm movement which was spacious and could excite players and singers considerably. He also had a very light touch so that delicate orchestral sounds emerged with much sensitivity. I never saw or heard him get angry but there was no doubt as to who was in charge. When I was working with him, his chief fault was this excessive power of generating excitement, which sometimes led to almost catastrophic results if the choir got out of hand. Certain things became memorable and remain so. That is, I feel, one of his shortcomings. There were peaks. With Toscanini, there were seldom peaks. The whole thing was a range of Alps. I recall, though I was not present, that Astra Desmond told me that when Coates was called upon to conduct Elgar's *Gerontius*, he knew not one note of the music. However, he gathered together all the soloists and friends and asked them to teach him the work. Astra told me that the 'moment', when it came, was the most shattering sound she had ever heard - and so it should be. She then told me that Coates 'nursed' the approach to this moment so carefully. I realised this was the secret and did likewise when it came my turn to direct this work. On the other hand, Sargent missed the effect completely in my view as he made an accelerando too soon and swiftly so that the climax was missed. It should sound like an oncoming railway engine, coming at you slowly, gathering momentum of its own that cannot be withheld. Coates was in every sense a Wagnerian conductor and, being brought up with Nikisch, he knew what a Wagnerian score meant. He attended one of my performances of *Faust* which I conducted at the Albert Hall and, very charmingly, he congratulated me. He told me he had learned from Sucher, and in one history, one can see the musical connections here. Everything that Coates conducted was on a Wagnerian scale and had the Wagnerian colour and outlook. This fitted a good deal of music - Elgar, even Dvořák, he did with success. The *B Minor Mass* was something of a travesty - thrilling to a considerable extent - and some musical friends in the Philharmonic Choir absolutely worshipped him for being able to 'tear the heart out of them' as they sang. Whether such 'heart tearing' is always in good taste must be considered. Some phrases from *Elijah* are still in my mind....but, of course, he pulled the music about, almost like elastic, to give the proper drama to the music for the Pageant performance production. The Baal choruses were terrifying to sing. The pace was unbelievable. The final Baal chorus was not two beats in a bar but *one*, so that the semiquavers of the orchestra could not be played at the pace, unless slurred. Likewise the 'fiery chariot' chorus was terribly fast and the choir were lashed into a frenzy of heat. Later, when I came to conduct the work with the LSO and my pace, while not as fast as Coates, was on the fast side, George Stratton took me aside in the artists' room during the interval of the rehearsal and explained that it was 'too fast'. I protested that nothing could be too fast for the LSO. He demonstrated the bowing across the strings and, in a flash, I saw the error of my ways and the obvious wonderful effect that Mendelssohn had in mind if the piece was played at the proper speed. From that moment I was conscious that my performance gained immeasurably by 'ditching' the Coates method of interpreting this passage. Bernard Shore, in his book about conductors, gives a true and vivid description of Coates. He was such a personality that anyone young and inexperienced, like myself, came under his influence, which was both good and bad. I had not the experience or the courage to question his musical vision. It took me a good time to sort out the questionable matters of good taste in his musical personality. A friend criticised him as 'attitudinising' - which was fair comment.

He was naughty on several occasions. When I asked him, at our first meeting when I was conducting, whether he would rather that I gave up the baton to him as I did not wish to presume that I would be expecting to conduct the rehearsals in his presence, he replied he was suffering from some stomach upset so would prefer me to conduct. When I next saw him a few days later, I perceived he had no knowledge of any stomach complaint during the past two days. Obviously, he only wanted to 'search out the land' and assess the conditions and ability of the choir. Had he told me this, I could at once have understood his attitude. It should have been a warning - I did not heed. He absented himself from some of the performances, although he had been engaged for the fourteen performances. Again it was a certain 'indisposition' given as the reason. I heard that on one occasion in Leeds at a Festival, he was 'indisposed' and could not conduct a concert which included the *Ninth Symphony* of Beethoven. He left the first part of the *Symphony* to some substitute or other. However, he was able to conduct the *Finale* and reap the reward that this choral *Finale* always gives to a conductor. I am inclined to think this 'indisposition' was a result of having read that morning a very bad criticism of a composition of his that he had conducted the previous evening. Coates had some talent for composition and tried to include some of his works in a programme. Personally, I had no high opinion of such music of his that I heard. But I respect anyone who has the mastery of an orchestra both as a conductor and composer.

The choir in *Elijah* was somewhat annoyed that Hammond conducted the performances when Coates did not appear, for they had formed an attachment to me which was somewhat evident. This reached a climax after the matinée performance which Hammond conducted. The entire chorus assembled in the arena and demonstrated, in no uncertain way, their devotion to my musical work. They called my name so insistently that I was called back from the exit doors, through which I was about to go out for the tea interval, and given a loud and vociferous ovation. This so unnerved Fairbairn and the Management that I was glad to get away into the fresh air and return only in time for the evening performance - I hoped, unnoticed. Hammond had been Coates' assistant and had prepared all the scores and band parts for him so knew the whole musical 'set-up' from the inside. At the dress rehearsal, Coates called out to him in tones which were heard by the entire cast "What do I do now? Have I finished with the big black book?" There were a great many pieces interwoven in the production from Mendelssohn's symphonies to an arrangement of the *Spring Song* danced by Markova in the ballet scene.

Those who have not witnessed these great pageant productions have no idea what 'liberties' were taken by both Coates and Fairbairn to produce a real Pageant production. It was not simply the dramatisation of the oratorio that took place, but both conductor and producer 'used' the work as a basis for their own performance and production. Just one instance will show what went on. The opening of Part Two is the denunciation of Elijah by Ahab. For the production in which the whole of the arena and orchestra stage was used for the performers, only the back small section was roped off to contain the orchestra and conductor. To get Ahab on the stage with his retinue, the stage was designed thus. Ahab was 'discovered on'. Seated on a throne at the apex of the stage, he was surrounded by his immediate court, some few attendants. He was to receive foreign potentates and their retinue, which was contrived by a procession from the front of the Hall, down the steps across the arena and up to the throne, where they arrayed themselves on either side of the King. Such a spectacle of colour and splendour had seldom been seen. The procession was startling from the first moment. It was led by a very tiny boy, followed by the most enormous figure of a sword bearer one can imagine. His height was further enhanced by being crowned by a plume of feathers some eighteen inches high, so that this figure, preceded by the tiny boy, evoked such astonishment in the audience that they broke into applause. I forget what symphony was played for this procession, but it was apt by being light and airy so that the procession was in no way a heavy or weighty spectacle. When the stage was completely full of these 'visitors' to King Ahab, he commanded that the ballet should perform. This they did for about fifteen minutes and then Part Two of the oratorio was resumed with the entrance of Elijah who denounced Ahab. The Queen's part *Hast thou not heard* is somewhat undramatic, being written for a contralto in the low registers. Here Coates and Fairbairn - and I suspect it was Fairbairn's insistence as he always maintained that the producer had absolute authority, even above Coates - transposed the part up an octave for more effective delivery. This was just a small but typical attitude to the score that Fairbairn ruthlessly used to his own ends. Purists, of course, wrung their hands in horror and denounced Fairbairn as a showman and a non musician. But the thing *worked* - though his reputation was a source of trouble in the profession. I myself, when I made overtures to Novello to stage Elgar's *The Kingdom* later on, had to assure them that Fairbairn would be having no part whatsoever in my production.

I must say that there was no aspect of the theatre that Fairbairn did not know about. He produced operas for Beecham in the early days and his knowledge of Wagner was immense. His wife was a singer of some reputation and sang Venus in Germany and was highly complimented by the Germans who could not understand how an English lady could sing in such impeccable German, until she had to admit that German was her *Mutter sprache*. Her maiden name was Toni Seiter and she called her son, in true Wagnerian fashion, Siegfried - a charming fellow who, with his brother, rendered Fairbairn service in his production.

Fairbairn consolidated the choir in the Fairbairn Choir and then later consolidated the whole affair into a democratic society with a Committee and a Chairman. Up to this point, the Choir and the whole production was a complete dictatorship. I have to record, with sorrow, with the foundation of the Society, with proper constitution, the rot set in. Even I recall with horror that the Society thought they could stage some production or other without Fairbairn. But I anticipate somewhat as this is supposed to be my own life story so I had better keep events in some sort of order.

[Author's note: I have in my possession a programme of The King of Glory - A Pageant of the Passion - produced by TC Fairbairn. Charles conducted all the performances of this Pageant which ran from February 15 to 27 1937. Fairbairn's wife, Toni Seiter, played the part of 'The Blessed Mother'.]

7 - RUTLAND BOUGHTON

A good many years have passed since the writing of this book first began and now it seems perhaps a good idea to write some reminiscences of people I have met - as it were 'on the side'; but making the whole tapestry of life when considered in context.

Rutland Boughton (1878-1960) seems a likely person to engage the interest of readers who have no personal knowledge of the man, except one who is often declared to be among one of the worthies to be considered when one writes about English music and English opera in particular. He was an odd character in the history of English music. He didn't 'fit in' as one should, by being a student at one of the colleges and going on to university or a cathedral environment. He was an operatic person, an operatic composer. But what an anomaly - an English composer of opera where we had no operatic tradition or even an opera house where English opera could be fostered. Covent Garden was the centre of operatic life, but imported opera. Except for the Carl Rosa company there were no operatic societies except amateur ones, probably begun by some enthusiastic person but which 'died the death' because of economic ruin for themselves and their founders. Bernard Shaw called Boughton 'the perfect Wagnerite'. But, unlike Wagner, he had no prince to support him or build him an opera house to his design, foster a school of Wagnerian singers and orchestral playing of perfection under Richter and the like. But Boughton was a Wagnerian in imagination and achievement, within his own limitations and the limitations from which he suffered because of the conditions that existed in his time. He always had operatic ambitions that would come to naught - until, by chance, everything happened as a miracle to put him in the centre of an operatic stage of his own design.

This was the performance of his opera *The Immortal Hour*. I venture to suggest that without the perfect conditions that presented themselves, as it were by a miracle, it would have had no success at all. In fact it ran consecutively for several months with capacity houses in the worst possible venue one could imagine and brought critics and the public alike to worship Boughton as the composer of the age.

What were these circumstances that so favoured our composer? They make a very strange catalogue of circum- stances indeed. The first performance in Glastonbury was in 1914. The music, both quiet and simple in structure, makes an immediate appeal so that, in the period of the First World War, it was just the soothing effect needed to put some serenity into the minds of people who had been greatly disturbed by the energies of the war. The fact that the war was waged in France made it more poignant for the families left behind as they had to endure the privations at home and the anxiety of their relatives fighting in a foreign land under what they had found out to be intolerable conditions of trench warfare. All this was in addition to the dangers on the high seas. So the effect of their relatives being 'away from home' made the situation in the opera more vivid than it would have been in peace time. 'Going to the theatre' in the West End could be considered something of a luxury which, in the circumstances, would be quite unacceptable. But to attend an opera in the English language, which could be followed (even if not wholly understood) and listened to without much call on the attention and intellectual stamina required for Wagner, was more to the taste of the music-loving public. There was, too, the 'snob value', which ranks high in the requirements of the intelligentsia. They had to go to one of the least romantic theatres in London, seek it out in one of the least romantic parts of London's theatre land (in fact, it wasn't in theatre land at all) and this in itself gave an air of 'know-all' about the venture - in short 'snob value'. From the producer's point of view, here was the perfect answer to deal with the war situation. It required no great symphonic orchestra for the orchestra pit. A handful of good players could cope with the score. The chorus did not require great masses of people with loud operatic range of vocal power such as is required for Verdi. The soloists need not be those grandiose persons of heroic build as required for Wagner, Verdi and the classical masters of operatic productions. A few singers of moderate vocal power, whose words could be heard and sung with musical expertise, was all that was required. The score need not be conducted by an operatic conductor as required for Italian, German or French music. A good musician would 'do' and, in fact, the composer himself conducted on many occasions. A two act opera, such as this, would allow the scene to be changed and the audience refreshed and both could be accomplished within the twenty minute interval. In short, one can ask 'what is an opera?' and the answer would be 'anything as unlike The Immortal Hour as can be imagined'. The opera can be sung by the same people night after night, without undue effort and fatigue. The singers were first class, the orchestra equally fine and the chorus sensitive and musically alert. The result was that at once Boughton became the operatic composer of the day....in England.

Before The Immortal Hour, he had already made a start trying to establish an operatic centre in Glastonbury, similar in ideals to Wagner's Bayreuth, using the Arthurian legends as Wagner had used the Nibelungen. So it was quite proper for Shaw to call Boughton 'the perfect Wagnerite' as Boughton founded an opera tradition in Glastonbury, wrote the libretti, composed the music, his wife designed the scenery and he produced the accompaniment - not with a symphony orchestra but himself playing the piano.

Now this practice was not imitating Wagner but following Wagner's ideals within the scope of village hall conditions. Boughton had no patron and the state gave him no help. To see Boughton as a perfect Wagnerite might seem childish but to ignore this vision was to see Boughton only as a trite imitator of a great master, with no effect whatsoever, whereas Boughton became a great operatic initiator for opera and music drama in England.

The contrast, which is so vivid as to be completely ignored, is to notice how Holbrooke imitated Wagner, trying to produce great imitations of the *Ring*, by using Welsh folklore legends. The result was abortive, as the Gold Ring of Wagner was not to be superseded by the brass ring of Holbrooke, although the music and the orchestration are first class.

The abortive attempts of Boughton to create festivals of English music-drama were heroic and it is sad to think that the English-speaking race cannot yet see that the originality of Boughton is akin to the originality of Stanley Spencer, who did not imitate the great Italian painters but was true to his own genius and produced works of great originality and lasting effect.

These aspects of Boughton are part of music history in England and I will leave the matter at this point. I have enlarged the situation so that readers may see the environment in which I found myself later on in the story. There is a further aspect that

I must bring forward and that is that Boughton was a rabid Socialist and belonged to the Communist group of Socialists of his time. Shaw we know was a Socialist by ideals but managed to live a very successful and rich life, as far removed from the Socialist tenets of his belief as is possible. Boughton tried to live by his Socialist tenets but, in the end, had to accept help from the 'Establishment' he so abhorred when, at the age of sixty, he was awarded a Civil List pension. In his defence I told one of my friends of this honour and reward that he had been given, only to be told, in no uncertain way by my capitalist and 'Establishment' friend, that it was in effect a disgrace as it proved Boughton was incapable of managing his own affairs in a more prudent way. Such is the great division in the theory of political rectitude.

Boughton's family became somewhat involved in my family relations as, eventually, my cousin married his daughter. This brought me into the circle - or, at least, the outer perimeter of the circle.

It so happened that I was conducting a performance of Elgar's *The Apostles* with a choral/orchestral society I had been appointed to direct. Unknown to me at the time, Boughton attended the performance and subsequently wrote a critique of it, making the point that I had excelled by making this oratorio a living drama for the audience, rather than a mere performance of a sacred oratorio. In due time, I read this critique which pleased and encouraged me greatly as it spoke of the very fact I had tried to portray - that this oratorio was, in fact, an operatic music-drama without a stage presentation. The fact that this article appeared in a railway socialist-minded paper was of little interest to me, although had it appeared in *The Times* it would have brought me some notoriety. The fact was that this critique had been written by a real musician and that far outweighed all other considerations. From that moment, as far as Boughton was concerned, I was a marked man, who could conduct an oratorio with sufficient musical understanding to make the drama live in the minds of the audience. Also I was capable of directing large choral and orchestral forces with great effect.

Later on, I found that Boughton was presenting a Festival of his works at Bath and I forget how it came about but, for a week's daily rehearsals and week's performances, I was engaged as Chorus Master. In lieu of fees I was given free hospitality at a guest house, as were the other persons concerned in this enterprise.

Boughton had such incredible charm and honesty of purpose that he generated great loyalty to himself and his enterprise, which included the best singers of the day in the field of opera and oratorio. Of these, some were great Elgarites - not least myself. He gathered such people as Steuart Wilson, Astra Desmond, Frederick Woodhouse and Elsie Suddaby. A few long-standing friends of Boughton, who were amateur singers, also had parts. The professional soloists were often to be heard in the Three Choirs Festivals.

It was fascinating to be brought into this musical environment. My personal relationship with Boughton was always on a most friendly basis. He was often 'difficult' and many considered him to be completely 'impossible'. Being a Socialist of the most rabid type, a dedicated composer of operas, a very self-willed person and something, too, by way of a genius, if by that term one accepts a person of original turn of mind, it is not difficult to see that he was not 'easy to get on with'. In describing him to my parents, I could only describe him as like a rat. This term was not used in any disrespectful manner. The attributes one associates with creatures are unique and not necessarily evil or vicious. It is unfortunate that the human race has not yet learned to accept all creation on its own terms but must define things in its own human terms, which is often quite out of keeping with reality. Many so-called dangerous and vicious animals are not so by nature, but only if provoked and thought of in human terms. I am inclined to think that female rats make good mothers to their offspring and probably male rats are good fathers and spouses to their partners. Boughton was swift of thought as such, vivacious both in thought and deed. In trying to produce his operatic works, circumstances made it essential for him to write out by hand all the vocal scores, pianoforte score, full score, band parts and vocal chorus parts. These were the days before duplicating machines had been invented or before photocopying was the normal procedure for supplying music for performers. The labour of writing alone was a gigantic task, which he accepted as a matter of course. He couldn't afford to engage copyists. Published music of his was almost non-existent. It is true that *The Immortal Hour* was accepted by a publisher, likewise the choral music-drama founded on a mediaeval play, *Bethlehem*, which was successful with the discerning musical public and had short seasons of performances in London and elsewhere.

My personal contacts with Boughton began in real earnest when he initiated his Bath Festival. (Later, under Menuhin, this became a fashionable and expert organisation.) I travelled by train to Bath and in the same carriage was a young man of about my own age who talked with animation about many things. When asked about my own interests, I explained with swelling pride about my engagement at Bath for the Boughton Festival of Opera, to which I was appointed Chorus Master. His interest was not quite up to my expectations as he was unaware of music to a great degree and had never heard of Boughton. I was momentarily deflated but soon regained my self-esteem when we arrived at Bath. He was going on further. I looked around for indications of the Festival and expected to see large banners in the streets, posters and such like. I saw nothing. I thought it wise to seek out the actual Festival Hall, which was called the Pavilion. Knowing Bath to be of Roman origins, I felt that Pavilion was probably in keeping with the classical name for an Assembly. Enquiries led me to the public gardens and cricket ground and there, amidst this rural setting, was the Pavilion. To my surprise and dismay I found this was merely a modern hall, such as one finds in the midst of a rural village or small town. I estimated that an audience of about 200 would be accommodated. Inside there was no evidence of a theatre at all, except for a curtain which divided the audience from the stage. The entrance was no different to that found in any village hall. Somewhat deflated, I found the lodgings. Here was a fairly large dining room and my bedroom was the usual sort of place one finds in any small guest house. Subsequently, I met Boughton, some of his family, Christopher Ede, who I found to be a most interesting friend, a cousin of mine and other musical friends.

We were ruled by a strict timetable with places and times for rehearsal and my job was to train the chorus in the new opera. The tenor was an amateur of good voice and much enthusiasm and Boughton had used him in past productions. Astra Desmond, renowned for her singing in the Three Choirs Festival with Elgar and Steuart Wilson, and a wonderful contralto whose husband, as an artist, produced the scenic effects, all contributed to a musical atmosphere which was unique.

Boughton himself directed all the events leading up to the performance and conducted the performances himself. There was a small orchestra, built round the Boyd Neel string orchestra which had, by then, made a name for itself and for Boyd. I concluded that Boughton, with his eyes on the future, had engaged the orchestra for this purpose and did so with the promise that Neel would conduct *The Immortal Hour* performances. The orchestra was made up of skilled players and I was instructed to play the bass drum, which had no great expert requirement beyond knowing 'where to come in'. This I was helped to do by my companion, Milner, a good musician who I believe gained for himself a good reputation as a conductor later. For the first performance of the new opera at Bath, Bernard Shaw came down, sat in the front row and listened attentively. He was about four feet from me so I could observe him during the long 'tacet' bars in my bass drum part. Sitting bolt upright, never moving a muscle, he was as fresh at the end of the performance as he was at the beginning. Somewhere in the second act, I had to go backstage to conduct the chorus in a fine unaccompanied section. I knew the music could be effective so in rehearsal I did my utmost to make it so. One of the performances was broadcast and I did my best to make the performance telling. At the end of the performance, Boughton congratulated me on the section, saying it was the best part of the performance and I was duly 'chuffed'. He did, nonetheless, express the opinion that this was out of keeping with the rest of the opera. I have tried to understand this situation ever since.

At the end of the season of performances, it was obvious that Boughton would be out of pocket by the enterprise. This was chiefly on account of the Musicians' Union who insisted that very week that they would put up their prices for orchestral musicians so that the original contract Boughton had made was for far less money than was now to be paid. Came pay day and a trestle table was erected in the hall with three persons sitting behind. The players had to file past the three and identify themselves, from the second person collect the fees and, in front of the third person was a pudding basin of adequate size to collect such monies as the players could afford to return as a donation to reimburse Boughton for the Festival expenses.

After this enterprise, Boughton set up a scheme to produce his operas in London in a modest way. He did all he could to engage my enthusiasm. This was forthcoming but I was very anxious not to be the victim of mismanagement or commit myself to anything in a financial enterprise for which I had not, in my mind, an adequate guarantee of success. I am happy to say that Boughton's enterprise evaporated. Later, Steuart Wilson had a court case which he won and on the strength of his award for damages, he used the money in a most generous and altruistic manner to put on a new opera of Boughton at the Winter Gardens theatre in London. Of all the theatres in London to choose, I would have thought the Winter Gardens the least suitable. Nevertheless he obtained good singers for the chorus and good soloists including Arthur Fear, a young man of considerable ability and manly beauty I had often seen and heard at the Royal Academy of Music where he was a fellow student. Steuart conducted, Christopher Ede (from Bath days) was the stage manager and stage director. Boughton was the overall producer. I was engaged to work as Chorus Master and this I did with determined ardour and I devoted my energies to this. During the rehearsals, Arthur Hammond had been engaged by Coates at Covent Garden for a short season to produce two operas, one being the first performance of Coates' opera *Mr Pickwick*, a subject after my own heart. Hammond asked me to go to Covent Garden to see him, the outcome of which was that I was to be Chorus Master and generally be responsible for the music of the Coates opera, which the composer himself would conduct. This seemed like an opportunity not to be missed, but I was tied up with Wilson and my allegiance to him was secure and binding. I therefore sought his advice. It was generous. He said he would release me from my contract with him but, at the same time, warned me of certain dangers in the new venture that I had not quite realised - but he would not stand in my way. I gave much thought to the dilemma and decided in favour of Wilson and not Covent Garden. On reflection, I did the right thing because Wilson became a lifelong friend. My Coates/Hammond association evaporated into thin air after the short season.

There was, however, a solution that put the responsibility beyond me. As the first performance of the Wilson/Boughton drew near, having trained the chorus to almost performing standard, I became a victim of influenza, which made it impossible to leave my bed - even to attend the first performance for which I had done so much work.

The results of these two enterprises were as naught. The Boughton opera was never repeated and likewise, Coates' *Mr Pickwick* died the death as the opera that did not 'take on' - and I never heard of it again. Strangely enough, the musical comedy of the same name became a great success in London with Harry Secombe in the name part and there were very many performances of *Mr Pickwick* in this context.

Coates seemed to find no adequate niche for his conducting talents and went to Johannesburg, South Africa, where a heart condition put an end to what had been, some of the time, a gigantic career in conducting.

8 - ROYAL CONCERTS

St Cecilia, being the Patron Saint of music, deserves some mention and, while I am not qualified to give a history of the St Cecilia concerts (for all these facts can be gleaned from various histories available to the reader) the beginnings of the present day Royal Concerts being connected with St Cecilia, might be of some interest.

My own connection can be called amusing and, at the same time, somewhat unrecorded in the annals of English music. In my youth, it was arranged to hold a St Cecilia concert at the Royal Albert Hall. For this occasion, a great number of amateur musicians formed an orchestra and a great number of amateur singers formed a choir. The whole affair appears, in retrospect, odd - to say the least - for the concert was conducted by Harvey Grace. Grace was a very erudite musician, who later became organist and choirmaster at Chichester Cathedral. His book on Bach's organ works is valuable and highly respected. He was also the editor of the *Musical Times*, a respected monthly magazine which contained valuable articles on current musical affairs and representatives sent in reviews of performances abroad. The advertisements had a special value to organists, giving vacancies of organists' posts and the goodly number of private professional advertisements of teachers and correspondence courses formed a valuable *corpus* for musicians.

The organists' world featured very largely in the magazine, most probably fostered by Harvey Grace. The Royal College of Organists reported not only its monthly events but also the names of successful candidates for the Associateship and Fellowship diplomas. By and large the magazine was looked upon as the house magazine of Novellos, who specialised in church music publications. In reasonably recent years, the magazine was issued in two volumes which constituted over the years a goodly account of the happenings in the musical world at that time.

Returning to the St Cecilia concert, it will be seen that the organisation, with Grace as conductor, was connected with Novellos in some large measure. The whole affair was amateur in the extreme - so much so that I myself played violin in the orchestra. The music was well within my capacities (which were not great) which gives some indication of the standard of difficulty of the very amateurish music performed. I recall with much clarity of mind that Plunket Greene was the soloist. Of all the soloists to sing at the Royal Albert Hall, I can imagine no one less suitable. He was an advanced age, in his seventies, immaculate in evening dress and of such expertise that he could 'put over' very vividly any song he sang. His voice was small by any standards but pure in sound so that it may have carried in the half-empty hall on this occasion. He turned to the orchestra to repeat an encore so that those behind him could see and hear his presentation which had escaped them as earlier he had faced the audience.

Soon after the end of World War Two, when there was something of a revival of patriotism as peace became a challenge to activity, it was brought to the notice of musicians that whereas the film industry and the variety theatre enjoyed Royal patronage at an annual performance in aid of charity connected with their profession, there was no recognised

Royal Concert. A committee was formed with members including various musicians and organisations that were active in those times and I was invited to attend the inaugural meeting. This was chaired by Steuart Wilson and no better chairman could have been elected. He had a keen brain, was a distinguished musician, well-known by all performing musicians, and he had a charm of manner which was very evident to us but of which he himself was completely unaware. His quiet sense of humour made any meeting pleasant and to the purpose. The King (George VI) and Queen were mentioned as the Royal Patrons one should seek and, if possible, try and arrange their royal presence at a concert. Steuart Wilson was aware of the strain of the war years on the King and Queen and felt that to call on them would be an imposition that should be considered with due regard for their great efforts during those years. Steuart turned to the meeting and said we ought to regard the heavy responsibilities of both the King and Queen, for "they are always opening or shutting something or other". The meeting pointed out that the whole enterprise really relied upon Royal Patronage if it were to be a success.

I forget the dates but I believe that the first Royal Concert was at the Royal Festival Hall recently opened by King George VI and that Queen Elizabeth II, in the year of her Accession, was the first monarch to patronise the Royal Concert. It was agreed that lots should be cast for the first participants and it so happened that the London Symphony Orchestra was the orchestra so engaged and the Alexandra Choir the choir. Malcolm Sargent was elected the conductor as it was felt that he was the outstanding conductor for such a concert that required more than the usual ordinary 'rule of thumb' organisation that had so often been the forerunner of lacklustre concerts of many such occasions. The programme was planned to include many British composers and it was proposed that I should conduct my own choir, the Alexandra

Choir, in a work for unaccompanied voices. I could see through the plan which was to allow only Sargent to perform orchestral/choral works or he would be deprived of the office of being the one and only conductor. I was permitted to conduct my own choir as an item, the orchestra having left the platform during the interval and my item to open part two of the programme. The engineering of this was of much personal hurt, but I was satisfied that my choir and myself were both represented and that must suffice. The choir also sang for Sargent the first movement of Vaughan Williams' *Sea Symphony*. For my item, I had to search for a ten minute work for unaccompanied choir. It was indeed a daunting and arduous search. I visited all the publishers and went through dozens and dozens of pieces. There were many unaccompanied heavy classical works or church pieces for choir that would 'do' for a service but not for what I felt would be a festive Royal Concert. After many hours, I came across Healey Willan's first class setting of a Song of Praise founded on *Lasst uns erfreuen*, the well-known chorale sung in many churches to *Ye Watchers and Ye Holy Ones*. This was exactly what was needed. The 'tune' was well-known, the setting adroitly done, the treatment of the voices expertly devised and the work ended with a good climax. Healey Willan's name was known to me as a church musician for many years and he had been organist at a church in Hammersmith with a fine musical tradition and a very fine Willis organ. In fact, I myself at one time aspired to the post, but was not successful in being appointed. I knew Willan had emigrated to Canada and I understood had made much of a fine reputation there. I was not aware of his age and feared he might be dead - not that this mattered as most good composers succumb to that eventuality before they get their music performed in this country. I wrote to the University of Toronto to make enquiries and found he was still alive and had, as I believed, made a high reputation for himself. I got in touch with him and told him I had chosen his piece for the Royal Concert and that my suggestion was accepted and that I was to conduct the work. I rather feared that as the composer was alive, it might be thought proper to invite him to conduct his own work. So I was careful to present him with the full state of affairs at once - ie that I would conduct the work. His response was most cordial and he arranged to attend the concert. Further he appeared with me on the platform and we were both presented to the Queen during the interval. The performance of his piece was quite first class and Titterton, the Secretary, said "He will never hear it like that again".

After the concert, the chief musicians and members who organised the concert were asked to a reception by Lady Ravenscroft who was the Honorary Treasurer of the Musicians' Benevolent Fund, on account of that organisation being the chief benevolent fund of the profession and who had, in effect, brought the Royal Concert into being. The reception was marked by many distinguished guests: Laurence Olivier, Charles Chaplin and Vivien Leigh being the most notable.

This Royal Concert was tied up with St Cecilia's Day, which had to be revised later on as the two celebrations made life difficult for those who wished to attend both the Royal Concert and the St Cecilia service at St Sepulchre's Church, Holborn - or, as it is sometimes called, the Church of the Holy Sepulchre. Personally I have always had a very happy regard for this Church on many counts.

Sir Sydney Nicholson, Organist and Choirmaster at Westminster Abbey, left that post and founded the School of English Church Music, which later became the Royal School of Church Music. At the time of its foundation, the School had a resident choir of boys and the men's voices were of students of the College, so providing a complete choir of trebles, altos, tenors and basses. Harry Barnes was the choirmaster and the

School was resident in a large house in Chislehurst. The School had a chapel with a small Harrison organ. I think regular daily services were sung in the School. The object was to train organists in the history and performance of the English School of church music as there had been no proper school for that purpose, although Trinity College of Music in London, (now one of the accepted Colleges of music education with such other academies as the Royal Academy of Music, the Royal College of Music and others) was originally founded in 1872 with this end in view. It broadened its curriculum to embrace other disciplines so that it has now become a conservatoire with no special interests except the general higher education in music. As stated, the School was created to train organists and choirmasters in the tradition of English church music and this was done by having teaching and experience provided by tutors within the School. It was also the intention for the Choir to visit churches throughout the country to try and encourage them to realise the tradition of English church music in services and to demonstrate what results could be achieved within their own parishes.

Once a week the Chislehurst School Choir came up to London to St Sepulchre's Church for a short rehearsal and to sing Evensong. This was to allow organists and choirmasters to see and hear Nicholson rehearse the Choir and accompany the services. These services were to me a revelation - not so much because of the expertise of the Choir or organist, for remember I was brought up in a good environment at St James, Muswell Hill and Highgate School. It was a demonstration of humility and awareness of a great man. I personally think of Nicholson as one of the great ones in English music. It was quite wonderful to see him taking a rehearsal of about twelve to fifteen people and playing a small organ which was installed behind the choir (before the now reconstructed organ with its ornamental case was rescued from the demolition of the great instrument which had been there before on the West wall). To see this great man, who had played and directed the music at Westminster Abbey, perched on an organ bench before a tiny, although musical, instrument, was a deeply moving experience which I never forgot. I met this same sense of modesty or complete lack of 'side', which had so moved me, once again when I saw Schweitzer at St Margaret's, Westminster, where he was giving a recital with the Bach Cantata Club. He was standing before the concert completely unselfconscious, looking into the audience to see if there were any friends he would recognise. These two experiences made a deep impression and brought forth a musical event later on which I shall relate as the opportunity arises.

This posed a great problem for me, although the answer was really quite simple. Certain occasions before the public demand a form of behaviour which is not acceptable, say, in church. The concert hall, which became eventually the centre of my musical life, demands a form of presentation which could be summed up in the axiom 'Modesty will get you nowhere'. On reflection, I recall with something like a shudder when I remember the occasion at Queen's Hall. I was engaged by the London Symphony Orchestra to conduct the great Bach *B Minor Mass*. I need not go into how this invitation was brought about. All the soloists had been engaged and I had two orchestral rehearsals - an unprecedented situation in those days. One rehearsal was with the soloists and orchestra and the second with the Choir (the first appearance of the Alexandra Choir I had founded) and orchestra. All seats were sold. I recall Lloyd George was in the audience. The occasion was the very imminent possibility of war, the time was 3 pm and the day was Good Friday. All this led to the concert being an immensely moving and awe-inspiring occasion. The final *Dona Nobis Pacem* was sung and played and directed by me with tremendous fervour, which made applause seem both unwarranted and unwelcome. I left the platform without bowing to the audience, in spite of the great applause the performance had generated, only to be barred from making my way from the podium to the exit by Mary Jarred, the most excellent contralto soloist, who indicated that I would not be permitted to leave the platform until I had made a conventional bow to the audience in response to the applause, which was prolonged and vigorous. This was a lesson I had to learn. Conventional behaviour is a reality that must be observed or the result may well be interpreted as bad manners, gaucherie or wanton misbehaviour.

Later on, when I had to take Sargent's place at the Royal Albert Hall to conduct some fourteen concerts, I found this exercise got the respect and goodwill of an audience at the end of a performance. In fact so adroitly did he 'manage' the audience and applause that he was often thought to be a 'showman'. I recall a Toscanini concert which my father attended. I had been out to supper as the guest of a distinguished conductor and I mentioned Toscanini. This was an unpardonable *faux pas*; one should never mention another conductor's name in the presence of any other conductor. My host was no exception and dismissed Toscanini as a showman. I was deeply hurt as I placed him above all others. With rather hurt feelings, I asked my father if he thought Toscanini a showman. Very uncharacteristically, my father did not answer at once, then said emphatically "No.....but it was a good show".

Here concludes the autobiographical section of this book.

Chapter 2

THE ALEXANDRA CHOIR

It is not my intention to write a lengthy and detailed history of the Alexandra Choir as that is not the purpose of this book. However, it is very important that some facts about this be recorded as it was one of Charles Proctor's major pieces of work during his life. The history of music in war-time London would not be complete unless it recorded faithfully and accurately the part played by the Alexandra Choir - for, behind the mere announcement of a 'Concert by the Alexandra Choir', there exists a story of one of the most courageous organisations of the times. The story, as it unfolded, was one of faith and courage, not only for those responsible for the organisation of the Choir but of the members themselves, who braved the dangers of the London Blitz at its worst.

After his death, I found two pages of an article which Charles had written about the beginnings of the Alexandra Choir. Subsequent pages have been lost - so his article stops in mid-sentence. The remaining information I have gleaned from other sources. I start by quoting the two pages that he left:

"There are so many misconceptions about the origins of the Alexandra Choir that perhaps these misconceptions might be put to rights if I outline the real story as it was lived.

I had for many years been the conductor of the Alexandra Choral and Orchestral Society, formerly conducted by Allen Gill. This Society was originally the Alexandra Palace Choral and Orchestral Society, being at that time connected with that place. It was housed at the Alexandra Palace..... where, in the large auditorium, monthly concerts were produced with a choir of several hundred singers and players. These programmes were of the usual run of choral concerts of their time, but Elgar's oratorio *The Dream of Gerontius* had its first performance in that hall under Gill. [It had, of course, received many performances throughout England by this time.] World War I shattered the organisation there and the place became a hospital for the wounded and no music was performed.

After World War I, the Palace was resuscitated to a degree but, by that time, the Musical Society had emigrated to a good-sized hall at the North London Polytechnic, Holloway Road. A good-sized stage with a good organ provided the Society with a venue for continuing its concerts on the same lines as before. It had a degree of success under Gill, in its new surroundings....but Gill became somewhat unreliable in his work, owing to age, and the Committee saw dangers ahead. They engaged me as a possible conductor, should Gill fail in his exertions. He started the new series unaware of the 'safety measures' that had been implemented....but, later on, he knew that 'in the wings' I was available to assist him. The first concert of the new season was Handel's *Judas Maccabaeus* - the second, Elgar's *Gerontius*.

Later, when it was self-evident that Gill would not be able to conduct the next concert, it was decided that the *Gerontius* performance should be allocated to me. *[Editor's note: Before Charles' first performance of* The Dream of Gerontius, *he went to the Three Choirs' Festival to hear the work and, to his great delight, Elgar himself was conducting it.]* This was such a success that gradually it became obvious that I should be appointed to succeed Gill. This was agreed. Under my direction, the Choir had a goodly success as I introduced more modern works, including Bliss' *Morning Heroes* and Dyson's *Canterbury Pilgrims*. The orchestra fell off in numbers and I insisted that, instead of bolstering up the small orchestra with further amateurs with only one rehearsal, this must be supplanted by a quasi-professional orchestra. Some two or three orchestral rehearsals and a final full rehearsal with choir was implemented. This continued until World War II.

Just before that event, a Handel Festival at Alexandra Palace was brought about, to celebrate the re-opening of the Palace and the re-tuning of the organ to concert pitch (A440) and its restoration after it had been damaged both wantonly and by neglect. This great revival of the tradition at the Palace was greeted with much delight by all amateur choral societies, for they saw the possibilities of a new life for the Palace. Sir Henry Wood was the conductor and two orchestras were brought in - one from the Royal Academy of Music and one from the Royal College of Music. I was the Chorus Master and had to take a rehearsal with piano, while Wood sat in the stalls. This led to far greater things than I then imagined. He seemed very satisfied with my conducting and we became quite friendly as a result. Lady Jessie and I were sitting together and she said, in her most commanding tones, that the organ, being played by GD Cunningham, was too loud. "Go and tell Henry". So I had the unenviable task of going up to the podium and saying "Sir Henry, your wife says the organ is too loud". He demurred at this, as he protested that Cunningham knew his job and the organ, but, in deference to Jessie, he shouted to Cunningham to play less loudly in certain places. I know from experience that the conductor's desk is the last place on earth from which to judge these things. The sound of the organ can go over the heads of the orchestra and conductor and reach the audience in ten times its loudness, unbeknown to the conductor, who is deafened by the proximity of the orchestra.

After this Festival, Wood wanted a choir for the Proms as the War had become an actuality. He engaged the Choir for three concerts and I was to share in the conducting. But, before that, I conducted the *B Minor Mass* at the Queen's Hall, out of the choir that was available to me from the Alexandra Choral Society and the Festival Chorus. This was the first appearance of the Alexandra Choir. I used the existing members of the Society, under my own Chairmanship, to pay my respects to the original Alexandra Choral Society who had declared that the Society *per se* was 'in abeyance' for the 'duration' (as it was put), referring to the War."

Amongst the 'more modern works' that Charles introduced to the Alexandra Choral Society were his own *Song of England* (November 1934) and *Choral Symphony* (April 1939).

In *The Last Years of Henry J Wood*, Lady Jessie Wood writes that the Handel Festival concert took place on June 3 1939. She also wrote: "During the preliminary rehearsals for this concert, Henry noticed how capably the young chorus-master, Charles Proctor, handled his singers."

In 1939, the Alexandra Choral Society having suspended its activities with the outbreak of World War II, Charles Proctor was approached by the London Symphony Orchestra to form a choir for a Good Friday performance of the Bach *B Minor Mass* at Queen's Hall on March 22 1940, to be conducted by

Dr Heathcote Statham. However, Dr Statham did not conduct the performance and it was conducted by Charles Proctor.

Shortly after this, Sir Henry Wood invited Charles Proctor to provide a Choir for the forthcoming Promenade Concerts and to share those programmes with him, to the extent of conducting half the choral items. (I have Sir Henry Wood's original letter, dated April 8 1940, in my files.) From the singers who had participated in the Good Friday B *Minor Mass* performance, Charles formed the Alexandra Choir for which he assumed entire personal responsibility, whilst enjoying the co-operation of the officers of the suspended Alexandra Choral Society. The male section of the newly formed Alexandra Choir duly appeared in the Proms in August 1940 in a performance of Brahms *Alto Rhapsody* (conducted by Sir Henry Wood) and Stanford *Songs of the Sea* (conducted by Charles Proctor). The whole choir then took part in a Promenade Concert on August 5 1941 in which they sang John Alden Carpenter's *Song of Faith* as part of an Anglo-American concert. Later that month, the Choir sang in Beethoven *Ninth Symphony* and the male section again sang the Brahms *Alto Rhapsody*. The full Choir was due to appear at another Promenade Concert on September 10 but, unhappily, it was at this moment that the remainder of the Promenade Concerts season was cancelled owing to the Blitz. Though the Blitz had the effect of temporarily suspending the musical activities at Queen's Hall, the Alexandra Choir's activities were unabated. Indeed, the Choir gave performances in aid of the 'National Air Raid Distress Fund', which had been set up to provide relief for those who suffered as a result of the air raids. Other performances were given in London churches, thus increasing the repertoire of the newly-formed Alexandra Choir. After a few months' suspension, during the period of the heavy raids, the Choir resumed its activities and appeared at the Queen's Hall again in April 1941 for a performance of Beethoven *Ninth*

Symphony with the London Symphony Orchestra, conducted by Charles Hambourg.

A former Alexandra Choir member wrote to me about the early days of the Choir. "We used to rehearse in a hall at the back of Lyons Corner House at Marble Arch but, as the choir enlarged, we had to get larger premises. We ended up at Hinde Street Methodist Church Hall opposite Trinity College of Music. During the war, we took part in a number of 'benefit' concerts. We travelled far and wide to do some of them but we always 'made it' and, in spite of the bombs and transport difficulties, we really enjoyed it."

In 1942, the Choir participated in the Sullivan Centenary Festival in the Royal Albert Hall, Charles Proctor sharing the conducting of the concert with Sir Henry Wood. The Choir also participated in the Promenade Concerts on three occasions - one of those being a performance of Beethoven *Ninth Symphony*. By now, the Promenade Concerts had been transferred to the Royal Albert Hall, as Queen's Hall had suffered severe bombing.

In September 1942, the Choir took part in a pageant entitled *The Cathedral Steps*, which was held on the steps of St Paul's Cathedral. This was an anthology of national poetry and music. The poetry was read by foremost actors and actresses of the day, including Dame Sybil Thorndike, Edith Evans, Leslie Howard and Marius Goring. The Choir was accompanied by the band of HM Brigade of Guards. Traffic around the Cathedral was diverted for two hours as thousands of people watched the spectacle which had a cast of 500.

A list of all the subsequent major concerts, given by the Alexandra Choir until December 1978 (when Charles retired), will be found as an Appendix at the back of this book. A glance at the list will demonstrate what a huge part the Alexandra Choir played in the musical life of the country - especially in London - for a great number of years.

One of the highlights of each year was the annual Carol Concert in the Royal Albert Hall. In addition to the 'standard' carol concert repertoire, first performances of carols were often featured - some written by Choir members (Mary Manson, John Turner) others by colleagues of Charles Proctor from Trinity College of Music (Carey Blyton and Leonard Smith).

The final Carol Concert, on December 17 1978, was a milestone for the Choir. It had had only one conductor in its thirty-eight year history. At the end of the concert, presentations were made both to Charles and to Rosemary. The Chairman, Frank Selby, in his valedictory speech, said: "We are sad about his leaving the position he has held since he founded the Choir some thirty-eight years ago. We have so greatly enjoyed, as I trust have our audiences, his leadership. We have benefited immensely from his deep insight into music, his devotion to the Art without superficiality, his authority without pomposity. Charles Proctor's qualities show themselves also in his compositions - and their impact on audiences and performers can be summed up in one word - sincerity." The Chairman referred to the gifts which the Choir had for the Proctors and went on to say: "We hope that these gifts will be permanent reminders of the feelings that fill the members of the Alexandra Choir today: respect, love and, above all, gratitude." The Carol Concerts always ended with the singing of Oldroyd's arrangement of the hymn *Ye Watchers and Ye Holy Ones* and, for many years, it had been Charles' custom to invite the audience to think of something or someone for whom they felt gratitude during the singing of this hymn. In his short speech of reply on this final occasion, he said: "....My over-riding emotion tonight is one of gratitude, for so many things and I invite you all, as I have done at each of our Carol Concerts, to find something in your own heart for which you feel grateful and perhaps are too shy and embarrassed to express - to join with us in singing the final item: *O Friends in Gladness let us Sing.*" Thus ended an era of an exceptional choral conductor.

The History of the Alexandra Choir is "a book waiting to be written". In 1995, Charles was delighted when he learned that the Royal Academy of Music had agreed to be the custodians of the Alexandra Choir archives. This had been arranged by Edna Norton and Marjorie Baldwin - two long-standing members of the Alexandra Choir. There were three enormous books of programmes, press cuttings and other material. Edna Norton added her own archive material to these and arranged for them to be professionally bound in red with gold lettering down the spines - a generous gesture which made fitting additions to the Royal Academy of Music Library. The archives are available for inspection by arrangement with the Librarian of the Royal Academy of Music.

Chapter 3

THE NEXT YEARS

I had great difficulty with the next years of Charles Proctor's life. It is not entirely clear in what year his autobiographical section ends. The period from the late 1920s until 1963 is very sketchy as I have few details about this and, though I endeavoured to find people who would be able to help me 'fill in the gaps', there were none. This did not surprise me, as Charles would have been 100 this year and many of his contemporaries have predeceased him. Such information as I possess is here recorded, but there are omissions. When I realised there would be something of a 'black hole' in my text, I wondered whether it was prudent to embark upon this work at all. This period of doubt did not last for long because I am convinced that the material I *do* possess is eminently worth sharing. There is some overlap with the autobiographical material at the beginning of this section. This is intentional, in order to give as complete a picture as possible of his activities.

* * * * * * * * *

On returning to England in 1928, after studying in Vienna, it became clear that it would not be possible for him to follow his chosen career - that of a concert pianist - for the reasons given in an earlier chapter. I find it somewhat strange that the record of his debut recitals receives such scant treatment from him. Let me remind you what he wrote in the earlier chapter: "I took some engagements in London as they presented themselves and I prepared for the coming winter season for recitals. This was engineered in such a way that I went to Vienna, then to Berlin, then to London in that order. About a month afterwards, the scheme was repeated as it was thought that no impact would be made by just one recital unconnected with another appearance." To have performed in three of the 'capitals of the musical world' in just over two months is 'no mean feat' and yet he writes nothing more about these particular months, or about the recitals. I have a small brochure which he produced giving his biographical details and press reviews of the concerts in these three cities. Clearly they were very well received. One quote must suffice - from the *Neu Zeit Charlottenberg Berlin*: "Marvellous agility - unheard of brilliance - richness of tone colouring." More light is thrown on this situation in an undated letter from Charles to his future father-in-law, Father Rennie, some years later. He had been asked to give a piano recital in St Jude-on-the-Hill church. He wrote: "It is YEARS since I have given a Pft recital.......I made a sort of vow to myself that I would not play the piano for money or applause. As these conditions are fulfilled in the present cir-cumstances, I feel quite delighted at the idea of playing. Further, I never wanted to play unless I could honestly feel that my efforts were 'WANTED' and here again S Jude's has given me the feeling after all that perhaps my efforts ARE wanted in the pianistic sense. For years I have toiled to gain a pianistic technique and then found 'no hands wanted' written large everywhere I tried to play in years gone by. S Jude's means SO much to me in providing me with a feeling that my efforts are so 'worth while' in a spiritual sense."

He took up conducting and was appointed Chorus Master to Albert Coates for the Fairbairn Pageants at the Royal Albert

Hall. He conducted several pageant performances there, the last of which was TC Fairbairn's production of Gounod's opera *Faust* with a cast of 1,000. The *Elijah* performances mentioned earlier ran from February 11 to 25 1935 As a result of this, the name of Charles Proctor became associated with spectacular presentations at the Royal Albert Hall, where he conducted some forty performances. He was appointed to the staff of the Royal Opera House, Covent Garden for two International Seasons, given under the direction of Sir Thomas Beecham.

His 'organist's career' began at All Saints, East Finchley, at the tender age of thirteen or fourteen! In a letter written in 1981 to a friend, who is currently (2006) the organist at that church, he wrote: "When I was at Highgate School, I became interested in All Saints as they had a good choir there. The organist, Dibbin, allowed me to play occasional services and I began by playing 'bits' while he was organist. I made his hair stand up as I was supposed to drule....or droole....in the key of G while the Choir recited the Creed on a monotone. I always prepared the next chord à la Stainer....and he saw to it that there was always present the note G therein. EXCEPT, very naughtily and KNOWING what I was about, I struck an F sharp Triad and resolved it onto G. He nearly had a fit...but it worked as you may know." Later, as a young man, Charles went to Wood Green and by February 1937, he was Organist and Choirmaster at St Saviour's Warwick Avenue. Around this time, he had lessons with HA Bate and in 1942, he obtained the FRCO diploma. His organ sonatas were written while he was at this church. (The church has since been replaced with a new one.) In 1943, Charles took up the post of Organist and Choirmaster at St Jude-on-the-Hill, Hampstead Garden Suburb, which position he held until Easter 1973. Here he met his future wife, Rosemary, who was the vicar's daughter. They were married at St Jude-on-the-Hill on July 21 1945. Father Rennie conducted the service and Rosemary was given away by her brother, Peter. A letter from the Churchwardens to Father Rennie reads: "History was made at St Jude's by the marriage of Rosemary Rennie to Charles Frederick Proctor, this being the first time in 38 years that such an occasion has occurred as from the Vicarage. And what a wedding! Our great church was filled. The ceremony was all that could be desired in both beauty and solemnity. It was plain to see the deep emotion that was very near the heart of Father Rennie - particularly when he saw his son leading the bride towards him, and when he administered the Sacrament to the newly-wedded couple. They have secured a home at 13, Eastholm." (They remained at this address until they retired to Winchelsea in 1975.) Rosemary was a sculptress and the couple were to share fifty years of great happiness - exemplified by their absolute devotion to each other and their shared interest in and dedication to their artistic endeavours. (Rosemary's other brother Michael had lost his life at sea in 1940, trying to save evacuated children from the mercy ship *City of Benares*, which had been torpedoed on its way to Canada. A newspaper report of the tragedy recalls: "He continually dived into the sea to rescue more and more children. When a warship was finally sighted, he stood up, trying to attract attention, then collapsed, falling dead into the waterlogged lifeboat." Little wonder Rosemary's wedding was a highly-charged emotional occasion for Father Rennie.) Two of Rosemary's works are in St Jude's church - over a door is a figure of Christ, in memory of her brother and, on the north wall, a bust, as a memorial to her father. In a lunette above St George's altar is a painting by Starmer which represents the last few moments in the life of Michael Rennie.

During his time as Organist and Choirmaster at St Jude's, he gave many organ recitals - generally in aid of worthy causes. Amongst these were four Bach recitals which he gave in 1948, specifically in aid of Albert Schweitzer's Hospital in Lambaréné. Charles had a great devotion to Schweitzer and this became clear to me when, in 1971, I typed a lengthy lecture which Charles was to deliver to the theological society of which he and Rosemary were members. The concluding passage from Schweitzer's book *The Quest for the Historical Jesus* was never far from him when he was working. It is worth reproducing it here:

> He comes to us as One unknown, without a name, as of old, by the lake side. He came to those men who knew him not. He speaks to us the same word: "Follow thou me" and sets us to the tasks which he has to fulfil for our time. He commands. And to those who obey him, whether they be wise or simple, He will reveal Himself in the toils, the conflicts, the sufferings which they shall pass through in His fellowship, and, as an ineffable mystery, they shall learn in their own experience, WHO HE IS.

During the War, Charles worked at the War office - though I am unclear in what capacity. It was some kind of guard duty as he was often there throughout the night - and more than once he told me that he had to carry a gun - "but thank heaven I never had to do anything with it!". He worked on his music during the long hours of the night. He wrote in one of his letters "Many of my counterpoint exercises for RCO were done 'on the job' at the War Office as I did them while on duty in my head then wrote them out in odd moments on MS paper and wrapped them round my truncheon for that machine had a long pocket on the trousers that would take 12 stave paper. That's how much of my *Organ Sonata No 1* was written."

As the previous chapter recorded, Charles Proctor founded the Alexandra Choir, which was associated with many of the famous conductors of the post-war era. The Choir took part in the twelve seasons of the London Symphony Orchestra in which Josef Krips conducted Beethoven *Ninth Symphony* in the Beethoven Cycle at the Royal Festival Hall. Sir Malcolm Sargent appointed Charles Proctor as his Chorus Master for the Royal Choral Society and, during the latter years, when ill health took Sir Malcolm from the concert platform, Charles Proctor deputised for fourteen performances at the Royal Albert Hall. The final concert of the Henry Wood Concert Society's Festival performance of *Messiah*, with a choir of 1,000, was conducted by Charles Proctor, with the Royal Philharmonic Orchestra. With the London Symphony Orchestra and the Alexandra Choir, Charles Proctor conducted most of the choral repertoire with some 200 appearances at the Royal Albert Hall.

Here I must insert a rather dramatic personal story concerning Charles and Rosemary - as told in *The Evening News* of August 18 1952. They had gone for a three-week 'quiet holiday' to Lynmouth, in Devon. This was cut short - by two weeks. They were staying at the Old Cottage Hotel on the Porlock side of the village. One day, it rained heavily and, after dinner, the river Lyn began to rise quite dramatically. The Proctors went outside to look at the swollen river. They crossed a bridge - which, even then, was shaking - and water was gushing across the road. Soon they were knee-deep in water and could not get back as the bridge had been swept away. They got to the only hotel on the eastern side, the Tors. Then came darkness and a night of terror. All night they sat sat listening to the roar of the river and the crash of boulders. In the morning, they found they were completely cut off from the other side. They watched as pitiful lines of the homeless trudged through the water, many with blankets wrapped around them. The Proctor's belongings were, of course, in the Old Cottage Hotel, the other side of the swollen river but the police got into the hotel and swung all their possessions across to them on ropes. An army truck then took them to Minehead where they spent the night in a house. Next day, they were the only Londoners to return from Minehead by train. The event was a national tragedy and many people lost their lives in the disaster. The Proctors were lucky indeed to have escaped.

In 1949, Charles was appointed to the professorial staff of Trinity College of Music. In a letter to a student who was preparing a thesis on Alec Rowley, Charles wrote: "I am indebted to Alec Rowley as he was instrumental in getting me accepted as a member of the professorial staff at Trinity College." Rowley had also been a pupil of Corder - Charles' Harmony professor at the Royal Academy of Music. Charles wrote of Rowley: "I am of the firm opinion that his services to Educational music are neglected and overlooked. He was one of the key figures in the building up of the Examinations' system in Trinity College." In 1952, Rowley edited for Lengnick five albums of piano pieces by ten composers, called *Five by Ten*. The composers were William Alwyn, Malcolm Arnold, Madeleine Dring, Julius Harrison, Elizabeth Maconchy, Charles Proctor, Franz Reizenstein, Edmund Rubbra, Bernard Stevens and William Wordsworth. This enterprising series introduces the pianist to contemporary compositions within a carefully graded framework, ranging from pieces mostly in the five-finger group in Book One to recital pieces in Book Five. By this time, Lengnick had already published a large amount of Charles Proctor's compositions. In 1963, when Charles Kennedy Scott became ill, Charles Proctor was appointed Conductor of the College Choir, conducting all the choral performances until his own retirement in July 1975. By this time, Charles was a Professor, Lecturer, Examiner and Member of the Corporation of the College. One of the most memorable occasions in the last few years of his time at Trinity College of Music was the Centenary of the College in 1972. Charles conducted the College Choir in a Thanksgiving Service at Westminster Abbey on July 10. The College had had many links with Westminster Abbey. Sir Frederick Bridge, Chairman of the Board of the College from 1909 to 1924 had been Organist and Master of the Choristers at the Abbey from 1882 until 1918 and Sir William McKie, who had been Organist there from 1941 to 1963, was still a member of the Corporation at the time of the Centenary Service. The choral music at this service included Britten *Hymn to St Cecilia,* Stanford's setting of *Psalm 150,* Charles Wood *Hail Gladdening Light,* Sir William McKie *We wait for thy loving kindness O God,* and William Mathias *Make a joyful noise unto the Lord.* The final hymn was *Ye watchers and ye holy ones* - the arrangement by George Oldroyd, a member of the College Corporation from 1925 to 1951. This was particularly appropriate as it was the hymn which concluded the Alexandra Choir's Carol Concerts at the Royal Albert Hall. The service concluded with a final *Amen,* specially composed by Dr Arnold Cooke, who was a member of the professorial staff of the College. I have vivid memories of that service and the College Bulletin for October 1972 recorded "The singing of the Choir was magnificent". It most certainly was! Two days later, in the Royal Albert Hall, Charles conducted part of the Centenary Concert - Elgar *National Anthem* and Beethoven *Choral Fantasia* - for which the pianist was Irene Kohler.

At the same time that he was on the staff of Trinity College of Music, he was also teaching in schools - Woodhouse Grammar School, Friern Barnet in North London (which is now a Sixth Form College), and at a Marist Convent. He was often called upon as an adjudicator for music festivals and competitions and this work took him up and down the country. In addition to his composing activities, he was both writing and editing books on music. (Details can be found in the Appendix of this book.)

As stated at the beginning of this chapter, I have few details of his activities during the period under consideration. However, in addition to the work at Trinity College of Music, with the Alexandra Choir and at St-Jude-on-the-Hill, Hampstead Garden Suburb, other bodies with which he was involved were:

North London Music Competition Festival - of which he was Chairman.

Hendon Music Festival - of which he was Chairman.

London Music Festival - of which he was Vice-Chairman.

London Society of Organists - of which he was a member.

The Incorporated Society of Musicians - of which he was a Member of the Council. From 1971 until 1977 he held the post of Treasurer.

The Royal College of Organists - of which he was a Member of the Council and a Lecturer. He was made a Life Member in 1981.

The Royal Society of Arts

The Performing Right Society - of which he became a member in 1946

The Composers' Guild of Great Britain

The Royal Academy of Music Club

Music Adviser to Alfred Lengnick and Co.

Patron of the Westminster Abbey Special Choir

Though I do not have further detailed information about these years, it is clear that Charles Proctor was in great demand in many areas of the music profession.

For the sake of completeness, I list his diplomas:

LRAM 1930
ARCM 1930
ARAM 1932
ARCO 1941
FRCO 1942
FRAM 1945
FTCL 1958
FRSA 1963

Chapter 4

Introduction to the Letters

The next section of this book is made up of material taken from the letters I received from Charles between 1970 and 1996. I have tried to extract those things which demonstrate what his life was like during these years and what he was doing in his many spheres of activity.

One or two words of explanation are needed. First, he always referred to Rosemary as 'RM' and to Winchelsea as 'Winches'. As with the autobiographical material, the grammar, capital letters and spelling, which may seem odd or wrong, are his - and, where appropriate, I have left things exactly as he wrote them. Invariably, he addressed people by their surnames - Densem, Brownbill, Maundrell. This was not meant rudely....it was just his way. For years I was 'Fellows'' (my maiden name) or 'Miss Thing'. At College, we were often 'Miss' or 'Mr Thing' - because he couldn't remember our names. I have left all abbreviations as they appear - VW, JSB, LVB, RAM, RAH, ISM, RSCM, RFH. To 'spell everything out' would detract from the originality of the letters.

Charles 'wrote as he thought' and his letters read as if he was speaking to me. They jump from subject to subject - and back again. Often it took some time to piece together the whole meaning of a letter from the verbal jigsaw that I received.

It is appropriate here to quote from a letter dated December 13 1968 as it sets out much of Charles' thoughts concerning the profession of Music - thoughts which run through all his letters to me as the very foundation of his life. At this time I was on the Committee of the Trinity College of Music Guild, an association for former students and diploma holders. Charles had been invited to propose the Toast of the Guild at its annual Dinner. I had been asked to obtain a copy of his speech for reproduction in the Guild Newsletter. Charles was most anxious that he should not be misquoted so he set out his speech in the letter to me. It read:

> If the purpose of the Guild is to bridge the gap which exists between the acquired knowledge gained in College and its practical application in the profession - then I give you the Toast with hope.
>
> If the purpose of the Guild is to make the professional musician feel at home in the environment of modern society - then I give you the Toast with gratitude.
>
> If the purpose of the Guild is to bring colour and romance into modern society, where the present tendency is to bring things down to the lowest common denominator - then I give you the Toast with exultation.
>
> If the purpose of the Guild is to foster camaraderie and make the single-minded aspirant feel he can belong to a Society which values his company - then I give you the Toast with fraternity.
>
> If the Guild can give students a feeling of being wanted by their fellows, so that they feel they can contribute something to the fabric of music - then I give you the Toast with great happiness.

If the purpose of the Guild is to be forward-looking, courageous, imaginative, helpful, benevolent and hopeful - then I give you the Toast - "The Guild".

There is no denying that things were not always easy for Charles. This situation obtained throughout his life and especially towards its end. One of the reasons for this was his uncompromising attitude to his profession. He often said "I consider loyalty to be the queen of virtues." Loyalty to one's colleagues or to a belief does not always result in 'success' - as the world at large knows it - but it does result in peace of mind. In 1984, he wrote "So much of one's life in the Art of Music is writ in water............ but I do not forget my own terms of acceptance - to look forward and to press on - not counting the cost, as the Scriptures have it." That sums up Charles' approach to all areas of his life - especially music.

Re-reading the letters, in order to prepare this book, was an exhausting exercise. The sheer volume of them was somewhat formidable. The contents were so 'tightly packed' with information, news, requests and details of his activities that I never ceased to be amazed at his energy and enthusiasm. This was true right up to the day of his death. When I came to prepare the List of Works (see Appendix B at the end of this book), I marvelled at his dedication and single-minded application to composition, which seemed to increase with every passing year - despite the fact that performances of his compositions were 'few and far between'.

I trust the extracts I have quoted will give readers an insight into Charles Proctor's busy and fulfilling life, and, more especially, into his personality.

THE LETTERS:

JANUARY 1970 - NOVEMBER 1996

From 1970 until his death, I exchanged letters with Charles. These were very frequent and very long and they have been invaluable in providing information about his life. Consequently, much of the remainder of this compilation is drawn from material extracted from this correspondence.

In 1970, Charles was living in 13, Eastholm, London NW11 and was engaged in a large number of musical activities. He was a member of the Professorial Staff of Trinity College of Music and on the Corporation of that institution; he took classes in Sight Singing, for Organists and Choirmasters, taught Harmony, Counterpoint and Composition, conducted the College Choir in its weekly rehearsals and for the choral concerts, examined diploma candidates in various musical disciplines and examined theses for both the Graduate and Fellowship diplomas. For many years, he was on the Councils of the Incorporated Society of Musicians (where he was Honorary Treasurer from 1971 until 1977) and the Royal College of Organists (for which he was also an Examiner) and, as an adjudicator, travelled the length and breadth of the country. He was Organist and Choirmaster of St Jude-on-the-Hill, Hampstead Garden

Suburb, a post which he had taken up in 1943. Throughout this time, he continued to compose.

The letters between 1970 and 1973 were concerned solely with the Alexandra Choir and the steps some of the younger members of the Choir were taking in an endeavour to attract new members and instil new life into it. (The membership was increasingly 'elderly'.) It was an uphill task which never really proved successful, despite our best efforts. In 1973, when I took on the Secretaryship of the Choir, I *thought* I understood the size of the job. With the benefit of hindsight, I had no idea just how much would be required of me. It was much bigger than anything I had anticipated. At the time, my 'day job' (on the administrative staff of Trinity College of Music) was very demanding and I could never get through all the work that was expected of me during the prescribed hours. I had to take home much work - that being the only way I could cope. The Alexandra Choir tasks added to this - and so my days began at 5.00 am.

In March 1973, after thirty years service, Charles retired from the post of Organist and Choirmaster of St Jude-on-the-Hill, Hampstead Garden Suburb and some members of the Alexandra Choir joined the St Jude's church choir for the Easter Day Evensong, his final service as Organist.

By now I had started my work as Secretary of the Alexandra Choir in tandem with Vic Carter, the retiring Secretary, so that by the time he left, in May 1973, I hoped I had everything at my finger tips. Charles' approach to the Choir was perhaps not in line with current taste. He insisted that "Our Society is *only* a choir - and not a Social Society". To him, the music was the all-important thing and he had no interest in social gatherings 'for the sake of them'. The idea of a Bring and Buy Sale or sponsored events to raise money for the Choir was not something he wished to contemplate. One thing on which he insisted (and with which I was in complete agreement) was the absolute necessity for detailed forward planning and that *everything* should be in writing.

In November 1973, a distant relative, Dennis Proctor, arrived at Trinity College of Music in search of Charles. Dennis was very interested in the Proctor family tree and his relationship to Charles was that Dennis' grandfather, Charles Cooke Proctor, was Charles (Frederick) Proctor's uncle. Charles and Dennis met at Eastholm where they pieced together details of the early Proctor family. A family tree exists going back to 1679 (though the earlier details are somewhat sketchy) and Charles was able to produce a photograph of Mrs. Proctor's Band. By now, Dennis and his wife and daughter were living and working in Venice, where they still live.

From time to time, Charles would write an Alexandra Choir *Newsletter,* giving details of the Choir's engagements - both past, present and future. It also contained personal news of both Charles and Rosemary and Choir members. The Newsletter for January 1974 contains the sentence: "*There is always something* is the likely title of my, as yet unwritten, autobiography." This was followed by a recital of the difficulties under which the Choir had worked at that time - "power cuts, transport problems, and general depression made an ominous gloom around our prospects".

David Toplis became a great friend of the Choir as he ran the Jupiter Orchestra, which was made up of music students, and the Alexandra Choir engaged this orchestra for some of its concerts. David was also the Orchestra Manager at Trinity College of Music. In 1973/4, Charles, David and I embarked on a most ambitious project - to put on staged performances of Coleridge-Taylor's *Hiawatha* Trilogy in the Royal Albert Hall - as had been done in the 1920s and 1930s. Charles had had much experience of conducting dramatised performances of this kind. He had dramatised and conducted (as an opera) Elgar's *The Kingdom,* a work not performed nearly enough - either now or then. (Sargent was of the opinion that *The Kingdom* ranked with *Messiah,* the *B Minor Mass* and the *St Matthew Passion.*) We were joined in the *Hiawatha* enterprise by Denis Brearley, a lawyer by background, who was, at that time, the General Secretary of the Incorporated Society of Musicians. On one never-to-be-forgotten occasion, Charles, David and I visited T C Fairbairn at his home in North London to take our discussions further. (Charles wrote about his work with TC Fairbairn in the autobiographical section of this book.) Fairbairn was very very keen that this should go ahead and the evening concluded with the smoking of the pipe of peace which had been given to him by Chief Os-ke-non-ton of the Mohawk Tribe when he took part in a *Hiawatha* performance in June 1929. Solemnly, the pipe was passed round us all and, ceremoniously, we smoked it. Fairbairn subsequently gave us all the material which he had used for the Royal Albert Hall performances all those years ago. There were small items of scenery and the enormous backcloth which had been specially made to cover the front of the stage of the Albert Hall. This material was stored in a depository and we had to take over the monthly payments of the storage fees. (These were not inconsiderable so, after a time, a friend, who was then Rector of Skegness, kindly agreed that the material could be stored in the basement of his Rectory - free of charge.) We booked the Albert Hall and entered into negotiations about the production with a charity who would benefit from the profits. For many reasons, the *Hiawatha* performances did not come to fruition - despite a great deal of hard work. It was a huge disappointment. We tried to find a home for the backcloth and other material, approaching Covent Garden, the Theatre Museum, the Victoria and Albert Museum and other similar venues. We had no success. When the Rector moved from Skegness, in September 1978, at our request the contents of his basement were removed by the local scouts and used for their Bonfire Night celebrations. TC Fairbairn died in the same year, aged one hundred and three.

At the beginning of August 1974, one of Charles' letters included this rather telling paragraph: "So much of one's life in the Art of Music is writ in water and I am, I think, guilty of indulging in a degree of self-pity in an unguarded moment, forgetting my own terms of acceptance - to look forward and to press on - not counting the cost, as the Scriptures have it."

It is interesting to note that by August 1974, the style of Charles' letters was changing. They were becoming more humorous and contained wonderful drawings of things referred to in the letters. Consequently, the style of my letters changed too. They began to include snippets of 'news' as well as all the matters concerning the Alexandra Choir. In a letter in January 1975, Charles wrote that he had received a long letter from 'Jimmy' Judd who was 'doing things' including conducting at the Hollywood Bowl. James Judd, now an internationally famous conductor, had been the rehearsal pianist for the Alexandra Choir for some time, having being a student of Charles at Trinity College of Music.

In September 1974, Charles had given a talk on 'What is a Musician?' and I wrote to him about this. One paragraph of my letter included this quotation from Edwin Fischer's book *Reflections on Music*. "In his best hours, the creative man is godlike. Out of the (musical) works and his own personality, something new may arise from which the Eternal shines forth in power and purity. For this alone, it is worth while to live." This quotation was to have resonances with things Charles was to say in later years when he began to expound on his musical philosophy.

July 1975 saw Charles' retirement from the Professorial Staff of Trinity College of Music. At his farewell performance with the College Choir and Orchestra, he conducted Holst's *Hymn of Jesus* and Brahms' *A German Requiem* in Southwark Cathedral on June 23. The Proctors moved from London to their final home - Bay Tree House in Winchelsea, East Sussex. His retirement from Trinity College of Music meant he had much more time to pursue other musical interests which he did to great effect in East Sussex.

In a Choir *Newsletter* in August 1975, Charles wrote about the concert organist Jennifer Bate. She was the daughter of the late HA Bate from whom Charles had learned so much in earlier years. Jennifer very generously sent me photocopies of letters to her from Charles which concerned some of his compositions. They were a delight to read - filled with 'Proctorisms' and wonderful pictorial illustrations of other subject matter of the letters. It is always difficult to obtain performances of new works and Charles was indebted to Jennifer for giving first performances of some of his organ works. In 1974, Charles had been impressed with her performance of his *Canzona, Choral and Passacaglia for Organ*. Jennifer invited him to write a piece for her. The result was the *Chaconne for Organ*, subsequently published in 1976 by Weinberger. She gave the first performance in London on July 1 1975 at St James', Muswell Hill and, in September of that year, she appeared in the BBC Promenade Concerts, playing Liszt's *Ad Nos* - the first time a Promenade Concert had opened with an organ work. In the same *Newsletter* Charles recorded that the Alexandra Choir had not featured in any way in the Proms since the death of Sir Malcolm Sargent. Things had changed at the BBC and despite countless letters, the door was apparently closed to further participation - not only by the Alexandra Choir, but other amateur choirs.

In another *Newsletter*, in October 1975, Charles wrote something which he was to quote from time to time and which is so true: "There are three kinds of people - 1) People who let things happen; 2) People who have no idea what is happening; 3) People who *make* things happen."

In 1976, Charles was taken ill with jaundice and was unable to conduct two concerts - one in St John's, Smith Square in London (which was conducted by Denis East) and the other in West Meon, in Hampshire, when Robert Hill, the then choir accompanist, took over. In 1977 Charles underwent an operation for the removal of his gall bladder. This was the culmination of - and perhaps partly the reason for - the preceding months of ill health.

During 1976, Charles had accepted the post of Organist and Choirmaster of St Mary's, Rye (the Parish Church) in East Sussex. It was a great delight for him to be back in the church organist's world, though his work was to prove taxing on many occasions - for instance, when children would attend the weekly rehearsal only to be absent on the Sunday morning as they 'had something else on'. His involvement in the musical life of Rye and surrounding areas provided many opportunities for performance and composition. The Alexandra Choir had sung in Rye Parish Church in the Rye Jubilee Concert in 1977 and, as a direct result of that concert, the Rye Harmonic Society was founded with the intention of promoting choral and orchestral concerts in Rye. It was a happy thought that the Alexandra Choir was largely instrumental in the formation of another Choral Society, in East Sussex, with similar aims to its own.

By now, the membership of the Alexandra Choir was dwindling and, despite recruitment drives, it did not seem possible to enlist singers. That, combined with the fact that 'regulars' sometimes let him down by their non-attendance, became an enormous anxiety for Charles. The strain of this was to take its toll on his health. In 1978, he was taken ill and his doctor diagnosed a slight heart condition. He was ordered to rest and not to undertake any engagements. The annual Alexandra Choir *St Matthew Passion* performance on March 11 that year was conducted by Robert Hill. Charles announced his intention to retire from the Conductorship of the Choir and his last appearance was the Royal Albert Hall Carol Concert on December 17 1978. It was fitting that, in addition to Geoffrey Morgan, who had been the Choir's organist for many years, the soloists at the final concert included two local musicians from Winchelsea - the mezzo-soprano Molly Townson and the pianist Mary Densem.

The letters between us, from which I have been drawing material, were long and detailed, containing, as they did, research into pieces of music suitable for concerts, orchestrations of various works, possible concert venues, consideration of correspondence from other bodies, choir finance, membership matters, and a hundred and one other things involved in running a choir. In May 1975, it had been decided that the services of the Concert Agent Ibbs and Tillett should be discontinued for the management of the annual Choir Carol Concert in the Royal Albert Hall. As I had experience of this work, it seemed unnecessary to pay a professional agency to do it. This made a financial saving for the Choir as Ibbs and Tillett's management fee was not inconsiderable. Results of my investigations into all Choir matters had to be relayed to Charles for his consideration and my subsequent action. Reading these letters again, some thirty years later, left me feeling quite exhausted, recalling what an uphill struggle it all was. I record this only to underline what a huge amount of time and work was involved for Charles in 'keeping the show on the road'. These last five years of Charles' time with the Alexandra Choir (when he retired in December 1978 he had been its Conductor for thirty-eight years) were, I am certain, the most difficult for him. Reasons were many - ill health being one of them - but I feel it must have been a source of great sadness to him to see the personnel of the choir reduced to often only about eighty members. When he founded it in 1940, and for many years afterwards, the weekly attendance was around 200. When I joined in 1966, singers arriving at the rehearsal in Hinde Street Methodist church basement at 6.25 pm for the 6.30 pm rehearsal, had difficulty finding a seat. By 1973, things were very different. There are many reasons for this situation but one of the most important of them was spelled out very clearly in the Newsletter of *another* choir in mid-1978. It read:

> "Difficult as it is for the average concert-goer to accept, it is now a fact that the income from ticket sales, even with a full house, is rarely enough to cover the cost of mounting a concert with a full orchestra and soloists, with ticket prices at a level that the concert-going public can readily afford. As a result, musical organisations are having to rely increasingly on the generosity of patrons in the commercial field."

That choir had received a great deal of sponsorship from 'big business' and others. Whilst its operation was on a much bigger scale than that of the Alexandra Choir, the 'same rules applied'. As a consequence, any choir has to look to its members as 'ticket-selling agents' but it is not always easy to persuade the members to 'do their bit' on this front. (I understand that this situation is as much an ongoing problem now as it ever was!) The Alexandra Choir had only individual Patrons who paid a relatively small annual fee. It never received patronage from 'big business' or other sources and, consequently, it relied on its own efforts to keep its financial head above water. The archives of the Alexandra Choir can be found in the Library of the Royal Academy of Music in London and are available for reference.

* * * * * * * * *

After the final Alexandra Choir Carol Concert in December 1978, the content and composition of Charles' letters became a joy to read. His letters show a side of his character that would surprise many. His sense of humour and inspired use of the English language (and spelling!) have to 'be read to be believed' - to the extent that I considered preparing 'The Collected Letters' so that others might share in the joy of them. But that is something for the future.

Now that the strain of the work involved with the Alexandra Choir was behind him, he began to involve himself more and more in local music making and he accepted my offer of continued secretarial assistance with numerous projects. At this time, I began to be involved in his compositions and in May 1979, when I had looked through a Latin mass which he had just written, he wrote to me "Thinking about the Latin Mass, I will revise those places you 'spotted' as being out of the style of the other places. I agree wholeheartedly....the fact is I did not set out on Page I to write in 4ths and 5ths but this became evident later on - so I must make it consistent. Thanks for your erudition." This scrutiny of his work I continued until his death and I found it completely absorbing and fascinating.

1980 was a very important year in Charles' life as he was awarded the OBE. The Investiture took place on December 2 1980 and it was an occasion of great joy for Charles and Rosemary - joy shared by all his friends and colleagues. It was clearly one of the happiest days of their lives and he wrote a 'round robin' letter to certain friends giving a vivid account of everything that was involved in the Investiture. Sadly, on that very same day, their good friend Lord Patrick Gordon Walker died.

In 1980, my husband, Howard, and I were married and Charles played the organ for our wedding. To our great joy, he wrote an outgoing voluntary for the occasion, the rhythm of our names providing a kind of *leitmotiv* for the piece. He entitled it *Marche Joyeuse* so that its use would not be confined to weddings. Later, he orchestrated it and, in November of that year, the Trinity College of Music orchestra performed it, under the baton of Bernard Keeffe. I was present when the orchestra played it and I wrote to Charles telling him how good the orchestral version had sounded and how I had noticed 'lots of extra bits' which he had added to it. He replied: "I was interested in your comments regarding the 'extras' I had put in the score. I feel it is *essential* in writing for an orchestra to think the music as if *composed* for the orchestra - NOT, repeat KNOT a mere transcription of the piano notes onto various instruments. I have failed many TCL papers on this score. Anyone can write this or that tune for an orchestral instrument but that is NOT Orchestration as I see it."

To celebrate his OBE, Rosemary gave Charles a present of a leather-bound red book which he used to write a journal, starting on May 1 1980. (The letter from the Prime Minister, informing him that it was proposed that his name should be submitted to Her Majesty the Queen for this honour, was dated April 30 1980. It became public knowledge on June 14 of that year.) This particular book proved a very useful source of information, some of which is incorporated with that extracted from the letters.

May 13 1980 saw the first performance of Charles' Latin Mass *In Nomine Jesu Christe* given by David Wookey and Hastings

Chamber Choir at St Barnabas, Bexhill. On the following day, the second performance was given at All Saints, Hastings. A third performance was given in Rye Church on June 24 and the fourth on the following day at Christ Church, St Leonards. These occasions must have been very gratifying for him as, though he was a prolific composer, he experienced the greatest difficulty in having his works performed or published. There are a number of references to works being returned by publishers who had not accepted them for publication. This is not an uncommon state of affairs - but it is a disheartening one for any composer. So to have had four performances of his Latin Mass in one month was thrilling for Charles.

In September, Allan Wicks, the organist of Canterbury Cathedral, asked Charles to write a 3-part *Magnificat and Nunc Dimittis* - with or without organ! - for Canterbury Cathedral.

Mention must be made at this point of the many clergy friends of Charles and Rosemary. They were both people of profound faith whose spiritual life was at the centre of their existence. They had a particularly intimate relationship with Father Hill who, at the time of their first meeting in 1966, was the Incumbent at Brede Church, not far from Winchelsea. By the time of Charles' 'OBE Journal', Fr. Hill had retired and was in a nursing home where they visited him. Another clergy friend was Canon John Williams who was the Incumbent at Rye Parish Church when Charles took up the post of Organist and Choirmaster in 1976. His relationship with Canon Williams was always cordial (not necessarily the case between organists and clergy!) and Rye Parish Church was a place of great happiness for these years. It was a huge shock both to the town, and to the Proctors personally, when Canon Williams suddenly collapsed and died in Rye on June 12 1981. His successor Canon David Maundrell was another good friend. (His Induction took place on January 19 1982.)

In January 1981, Mary Megson died. She had been the Secretary of the Alexandra Choir for many years and was held in great esteem and affection by Charles and Rosemary.

Charles spent much time either painting or composing and his output was prolific in both areas. One of the significant works he wrote during 1981 was the *Duo Concertante for Piano and Organ*. Mary Densem (a neighbour in Winchelsea and a close friend of the Proctors) and Clifford Foster (the organist at the Methodist Church in Rye) gave the first performance of this at the Rye Harmonic Society concert on June 27 1981. Charles was gratified that he had such people 'on hand' to perform his new works. Another was Molly Townson who, with Mary Densem, performed some of his vocal works. A letter records that his three-part Latin Mass was to be premiered by the Rye Singers at the Festival Service on September 6 1981 and might be performed again by that same group at the Roman Catholic Church in Rye in October. Lesley Brownbill, who conducted the Rye Singers, was very helpful to Charles in 'matters musical'. In addition to her work with the Rye Singers, she was a soprano soloist in her own right and she performed one of Charles' *Vocalise*, (for clarinet, piano and soprano) on May 30.

Such performances were 'highlights' for Charles because, throughout his life, he had written music for many different instruments and ensembles but it was always extremely difficult to secure performances. He wrote "It is the most depressing thing to write music which is not performed.....and I should know". He made innumerable references to sending original compositions to people (other than publishers) who either did not even acknowledge them or merely returned them without comment. Such disappointment is hard to bear - as anyone who has ever been in this situation will know. The disappointment for Charles was two-fold - not only were the recipients not interested but they lacked the most basic common courtesy - something by which he placed great store.

In October 1981, Charles was asked to write an article for the Newsheet of the newly formed Albert Coates Society in America. Coates was due to celebrate his 100th birthday in 1982. Charles was an eminently suitable person for this task, having worked with Coates for a number of years.

In that same month, Charles gave the Address at the Memorial Tribute in St Peter's, Vere Street, London W1, for David Toplis. David had committed suicide and his death had been a tremendous shock to everyone.

With a number of deaths of their friends, 1981 was an *annus horribilis* for the Proctors. Bay Tree House was very cold in the winter months and Charles records that he had to wear mittens to keep warm when he was working in his music room. The cold, combined with the emotional effects of the loss of their friends, led to ill health for both of them during this period. Hardly a letter went by without a description of one or both of them being unwell enough to have to stay in bed for some days - previously a most unusual occurrence.

The Alternative Service Book started to appear in Rye Parish Church and this was not something which was to Charles' taste. Anyone who knew him will realise what an understate-ment that is! His preference was for 1662 and 'all that goes with'. He found the use of modern-day words very unpalatable. He felt that it added to a lack of reverence and it prompted him to write "Over the years, I have thought that if I could put into one sentence my philosophy for the 'good life' it would be a 'sense of reverence'. I could not go so far as Schweitzer with his Reverence for Life....but a sense of reverence *per se* seems to me to be an absolute MUST if one is to run a decent society.

I always try to get the Rye children to try and show some reverence for Church but it is very difficult when the grown-ups seem to regard Rye Church as a railway station." He added "I have left instructions that the Prayer Book version (of St Paul's Letter to the Corinthians) is to be read at my funeral - or I shall get up and walk out!"

Here I must quote from a letter Charles received, dated January 21 1982, from the then Bishop of Lewes, Peter Ball, who had participated in a service at Rye Church when Charles had played the organ. Bishop Ball wrote: "It was lovely to see you the other night and I was thrilled to hear your *Célébration*........The music made me feel that there was a real difference between pomposity and dignity and there was splendid dignity coming from the organ. I do feel highly honoured to be sent a copy of your manuscript both of *Célébration* and of your *Mass* at the Rye Festival and I shall treasure them and share them with some of the people here who love music as much as I do. You must know that it is one of the thrills of coming to Rye to know that everything in the musical line will be done with sensitivity and grandeur and thank you for inspiring us all in this way." That letter must have given Charles great pleasure, especially in the light of the changes that were manifesting themselves in the services at Rye.

In May 1982, the Proctors went to Canterbury Cathedral for the visit of Pope John Paul II and this was clearly a source of great pleasure to them.

October 1982 saw Charles adjudicating in Buckingham at a Festival and later giving a talk on adjudicating to the Hastings branch of the ISM.

At the beginning of 1983, the Proctors were thrilled to receive the news that their friend Dr Anne Hunter had been awarded an OBE. Dr Hunter had been Rosemary's doctor and she and her husband Brian were close friends. Brian later became their solicitor.

In the same letter, one paragraph was to be of huge significance. The publisher, Oecumuse asked him if he knew of anyone who could prepare his music for print. He wrote to me about this: "At the moment, the position is that Oecumuse will not publish any work of mine that is not so copied and he has a SACK of work that awaits such an one in his files as 'accepted' for publication.....so I feel frustrated as it seems that the outlook is rather bleak. Let's hear your reactions." I knew of no one who might do this so I offered to take on the task myself - little realising what a massive work it would be. The implications of this are covered in the Preface so they do not need to be repeated here. Suffice it to say, this work engendered another huge amount of correspondence but no reference will be made to it as it was purely technical and solely concerned with matters musical affecting the compositions.

Charles did not drive, but Rosemary was always happy to act as his chauffeur. The car was essential to them - not least for the trips to Rye Church for choir practice and services - a very frequent journey of two and a half miles. The car was not always reliable and, being rather elderly, often gave cause for concern and was a financial drain in terms of repairs, which were required rather too frequently.

In these later years of his life, Charles' hearing began to deteriorate, but it was 'not a subject for discussion'. The necessity to speak distinctly and slowly was clear but not everyone realised and this left him in embarrassing situations when he had not heard what was said. This happened more than once, especially when people would talk to him while he was playing the organ. (Anyone who has played the organ in churches is used to the fact that people come up and hold conversations whilst you are playing, perhaps, the outgoing voluntary. It does not seem to occur to them that every inch of concentration is needed for the task in hand. It is not always possible to hear what is being said - even for those *without* a hearing problem - so for anyone thus afflicted, it is an impossible task.) At Rye Church, though there *were* microphones, often they were not switched on, so Charles would have had no idea what point in the service had been reached and whether or not he was required to play had Rosemary not stood alongside him to guide him through the service. This made life very difficult for him - and for others who did not realise the problems.

Charles' interest in painting was immense and, as far as I am aware, he was self-taught. He had a particular love for the works of Monet. He wrote of him: "All he stands for is all that I can hope for....as far as painting is concerned." He ended that letter: "The happiest days of my life were spent reading *Impressionism* by Phoebe Pool (Thames and Hudson). I learned for the first time about all this....I only knew WHAT I liked....and then found out who done 'em....and I found my instincts were right all along. It was a revelation and this book is one of my most treasured possessions."

Charles was invited to give an organ recital at Lydd (in Kent) on September 16 1983 as part of 'the year's celebrations of the 700th foundation'. In this same month, I prepared the first of the many pieces of music for Oecumuse. Charles wrote to me: "I cannot tell you how delighted I am that you are being so kind as to do the Oecumuse things...for with the market being closed for publications these days - both Lengnick & Weinberger to my certain knowledge, likewise Cramer and the like - having as I now have TIME and space in which to compose, it was a terrible shock when Brunton [of Oecumuse] told me that 'unless......' he would not accept publication. It is wonderful to find that you are really capable of doing this work which I find quite impossible and only a real musician is capable of." At this time, and at her request, he had written a *Sonatina for Piano* for Rosalind Runcie, the wife of the then Archbishop of Canterbury, Robert Runcie. Charles was thrilled to receive this commission.

William Walton died in 1983 and Charles wrote "I am sorry Walton has 'passed on'. I think his Symphony I is the most powerful work written this century by anyone. I heard the rehearsals of it in Queen's Hall."

A new trombone stop was added to the organ at Rye Church in memory of Canon John Williams. It was dedicated at a service on Sunday April 24 1983 and Charles wrote a *Dedication Peal* for the occasion. Throughout the organ-building firm of Hill, Norman and Beard, it was known as 'Charles Proctor's Trombone'.

In April, Geoffrey Morgan wrote that he hoped to play Charles' *Canzona, Choral and Passacaglia* in his Westminster Abbey recital on July 28.

In May, Charles adjudicated at Gillingham and Eastbourne - the latter with 'Cranmer and Gipps'. "Accordions - wonderful high standard. A revelation in this field for me." Charles learned that his Broadwood grand piano, which had belonged to Mary Manson's mother, previously belonged to a lady who was a pupil of Careno and d'Albert and Paderewski. (Mary Manson had been a musical friend of the Proctors and a member of the Alexandra Choir for many years.)

A letter recorded that Holman Hunt had lived in Greyfriars - a large house in Winchelsea which at that time was an Old People's Home. That was of interest to Howard and me as we had visited Greyfriars on a few occasions - for fêtes and the like.

"This July I have to retire from RCO Council unless re-elected. I've done about 25 years as a Councillor, Examiner and sometime member of the Exec. Committee. I hope I may be re-elected as I like going up there." Sadly he was not re-elected.

In April 1984, at the AGM of the Rye PCC, Charles reported that the RSCM was planning a Festival in May at Rye and that, on May 5, there would be a Festival Service with a choir of about 300 singers drawn from several parishes in the district. The Choir would be conducted by the Director of Music at Chichester Cathedral, the Bishop of Lewes would preach and Charles would play the organ.

Charles had a very high regard for Albert Schweitzer. He quoted from the final paragraph of *The Quest for the Historical Jesus* :" He comes to us as One unknown....to those who obey Him...they shall learn in their own experience Who He is." Charles goes on to write "That is why I hold Schweitzer so highly."

The nuns at Edgware, whom the Proctors had got to know, asked him to write a *Sanctus* and *Benedictus* for them - which he did. Though they were using Charles' Winchelsea Communion Service music, they said they found these movements 'a bit tricky'.

Charles wrote that Stanley Warburton, the Secretary of the Turner Society, had written them a "lovely letter introducing himself" and the Proctors much looked forward to making his acquaintance. Later in the year, they heard that he had been made Chairman of the Turner Society.

In May, he ran into Richard Popplewell after an RCO meeting in London and he invited him to visit the Chapels Royal. "It was a wonderful experience for me with organists on the board going back to 1400." He had a fine time playing both organs in both chapels and listening to the boys' practice, which was excellent - "a model for all boys and practices". He asked Richard Popplewell if he could give them £5 "to get ice creams" and, subsequently, the boys sent him a 'thank you' letter, signed by them all. Such things gave Charles great pleasure.

Also in May, Charles gave two organ recitals - one at Rolvenden (St Mary the Virgin) and the other at Hastings (All Saints).

His letters contained many *non sequiturs* - one such read: "We were sorry to learn of Betjeman's death. He was at Highgate School at the same time as me." and, in the same letter: "My definition of a great work: It must arrest and hold one's attention".

Later that month, Charles went to the St Paul's Cathedral OBE service and in June Barry Brunton came to Rye and recorded Charles' organ music. Later, in August, Brunton agreed to publish three songs which Charles had written to words by Madeleine Chase. Brunton also accepted *Orpheus* and *Four Vocalises*.

"I am reading again Pissaro's letters to his son, Lucien. Manson's father was responsible as Director of the Tate in getting the Impressionists there. Lucien was a great friend of Manson and Mary knew him well - and they all came to Rye for a holiday."

All through this period, painting occupied a huge amount of

Charles' time and he painted a vast amount of pictures. Many of his letters include details of the completion of the painting, the subsequent amendments made when it was hung and, consequently, showed certain things in a different light. He spent as much time 'in painting' as he did 'in music' - but there would be periods when "Painting is OUT" or "Music is OUT".

In August 1984, Oecumuse staged an Exhibition of Charles' publications at Rye Church, concluding with an organ recital in the evening given by Alan Childs. At this time, Charles told me that he was making an arrangement for organ of Handel's *Fireworks Music*.

In December, he found his piano score of *Electra* which he had used at Covent Garden with Beecham about forty years previously. He had been on the staff at Covent Garden with Beecham for two international seasons. He noted one of Beecham's quotes: "A Musicologist is someone who can read music but can't hear it." In this same letter, Charles records that Sir William McKie had died. Amongst his many appointments, Sir William had been Organist of Westminster Abbey (1941-1963) and a member of the Corporation of Trinity College of Music.

Later that month, "June Nixon, a former pupil of mine, is now organist and choirmaster at Melbourne Cathedral." At this time, Carolyn Simpson, his assistant at Rye, informed him that the work at the Church was too much for her with all her 'other commitments'. But, on a happier note, the same letter records that he had had a letter from "my USA fellow student who has already given one performance of the *Duo Concertante*".

In January 1985, Charles referred to his autobiography. He was going to continue working on it but felt "it seems too much looking backward". And then, their beloved cat, Pansy, died. Pansy had featured in many letters - and drawings - and was a very dear pet to both of them. This was another cause for great sadness.

Another letter in January read: "I played the Toscanini recording of the Prelude to *Parsifal* yesterday. The FIRE and intensity of Toscanini had to be heard to be believed. It is the nearest approach to the Holy Ghost I have ever encountered. It was terrifying. And this record was made when he was 82. I always thought Coates and Wood were very full of energy ...but it was physical.... whereas Toscanini was entirely mental and spiritual. This comes over - to me at any rate - in ALL his records. I read of an author, Stephan Zweig who, watching Toscanini in the pit at Bayreuth, had to leave...he couldn't bear to be so near such a manifestation of power."

At the end of the same letter Charles mentioned that he had heard from the wife of Christopher Ede that he was suffering from a disease which was affecting his memory and actions and no cure was possible. Christopher Ede and Charles had produced Elgar's *The Kingdom*, as an opera, in the year of Edward VIII's abdication. Charles also wrote: "I appreciate your offer of typing the Autobiography for already I have several pages written and am making this my TASK for the future times." Interestingly, he made few further references to this and I was never to start on this project.

In his Organist's Report to the Rye PCC in 1985, he recorded that the Annual Concert of the Rye Festival Choir (commemorating the fiftieth anniversary of Elgar's death) had been given with the Hastings Youth Symphony Orchestra in June 1984.

In April 1985, Charles needed permission from the publisher, Weinberger, to make a 'cello arrangement of *Epicedion*, which he had written for the Brymer Clarinet series for Weinberger. He wanted to send it to a 'cellist, Faye Clinton, who had written to him, 'out of the blue', saying she had performed his *'Cello Sonata* for her Suggia award, was to play it again and wanted to discuss it with him. But later that month, he received a disappointing letter from Weinberger "We have recently come to the decision that we are unable, for the foreseeable future, to proceed with a third series of Brymer books. Sales have not been good so return your ms." Yet another disappointment! At the end of the month he wrote that he had sent his *St Augustine's Prayer*, which he had dedicated to Canon Dr Deryck Ingram Hill at Canterbury, to Barry Brunton at Oecumuse for his consideration.

In July, he was as busy as ever and wrote: "The new piece, the *Triptych* is coming on and I am well into the finale." Later that month: "I have finished my *Trio* for oboe/clarinet, 'cello and piano and am going to send it to Clinton. [the 'cellist]"

Charles received an invitation to adjudicate for the Hastings Concerto Class in 1986. He went on to write that he had been re-reading Honegger's book *I am a Composer*. "There is so much of my own thoughts there I feel somewhat encouraged.....especially regarding his PESSIMISM."

In October, he mentioned problems he was having hearing what the Vicar said at Rye Church as "either there were no microphones or, if there were, they were not switched on." This was to become a major problem for him over the coming years.

The Proctors were great friends with Sir Ralph and Lady 'Ba' Millais. Ralph was a member of the 'great' Millais family but had been unwell rather a lot in recent years. He and Charles got on very well together and Charles much enjoyed his visits to the

Millais household and his opportunities of spending time with Ralph.

Charles' painting exploits exhausted him and he would often go off on his own for two nights to 'get over it all'. The same applied when he had finished working on a musical composition.

In November 1985 'Gramps' had died under very sad circumstances. 'Gramps' (Mr Grammans) had been a wonderful support to Rye Church as he could 'fix anything' - including things that went wrong with the organ. He and Charles got on very well and Charles was indebted to him for such practical help on so many occasions. The Proctors were very sad to learn of his death as "we were alike in so many ways." The manner of his death - "he took matters into his own hands" - compounded the sadness.

In December 1985, Charles wrote: "I found a copy of BJ Dale's *Piano Sonata* in a junk shop. I have never had a copy and always wanted one - so I paid the 50p for it! I must outline my connection with this piece. BJ Dale was the fine pupil of my Academy Professor, Corder. Although when I went to Corder, Dale was himself a professor at the Academy. When the piece was written in 1905, it was hailed as the greatest sonata for piano since Beethoven. Corder told me some points about how it was written and how original some of it was, but behind all this I could see Corder's influence as most potent."

In January 1986, Charles made a rare reference to his autobiography. "I think you did offer to type my autobiography ....in a weak moment. Does that offer still stand? I have done about 15 pages for Chapter 1 which takes me from DAY 1 to entering the RAM." Later that month: "*Parsifal* was one of the most potent effects on my whole system when I first heard it, conducted by Goossens. The music was such to throw me completely off my balance - almost to hysteria........"

On this same subject, in a lecture on Church Music, Charles wrote: "Certain aspects of music stir one's soul; our own reaction that passes unheeded by someone perhaps sitting next to you. This stirring of the soul can be soul-shattering."

These may seem somewhat excessive reactions but as I typed them, I was reminded of something I read in Charles Reid's book - *Malcolm Sargent - A Biography* (Hodder 1968). It is worth quoting the paragraph here:

"For his case, as an adolescent, was rare. One spring evening, he found himself confronted by the slow movement (*largo e mesto*) of Beethoven's Op 10 no 3 piano Sonata. The crux of the confrontation was the return of the main subject with the added chordal weight. At the third bar of the recapitulation, a re-shaped bass line upheaves a dissonant F octave against a G of a diminished triad. It was this 'upheaved' octave, incomparably more mordant than anything hinted at in the exposition, that savaged the boy. He played the crucial bar a second time. Then he jumped up from the piano, and, leaving the house, walked blindly uphill through the dusk. His heart pounded. His head was in tumult. From the tumult one plain thought emerged. Music was a terrible power; a power not to be endured. Sitting down at the roadside, somewhere on the grassy outskirts of the town, he wept and prayed to God that he should not be musical any more. Music was a burning, possessing force, a thing to fear and run away from. It was a torment. He prayed God to deliver him from it lest he should be driven mad. Telling of this long afterwards, he reflected: 'I didn't go mad. One adapts oneself to shattering experiences.'"

Charles' letter went on: "Also, I am of the opinion that Wagner took from the slow movement of Beethoven's *Eroica* the wonderful ascending horn passages...... Do not forget, the opening of Beethoven IX nearly transfixed Wagner and I believe he copied out the whole of the Symphony for his own delight."

In February 1986, another disappointment - "I have just been 'let down' over what I had hoped would be a MAJOR performance of something of mine....but that is not unusual....I am afraid." He gave no details - such was the man. In the same letter, on a happier note, he recorded that he had received his timetable for the Hastings Festival and that he would be adjudicating with Dr Ruth Gipps, which pleased him.

Charles had heard 'on the grapevine' that his *'Cello Sonata* had been played in a lunch time concert in Chichester. The 'cellist had told Charles that she was going to perform it - indicating that it would be in February. He had written offering to take her through it, if she so wished. Not only did he not receive a reply, but the event had now happened. The way he had heard about this performance was entirely coincidental. "I had a delightful letter from one of my Marist school girls in Ascot I used to teach...she was typing out the programme for the concert and saw my name - so wrote to me - as she was helping the Organist's wife with the programme as she is the Dean's secretary. So she gave the letter to David Maundrell as she heard I was org. at Rye."

"Mary Manson is in a poor way and can't play now so is selling her piano upright Broadwood...as she sold me the grand I have when she sold up most of their home when going to live in Surrey."

In this same month, I had written telling him that I was going to play his *Alla Gavotta* in a concert and he responded: "That piece came about as my professor at RAM used to play a *Gavotte* by d'Albert who was a terrific pianist. My professor thought well of that piece...and I didn't........so I thought I will write a similar piece...and I done it....and it's *far* better than d'Albert."

In March 1986, Charles sent me a leaflet for the Tenth Annual Concert of the Rye Harmonic Society - shared with Stowmarket Schools Concert Band - which was to take place on June 21. Another letter told me he had done two days of concerti adjudicating at Hastings with Dr Ruth Gipps. "We get on well together - which is the chief thing. The first day was something of a fiasco. Only one in the morn and 22 in the afternoon and evening - so there was a lot of wasted time. So many candidates had withdrawn or just didn't materialise without telling the management, But yesterday we made up for it as we had a full morn and afternoon. 7 to hear in the evening session. Suffice it to say about 5 were excellent and one outstanding ....who will in my opinion get the PRIZE tomorrow eve."

"I see Hanson [Geoffrey] is doing his THING at QE Hall. I must say I admire his enterprise and will to DO...and create. That is all as it should be. I always say if my things are no good...that's not my problem...God should have given me greater gifts...I am only responsible for using wot I have with craftsmanship which I can improve by work. THEN wot happens to my work is not my responsibility."

At the end of March 1986: "I've got my cheque from Hastings. THREE times what I earned in a YEAR with 2 practices and 2 services at my 2nd church at Wood Green."

In April 1986, he wrote: "Sunday - just back from church.

Fortunately nobody asked what was that lovely piece you played after Service..........being the MacDowell 1620....for I should have been tempted to reply...'I don't really know - the congregation were making so much noise after the service that I didn't hear it!!!!!'" (He had made an organ arrangement of AD 1620 from the Sea Pictures of Edward MacDowell.)

He had been teaching at St Thomas C of E School in Winchelsea since 1976 - one visit each week for one hour and full choral Mass at all festivals - once a month at least - in church.

In August - "Dr Vidler is out of hospital and the Mugridges wanted him to go to their place at Robertsbridge but SHE is unwell and they have no servants so the prospects are not happy." Later - "I am in the throws of LUMBARGO, as Sauer called it. Yesterday necessitated spending much of the day a bed, au lit, and all that goes with."

September 1986 - "As we are somewhat bored with the CP Mass at Rye, I altered the words of the NEW PARISH MASS card done long ago by Brunton...to the modern parlance of the ASB and asked if he might care to alter and publish this new version....or I could, with his permission.....alter the words by hand on the existing Oecumuse cards. His reply is rather revealing: 'ALAS......we gave up publishing Series III/ASB Rite...we found that the time, form-filling insisted on by the C of E Copyright....not justified on financial grounds etc.etc.' So you see the C of E has killed publication of Rite III as far as he is concerned."

"I am still enamoured of VUILLARD, the French painter I told you about. When I saw his book for the first time, I was 'startled' as I saw so many colours and treatment and subjects so like mine. It is quite startling."

"I am afraid the Alex might fold up at any minute the way things go these days."

Towards the end of the month, he wrote: "I enclose the latest HC I have written for Rye which is in the process of being tort. We have done my Winchelsea music so often that I thought I would try my hand at this Alternative. In spite of Brunton not willing to publish it."

In October 1986 - "I told you I am doing a recording session with Aitschison at Rye of organ music which is taking my interest in practising these days. The Vicar had mislaid the date and booked a meeting in the Upper Room and bell practice in the tower......"

Early in 1987 - "I have always said, and still say, that a performance should be an experience so that one can't feel the same after it....something has been done to one's spirit. I read once that Sargent, when he had attended a Toscanini concert in London, had to walk about the streets for hours by himself to regain his equilibrium. To hear Schweitzer play the Bach *Passacaglia* - to me anyway - makes everyone else seem as though they didn't know what the music is all about....whereas Schweitzer DOES."

"Many of my counterpoint exercises for RCO were done 'on the job' at the War office as I did them while on duty in my head then wrote them out in odd moments on MS paper and wrapped them round my truncheon for that machine had a long pocket on the trousers that would take 12 stave paper. That's how much of my *Organ Sonata No 1* was written."

At a service when he had to play two hymns that were not to his liking, he wrote: "Two hymns to my detestation. (Appleford and the other a sort of spiritual thing with a chorus.) Both are in the *Tonus Vulgarus* Mode 85043."

He had lent me his copy of *Arthur Honegger: I am a Composer - Interviews with Bernard Gavoty*. I had typed out what, to me, were significant sections and, when returning the book to him, I sent him a copy of my typed extracts. He wrote: "Thank you for the Honegger transcription. I agree with you.... the book is too valuable for a lot of talk by anybody else. I would have preferred to have had a book as you yourself have made in this transcript."

In April, writing about his suite of pieces for organ entitled *Fêtes des Jours* , he said it was by a foreign composer, Pinchot Salinsky.

On May 9 1987, the RSCM held a Festival service at Rye Parish Church to commemorate the Diamond Jubilee of the RSCM and the 40th anniversary of the death of Sydney H Nicholson (1875-1947). Charles had had much to do with the organisation and played the organ for it. On May 11, he wrote: "It is seldom one can look back on any event with complete and utter satisfaction. I could on the Centenary service of Trinity at the Abbey and yesterday was just such another. The day was sunny and fine, the music was magnificent ....the choirs all knew their stuffs. There wasn't a hitch from beginning to end. Popplewell was absolutely first class and and there was no evidence of 'aggro' anywhere...in fact it was just perfect."

Later that month, he wrote a hand-written letter (an unusual thing) from Goose Cottage Trevarrian, near Newquay in Cornwall where they were on holiday. On the way there, they spent the night at Buckfast and Charles played the organ in Buckfast Abbey. "Had an hour on Buckfast organ with Fr Sebastian. I played my *Passacaglia* and Bach *Fantasia in G*. Suffice it to say the *Passacaglia* sounded exactly as I had imagined it when composing it. Wonderful resonance in the Abbey and the sound was like molten GOLD!! Fr. Sebastian became for us both a true friend!!! He is the resident organist and played some of his compositions which I liked very much. Rather in the Dupré style." Later in the same letter he wrote: "We are planning to have a real lazy holiday just around about here without going about much. After Buckfast we both said 'We might as well go home now. We have had our refreshment (holiday).' It was so wonderful."

As a result of the visit to Buckfast, Charles wrote an organ work entitled *Resurgam*. This is a huge composition of some forty-seven pages. At the front of the copy, Charles gave a short explanation of the piece.

> Dedicated to a modern miracle, built on ancient foundations, BUCKFAST ABBEY. The Abbey was founded in 1018. The Cistercian Church and Monastery were built in 1150. Dissolution came in 1539. From that date until 1882 no monks were living in the Monastery. They returned in 1882 to live there and rebuilding began in 1907. At no time had there been more than six monks rebuilding the Abbey during the period 1907 to 1922 when it was opened. Consecrated 1932 and completed 1938. Dedicated to St Mary the Virgin. In the Lady Chapel is a statue, reconstructed from the design of the ancient seal, incorporating a part of the statue found when the monks were rebuilding the present Abbey.

> The overall plan of the *Resurgam* is indicated by reference to the Roman Numerals. The original foundations were discovered (I-XVI) and the structure visualised. The Interpretation (XVII-XXV) carries the inscription *Labor omnia vincit* in the composer's original MS. Reference to the finding of the fragment of the original statue of the Blessed

Virgin Mary is signified by the inclusion of the melody associated with the words 'Virgin born we bow before thee', set for the festivals of St Mary the Virgin; here quoted above the Ground Bass (XXVI). Reference is made to the French Melody sung to the words 'Let all mortal flesh keep silence' (XLV-LI). Above the High Altar hangs the great CORONA (LII-LXXII). The Ground Bass in the manuals, above the Plainsong Melody 'Adoro Te' (LIII), on the Pedals. The final chord contains all the notes of the Ground Bass played together (LXXXII).

I quote that note to demonstrate the amount of work that went into this composition and the immense inspiration Charles had drawn from the story of the rebuilding of Buckfast Abbey.

By now, I was working for the charity Christian Action, whose Director was Canon Eric James. Charles was an avid reader of all Eric's writings which I was able to send to him. Eric's output was vast including as it did sermons, lectures and books. In July Charles wrote: "I finished reading Canon [Eric] James' Shakespeare Sermons....All I can say is that he is to us the greatest "UNDERSTANDER" of Shakespeare we have read....with John Masefield. It is a sad experience to us that what is truly great.....is in itself so sad. For myself I cannot trust myself to quote a single line of Shakespeare without shedding tears...likewise I had to write a quotation from Canon J, which is so Shakespearean, to hand to Rosemary as I couldn't trust myself to speak it....even to her."

In August, at three days notice, he had received a poster of a concert at St Peter's, Bexhill which was to include his *Duo Concertante for piano and organ* played by Jonathan Marten, organ and Kevin Smith, piano. The performance was fine but balance was wrong. "I do wish people would ask me to attend a rehearsal....I could have put things to rights in a moment."

He had sent a copy of *Resurgam* to Fr Sebastian in Buckfast. "I still haven't heard a squeak from Fr. Sebastian in Buckfast - which almost makes me say 'NEVER AGAIN' will I offer unsolicited gifts of my work."

Later in August he received a letter in his capacity as Vice-President of the North London Festival - "of which I was Adjudicator and Chairman for many years."

At the same time, he received a letter from Norman McCann, the Curator of the National Music Museum (56 Laurie Park Gardens, SE26 6XJ) about the possibility of lodging material with the Museum after Charles' death - material concerning Charles' professional life and his Alexandra Choir.

At this point, the letters make many references to his difficulties in hearing, especially at church, when there were no microphones working.

In October, he wrote: "We are now putting into rehearsal A NEW PEOPLE'S MASS by Dom Gregory Murray. He is a monk at Downside and I met him once...He is an FRCO so is a good musician. But later, he wrote: "We did the Murray Mass *Sanctus/Benedictus* today - a less inspiring setting of the Mass I cannot conceive but everyone seems to like it...."

"Tonight we have a lecture on the Military Canals here which of course RENNIE engineered." (Rosemary Proctor came from the Rennie family.) However when they got there, (National Trust at Winchelsea) there had been a 'misunderstanding' in the programme and the lecture was on Martello Towers!

"I have given music etc. to a certain conductor and he hasn't acknowledged the gift or done anything about anything....and what opportunities have come his way via his connection with the Alex."

In the hurricane of 1987, the windmill in Winchelsea was blown down "and is a heap of rubble.". This had been one of the Proctor's favourite places - either to sit, to paint or just to walk for an 'evening constitutional'.

"On Sunday we visited Dr Alex Vidler, who now 88 years is in a home near Rye."

"I've sent *Passacaglia* to Bate, Canterbury, Winchester and Chichester and Ely. I wonder if I shall get a reply." On October 30 - "Canterbury said 'he hopes to play it - the *Passacaglia*...MIGHT do it', but as I wrote, at his behest a *Mag* and *Nunc* and after 3 years he hasn't done it....I haven't much hope."

"Sir Brian Batsford wrote asking Rosemary the date of the bronze bust of him which she had done and which he owns. It was displayed in the Martello Bookshop in Rye. Batsford had been a friend of the family at St Jude's before he was an MP and is an artist himself, in watercolours."

In November, he wrote disappointedly: "It is no use writing to my friend the monk as I doubt if he can write or even sign his PC, stamped for return to writer, in answer to the query if he ever received the package of music I sent, although from a Sister Benedictine, I have heard by post that he has...." This situation, which all too common, caused Charles tremendous sadness - not least because of the lack of courtesy. He used to say "What more can I do? I wrote the piece, bought a copy and sent it to him with sae for return or acknowledgement of the music.....and still nothing."

Also in November, Charles wrote that he had been asked, some months previously, to give a talk on Church Music to the Borderline Society run by Canon Harvey. (Membership was made up primarily of retired clergymen but the Proctors were to become members, and the monthly meetings gave them great pleasure.) He had heard no more. Though Charles' name was on the list, no one had confirmed it to him - the Secretary was supposed to have written with the details and particulars of the Society. This kind of situation was not uncommon but was one with which Charles found hard to cope. He tried to be conscientious, business-like and prompt in his own correspondence and expected the same of others.

Charles was to give two substantial lectures on Church Music to the Borderline Society. Three most important statements from these lectures must be recorded and this would seem the most appropriate place for them. The music of JS Bach and Beethoven was a much a part of Charles' life as the air he breathed. His devotion to the music of both these composers was total. He said:

"JS Bach was the product of the Church - the *chorale* being the soul of his *persona*. Beethoven was the product of humanity and represented humanity with its aspirations towards the unknown and the very limits of its soulful aspirations."

"Who would dare say that the Beethoven quartets do not express the aspirations of the soul of man in greater measure in music than any known musician of any era?"

"To think of the *Ninth Symphony* as being anything less than sacred it out of the question."

A few days before Christmas, the Proctors took Dr Vidler from his nursing home for lunch at Bay Tree House.

Early in 1988 Charles wrote: "Densem rang to ask me to give an organ recital in July HERE as part of the Charter Celebrations HERE... (700!) Date July 18. 700th Anniversary of the granting of the Charter to Winchelsea."

By now Charles was eighty-one years of age and I never ceased to be amazed at his work load. In addition to the weekly choir practice and Sunday services at Rye Parish Church, and weddings and funerals at that same church, he would attend local meetings of the RSCM, travel to London for meetings of Trinity College of Music, the Royal Academy of Music and the Royal Society of Arts - all of which he was a Fellow - prepare and give talks on musical subjects for local groups, prepare and perform organ recitals, undertake adjudicating for Festivals, pay his weekly visit to Winchelsea School and prepare and direct a full Choral Mass once a month - in addition to his prolific output in both painting and musical composition. He was an avid reader and often referred to his current reading. On top of all this, he typed the lengthy letters to me (sometimes two or three a week) and dealt with all my queries about the music copying on which I was now engaged and which demanded much detailed work and correspondence. Finally, there was his work on his autobiography. His letters began to contain many references to the fact that many of his friends and contemporaries were either unwell, in nursing homes or had died.

In January, he wrote: "My friend Christopher Ede has just died.... he was going 'senile' for the last 2 years.... so it is a relief. It was he who helped produce KINGDOM so another link with the past is broken."

In March 1988, Sir Ralph Millais was eighty-three. His health was rather precarious from time to time so although he had proved to be a great friend of the Proctors, Charles did not see as much of him as he would have liked as Sir Ralph was not always capable of receiving visitors.

About this time, Charles made an arrangement of his suite *Fêtes des Jours* for two pianos, six players - for performance at a party at Mary Densem's.

In April, he had to play for the funeral of Mrs. Johnson "aged about 99. She had been a great friend of Mrs. Rennie and knew my mother too. So it was a break in the circle of friendship of so many years."

He loaned us his pamphlet about the Curé d'Ars.... "he is my Patron Saint".

He wrote a piece called *Veni Creator*. "It has 2,300 notes - therefore I shall refer to it as the Tetley piece - who always refer to their 2,000 perforations."

Charles prepared the programme for the organ recital he was to give in Winchelsea on July 18. The programme was to end with the *Lord Warden's Rondo* - a work commissioned by Canon John Williams, late Vicar of Rye, 'for the visit to Rye Church in 1980 of the The Queen Mother as Lord Warden of the Cinque Ports, and played by the composer on that Royal occasion.' (Queen Elizabeth The Queen Mother had succeeded Sir Robert Menzies as Lord Warden of the Cinque Ports. In an Alexandra Choir Newsletter two years previously, Charles had written: One of the most impressive services I have ever played for was the Memorial Service to the late Sir Robert Menzies who, as Lord Warden of the Cinque Ports, was remembered at Rye Parish Church. The attendance of fourteen Mayors of the Cinque Ports and the Associate ports was colourful in pageantry. His widow (Dame Patty) and the Australian High Commissioner were present. A similar service had been held in Westminster Abbey that week.)

His letters often expressed his continual disappointment that people didn't even acknowledge things he sent them - let alone play them!

In May, Stanley Warburton, the Chairman of the Turner Society, came to stay as he was giving a lecture on Turner in Rye.

"Del Mar - conducted Southampton Orchestra at Rye. He was delighted that we knew his father and uncle as well."

By now, Sir Brian and Lady Batsford were resident in Winchelsea and both were excellent artists. At the end of this month, Charles wrote: "It is interesting to learn ...... which we didn't know..... that Sir Brian Batsford ...of the famous books on Art etc.....whom I thought was nothing but an amateur....very good artist....is one and the same BRIAN COOK....he changed his name to his mother's family name when he became connected with the BATSFORD BOOKS. A friend here gave us the best snow scene of Lamb House, Rye as an Xmas present by Brian Cook. Now we know he is the same that lived for some time in Lamb House. He became MP and Chief Whip and now lives round the corner from here. When he came to see our pictures last week he said they reminded him somewhat of CAILLEBOTTE - someone I had never heard of. Then when we went to see them last Thursday, I found he had a large book about him...and so we have it on loan....He is of the Monet school and it is nice to learn of another Impressionist we had not known about at all."

In June 1988, Charles was invited to Trinity College of Music for the farewell event to mark the retirement of Meredith Davies as Principal. Charles also received an invitation to a reception, following Evensong at Canterbury Cathedral, "to mark the retirement of 'Wicks'".

In July 1988, the Queen Mother visited Winchelsea as part of the 700th Anniversary of the Foundation of Winchelsea. Charles wrote that " the old people from Greyfriars were lined up to see the Queen Mother." The fact that some of the residents were almost certainly younger than Charles did not seem to be acknowledged!

After an organ recital he had given, he wrote: "My recital went well - about 80 people attended and the Mayor in chains!"

In November 1988, Charles sent his *Commemoration Passacaglia* to Barry Brunton at Oecumuse. This piece had been 'composed to mark the Church and Town Celebrations of the 700th year of the Foundation of Winchelsea, Sussex AD 1988.' Later that month, he went to the Royal Academy of Music for the Fellows' Society.

"No word from two organists about the *Resurgam* copies I *bought and sent them.*"

At the beginning of 1989, he was doing a huge amount of painting. His letters would tell of the number of times a 'completed' painting would be hung - and then taken down for many amendments. He found this work extremely exhausting - but also very satisfying.

At this time, there is a reference to the Borderline Society meeting at Bay Tree House. Each meeting would include a talk, usually given by one of the members. The subjects were many and various. Charles gave some of these talks during the course of their membership.

In March, the Proctors were reading Noël Coward's Diaries. "One rather cynical sentence caught my eye 'NO GOOD DEED GOES UNPUNISHED'".

"Sir Brian Batsford is very ill in the St Leonard's Clinic where we expect he may not survive. This, and coming to the end of the Noël Coward book last week, has made us a wee bit serious minded." "Rosemary went to see Vidler in Rye Hospital - who is well and very intelligent still but she says he is 'very tired' and 'ready to go'".

In April, Charles wrote: "We had the Rye AGM at which the Rector announced his retirement from September next." Changes of clergy are always something of an 'unknown quantity' for all church members but particularly for the organist as, until it is clear what the musical tastes of the new incumbent will be, it is a somewhat unsettling time. This is true for all organists (unless their tastes in music are extremely catholic!) so this new situation hung like a 'sword of Damocles' over Rye Parish Church as far as Charles was concerned. At this time, there were difficulties within the church....other choirs going to join in things.... didn't know what the music was...... their choirmaster away - so organising musical events was always fraught with difficulty.

The Rye Newsletter for May 89 announced "We celebrate the 700th Anniversary of the first known Mayor of Rye in 1289."

The Proctors read *Edward Elgar, the Windflower Letters*: letters from Elgar to Alice Stuart Wortley, daughter of Sir John Everett Millais. Sir Ralph Millais knew her very well indeed. (No Wortley letters have survived.)

In June a Mediaeval Week was held in Rye 'to mark and honour 700 years of Mayoralty of Rye'. In this same month, Charles recorded: "We have not seen Dr Vidler lately now he lives at Tenterden...."

"Bexhill RSCM festival - 24 people said they would be coming and all my rehearsals were geared to getting the choir up to the required standard of knowing the music. In the end only seven - repeat seven - of the 24 came!"

In July, the Proctors visited Falkington Manor House, "being the Centenary of STACEY-MARKS the picture dealer in Eastbourne we have known for years."

Another rather sad letter included the comment: "I am quite sure that the poor notice of *RESURGAM* will be a great relief to all organist friends (?) of mine who have been looking for a valid excuse why they should not play my music."

Things cheered up later that month. "We had for the evening Sebastian Brown, nephew and his wife. Seb. Brown was one of the three children who came to Rye with Lucien Pissaro and the Manson childer with Manson père and Brown père. The point is Seb. has been a lifelong friend of the Mansons. He is a musician of such erudition as passeth all comprehension. He has orchestrated *Kunst Der Fuge*, was a pupil at RCM with Manson, knows everybody and has spirited ideas about everything. To the musician he is an enchanting companion...to a non-musician I would suspect being a crashing BORE. I don't think most people have the faintest idea what he is talking about.... and I think he felt rewarded that he had for the evening one who could understand, even if not agree with his thoughts. He has edited *Kunst* completely.... for performance, done by BBC 1970 now just published.... and re-arranged the fugues in a different order and orchestrated it. He has made an arrangement of the great *G Minor Organ Fantasia and Fugue* for String soloists and *tutti* in the form of a *Grosso Concerto à la mode*...and his erudition is overwhelming. He seems to have held no Academic position or got any qualifications....teaches privately, coaches.....plays ALL string instruments and understands classical Fugue...to despise Tovey....who 'knew everything' as Joachim said. When Vaughan Williams criticised his RCM fugues, Seb. explained that the top voice was not the Treble clef but the Tenor, as stated in the given phrase subject....He is the sort of person who would find fault with Einstein if necessary....anyway we gave them a lovely supper in the swing chair. I said hardly a WORD.....it was not necessary." (Sebastian Brown had written a book entitled *Enigma Resolved* - a full solution of the Enigma in Elgar's *Variations on an Original Theme.*)

In early August, a letter records: "Yesterday was one of the most interesting days we have had. The Centenary of Conrad Aiken. At 11.15 we forgathered at Jeake's House Mermaid Street some 30 persons and then the Mayor unveiled the plaque withdrawing the two flags, USA and the Union Jack and made a speech. We then went inside to have sherry and about 12.15 we all traipsed down or up as the case may be to the Hope Anchor Hotel for what we thought to be a Buffet Lunch. You know what THAT is....But no....a SIT DOWN LUNCH. Cold meat etc and lovely sweets and much wine. THAT was all - no speeches. About 40 people or so on some six or seven tables. Mary D and Molly T and of course a lot of Aiken's family, as the Conrad Aiken we celebrated had had three wives. We were able to arrange seating with exchanges so that we all had at some time or other someone to talk to we liked to know. The whole affair most friendly and well done. Then we all traipsed up to Playden Church for an Exhibition and the Recital....which consisted of a biography well spoken....then Molly read extracts from the Books and Mary D played his piano compositions on the piano. These are gentle Jazz compositions of a tuneful nature and made a nice counterfoil for the readings. Then the Rector of Playden read an extract and to end with, Molly sang my song *All Lovely Things* [words by Conrad Aiken] which is in short a sort of Requiem anyway...then they played a tape of Conrad reading some of his work...then applause for the son who thanked everyone....a most moving occasion...Kisses all round and we came away."

Later in the month, Christian Action, the charity for which I then worked, had its 'office outing' - to the Proctors in Winchelsea. I must explain that the staff of Christian Action was only Canon Eric James and me! Charles and Eric had recently renewed their acquaintance (having originally met at Southwark Cathedral many years before) and both were eager to meet again. Their respect for each other was great.

In September, the news that everyone awaited came. "We have been vouchsafed the news of a new Rector...a Mr. BUXTED whose induction takes place in Rye on December 11." (That was not entirely accurate.....the new Rector was Paddy BUXTON.)

Very soon, another letter from Charles read: "I have had a very nice letter of 'co-operation with music' from the Rector Designate. He sends me the draft of the Carol Service he wants as he is instituted on December 11 and his first service is December 17 with the Carol Service that evening."

"On September 15 we go to Hastings Art Gallery for a Private View of Lucien and Orvido Pissaro's work. There we shall meet Sebastian Brown again...who was one of the 3 children with the Manson 'girls' in Rye about 60 years ago. PS William A G Buxton, Rector Kingston Buci, Shoreham by Sea, Sussex, aged 56. Late ordained!! Previously with Commercial Firms."

Later: "We went to Burwash and had tea with Sebastian Brown

at his new home. Tell G Hanson this - I am trying to learn the *Passacaglia* (Winchelsea) and find it very hard going....so if any of my friends are hoping to play it for my centenary celebrations, they had better begin practising it now!"

On September 21 1989 [Rosemary's birthday], the Proctors attended a recital by Ronald Smith. "In a word, Smith is a Great Pianist to be regarded in the same street as Petri, Ogden and the like. His technique is prodigious and his interpretation of the first order." They went back to see him after the recital. "He was delighted to see us and told me I hadn't altered these 20 years....which was when we met him here in Winchelsea at my friend's house, Alfred Bulley....and I believe he came to Eastholm once too." Not long after the recital, Ronald Smith and his wife went to tea with the Proctors.

"We are reading the 3 vols of Van Gogh's letters and have done Vol 1, so will collect the next 2 vols today. It is not only his paintings that are so wonderful....but probably to be expected....his mind that is so wonderful."

In a lecture, he had written: "What it means to *me* is the essential thing about art. Van Gogh, Stanley Spencer, Constable, Turner - they all mean different things to different people but what it means to *me* is the essential thing to me. This is true of experience in art and religion."

This reminded me of something he once said to me when I was bemoaning the fact that I had been trying to explain to a friend how Bach's *St Matthew Passion* was 'one of the wonders of the musical world'. My friend (whose acquaintance with the work was minimal and whose musical tastes lay elsewhere) could not see this. I was very upset - I could not understand how someone could not share my opinion of this work. I related this to Charles who, in his measured way, said to me: "Jane, you've got to *come* to art - and religion." I have never forgotten that wise comment.

In October, the Royal Society of Arts made him a Life Member.

In December, Charles wrote: "We had to tea, yesterday, our new 'intended' Rector with his wife.....he seems to enjoy the prospects that we are to be colleagues and that the services really depend on the Rector/Organist idea. I feel pretty sure we shall all get on well together."

The Proctors' first impressions of Mr. Buxton were of a very efficient man. "He likes to be known as 'Paddy'. He was in residence at the Rectory on Wednesday previous week, Inducted yesterday....but I have in writing, typed in triplicate, copies to Wardens and CP at the foot...of all the weddings to Sept as booked. All hymns until the New Year, Form of Service on Xmas Day...."

Three letters in late December and January 1990 echoed the same sentiment. "Everything at Rye is different and better. Very efficient etc." "We get on so well together...." "Rector came 'to discuss music in toto regarding the Church of St Mary the Virgin'. I can say it was all very satisfactory."

But there was another cloud on the horizon....."Sir Ralph Millais in hospital with a further haemorrhage."

In March 1990, he wrote of the new Rector: "He has exquisite charm....but underneath an IRON will...."

The Proctors had been burgled but, in their usual very private way, did not want to discuss it at all. Charles had 'phoned us to tell us and he thanked us for our concern. "I am happy to say that on the whole, by and large, for richer, for poorer, in sickness and in health ...etc...we have both managed to gain our equilibrium to a great extent. I think most of the business of the affair is now concluded as far as we are concerned and this has been done in great measure by RM who has more certain knowledge of things and conditions than I have. This being so we are now of the opinion that the matter from now on is to be considered closed....and no further reference will be made to it."

"We have instituted a monthly conference of an hour or so between Rector and his Director of Music....an unheard of affair. The recent outcome is that we are drawing up a proper contract of my job and salary. Anyway we are on MOST agreeable terms."

"Went to Brian Batsford's house. He is improving but it is sad to see this big man who was so prominent in business and as an MP trying to connect his thoughts and also follow conversation intelligently."

"Bosendorfer sent me a card - as I s'pose they got my name on their books when they sent me a piano anywhere in London FREE if I was playing at a concert....as I used to do."

In April: "I am enjoying reading St Eustache Cathedral book and re-reading about Marchal....in the book in memoriam about him. When I heard him at the Alex Palace...I wasn't at all keen. I had heard Dupré there and nothing could have been more wonderful.....but when it came that Marchal played, it was even BETTER....so you can relish the esteem in which I hold him in mind."

In May: "I slept rather uneasily after I had the report from Josie [Kane] re. the Alex and their affairs....so last night I concocted a letter urging them to consider various things. This morning I wrote the letter and sent it to Josie....in case they had a meeting or rehearsal and especially as last THURSDAY they had the resignation of the conductor....." (By this time, Josie Kane, a long-standing member of the Alexandra Choir, had taken on the administrative work connected with it.)

After so many 'disasters' in church affairs - both nationally and locally - about which Charles so often wrote to us, now he wrote: "Five years ago I gave the C of E 25 years to live....now I give it the remaining 20". This was after attending a QUIET EVENING. Though it was open to a large number of churches (an ecumenical event) only twenty-five people were present. The content of the evening left 'much to be desired'. "It was quite the dullest and most amateur affair I have ever attended."

"Mary Manson is in a poor way but we are going to see her and her sister on Wed. next. She has lost most of her memory we think. RM went to see Dr Vidler at Tenterden yesterday and he was unaware it was Ascension Day...in fact RYE had no celebration as the Rector was away and no provision had been made for the Festival. Though I did mention it at our monthly 'meeting' when he came last. So I suppose with the new theology, Ascension is now OUT".

"I am enjoying the Curé d'Ars book very much and so much is what I personally think is so lacking these days.... The Author speaks of Religion without God, manifest in the time of the Curé...as in our time. Divine service is nothing more than a coffee morning with a few hymns and prayers."

Later in the same letter: "I've now read with much pleasure the Curé d'Ars book through and RM is now doing so. It is the sort of book....if I were a Bishop....I would give to any priest I was inducting into a Parish. How to do the job is most clearly shown in the life of the Curé...and in this book it shows through."

A Song of Farewell

The Alexandra Choir was preparing a concert to mark the fiftieth anniversary of its founding. Charles' opinion was sought and he suggested they might like to consider a Thanksgiving Service but the choir thought that would have to be the following year. The members wanted to concentrate on the concert planned for 1990.

In June, he wrote: "There seems to be many problems surrounding the Alex......Josie Kane rang up to ask me to contribute a Foreword for the programme for the St Paul's, Baker Street concert (June 30) and I took the liberty of suggesting that if we got a cleric to say a prayer and give the blessing as a finale to the concert, and ended with *Ye Watchers* as we did in the Carol Concerts, we could end the matter of the Service at a blow and get shot of all the possibilities of a DISASTER - so she is putting the matter to her Committee. Also I gather the numbers of the choir are now but 60 persons.......so the less said and done the better."

Later that month, he wrote: "The Alex business affairs seem to be more precarious by the minute."

"Mary (Manson) is 'on the way out' and now in a second...hospital...so all is not very happy there I am afraid...she wants to 'go'".

He related one of the many 'frustrations' with the Church Choir with which he had to contend. "We had a full choir on Friday (at the rehearsal) with all the boys and girls also a good lot of adults so much so that we did Excellent work. On Sunday, my main lady was away, and two others not there on Friday arrived, only one child.......the others were at the Boot Sale down the road. The head boy was absent. The Mozart *Ave Verum* they did so well on Friday came apart towards the end - though I covered it up on the organ."

In early July he wrote: "I am glad the Celebration (50th Alexandra Choir concert) is now all over and done with.....I was a little taken aback when I suddenly realised it was 12 years ago that I left the Alex. It is very sad to think how things have changed in the music world in that short time....with Alex, Trinity, RCO, ISM being hardly the same institutions as we knew them...and few, if any, for the better!!!! Let alone the C of E."

He was arranging a rota of organists to play during a Flower Festival in Rye Church. He himself was giving nine organ recitals during the Rye Festival. "I am glad that all the spaces have now been filled. But it has taken a lot of organising - especially as I know so many of our 'friends' don't trouble to read letters! They pride themselves on this aspect of their originality and genius...."

In August, he wrote: "We were going to Worcester Three Choirs festival. That's where I saw Holst and Elgar and heard him conduct *Music Makers*."

In September, there was a meeting between a Hill, Norman and Beard representative, the Rector and Charles about the new Nave Organ.

Later that month: "It is not easy at Rye..... one has to be on guard all the time to check everything according to our church knowledge experience........although one mustn't mind making enemies in business........it is essential to get on with parish folk who have to do all the work week in and week out...."

Arthur Jacobs visited the Proctors as he was compiling a radio programme about Sir Henry Wood and also preparing a book about him.

"The essential of Schumann is the *Sehnsucht*....or 'longing'......as one feels as 'homesickness' when away from home alone. This quality is so much...in fact ALL of Schumann I learnt from Sauer and being in Germany as a young person. You get it all in Lisa della Casa's singing of Strauss' *Four Last Songs*....Lotte Lehmann had this quality. I heard her often in Vienna....and Toscanini attended her RECITAL........and she sang in *Fidelio*..........so you can understand that she had the quality I so often find lacking these days."

"We have our TEAM Service at Playden on Sunday...but the 'Fixtures book' prints RYE, likewise the Winchelsea magazine........no one had been told of the change of venue."

"I had thought that the Rector was not according to C of E cloth in the sense that we know the C of E happenings...but he was giving out A&M Hymn books...then I told him he was mistaken as we had chosen hymns from *Junior Praise* so he had to recollect A&M and give out *Junior Praises*. I then said 'where are the hymn sheets of the first hymn?' ....words I didn't know though tune was in A&M.....he then flew back to the Rectory to find them and realised that he hadn't 'run them off' as only he and I had the master copies, so we consulted and we had to choose another hymn from *Junior Praise*. He was in a bit of a 'tis' as it was then 5 minutes to 3. pm....I suggested 'All things bright and beautiful' which he didn't like as being 'Wckie' - or some such expression...so we had 'Praise my soul' ...ALSO on Sunday morn, we hadn't the choir hymn lists although I had mine as again he 'hadn't run them off'...so he had to bring them to Evensong....I am not telling you this out of malice a forethought or whatever the saying is but to let you know the hazards that beset us week by week STILL."

October: "The Organ is 'on ice' for 6 months...their ideas all round are silly anyway."

Charles wrote that Ludwig Lebell, who had been a 'cello professor at TCM, had been in Bruckner's Harmony class.

In November, Charles records that the Borderline Society was 'going strong'. This was obviously a great source of pleasure for both Charles and Rosemary.

December: "....... is such a pain in the neck by not reading letters, replying or even 'phoning....so we are 'going ahead' as far as possible without trying to consult them." Sadly this lack of communication was not an infrequent occurrence.

"Yesterday we had Peter and Valerie [his brother-in-law and wife] from Ascot for the day...arriving about 11. am and leaving at 3.30 pm We came to the conclusion that the distance of some 2 years between visits is about right."

"We are now on our third - repeat *third* - Church Treasurer since the advent of a certain person."

"Our Borderline Society has arranged that each member shall write as an 'exercise' a letter to the new Arch Bp telling him wot each member 'wants' from him in his new office. I've done mine....and it reads rather amusingly....between the lines. When the letters have been read, there will be a discussion about the situation. The letter will NOT be sent to the Arch Bp of course as it is a private Society and this is merely an exercise."

Charles sent me details of Sebastian Brown's book *Enigma Resolved*.

"I have decided, and am in the middle of, making the *Elegia* into a short score with a view to use by Military Bands. So I'm making a version in 4/4 time instead of 5/2 time as in the *Organ Sonata.....*"

January 1991 - Rosemary had been taken to hospital - suddenly. "Our biggest problem has been to overcome the suddenness of the whole affair. I am not going to give you any unnecessary details but suffice it to say that I was told to ring the Dr. one morning as she wasn't feeling well for no accountable reason. The Dr. arrived about 5. pm and made arrangements at once and the ambulance arrived to take us to Hastings within the hour. Certain 'tests' are being given and treatments and I have been there daily except when she said I wasn't to come. Her chief anxiety is that I am alright. I can assure her that everything is under control here and I can get a reliable taxi person without any trouble all day and even night if reqd. I am happy on travel etc. Her chief anxiety is that no one shall know....but persons here saw the ambulance so they 'know'. But I have only taken the Millaises into my confidence and I had 'words' with Lady M yesterday and she quite agreed with my wishes that she must on no account 'offer' to do anything for us...but if I ASK her to do anything she will do so without demur. She kept on asking if there was ANYTHING she could do...so I made the above statement and added 'that is the highest compliment I can give you....'.....she saw the point completely. I told the M's not to tell anyone hereabouts...but it has 'got around', as things do in a 'village like this' situation. One has to be very firm with people...and RM felt at the time I was ill that it only makes it more difficult for us if anyone 'encroaches on our privacy' even with the best intentions."

I sent them Eric James' book *A Last Eccentric - A Symposium concerning The Reverend FA Simpson; Historian, Preacher and Eccentric* (Christian Action 1991) which they both loved.

February 1991 - Charles had sent to some of his musical friends details of Sebastian Brown's book *Enigma Resolved* . "I've had nice letters from Prof Ivor Keys and Prof Ian Parrott saying they are interested and hope to get it into their university libraries."

"I am in touch with the Commandant (of Kneller Hall) about the *Elegia*. They are going to Banderlise it themselves and will let me see the Banderlised version when available." (A new verb invented by Charles!)

Later that month: "Although we are glad the Gulf War is over...we are sorry to hear that the tank that was accidentally hit by the USA in error...had a boy from Rye Harbour who was killed. It makes things seem more near at hand when we hear that story."

"I sent notice of the Elgar Brown book to Geoffroy Millais and he is ordering a copy....as being 'up his street' as he is an ardent Elgarite.....getting back from Carice the Wortley picture by Millais for his dad which Elgar had as Lady Wortley was of course Sir Ralph's Aunt and at whose house Ralph met Elgar several times. She is the 'Windflower' of the *Concerto* of course."

March 5 1991 - "I had not heard from .... in response to a Business Letter ......so RM 'phoned up... 'what with one thing and another, you know how it is'. Considering we had confided personal information...we were a bit cheesed off at the negligence....witch goes to shew......."

March 14 1991 - "We had the funeral of the lady opposite on Monday...Tuesday the funeral of Batsford at Rye. Today we had the funeral at Rye of the 18-year-old boy killed in the Gulf War. I played the Schumann *Funeral March* from the 5et. I have written out the arrangement and will submit it to Brunton."

"Did I ever tell you I sang the solo from Spohr's *Last Judgment*,

'As pants the hart' as a school boy at Highgate Chapel at Evensong - anthem?" (Louis Spohr and Charles had both been born on April 5.)

Throughout all the letters he is either 'In Music' and 'Out of Painting' or 'Out of Music' and 'In Painting'. Whichever he was in, a huge amount of both physical and mental effort went into the work and he was always exhausted at the end of it. He would often go away for a night or two to recover his equilibrium.

In March 1991 he had been invited to give a talk about Schweitzer to the Borderline Society in the following September. He worked on it straight away and soon had it complete - for me to type

In May, Sir Ralph Millais was not well again. In that same month, Charles went to Eastbourne on his own for a break. While there, he went to the small theatre for wrestling where he obtained a photograph of the wrestler *Big Daddy* - and got the wrestler to sign it for Rosemary. I continue to be amazed at this!

"On Friday we had the Rye Choir as usual but so much absenteeism........for no accountable reason except people had other things better to do........although for Whitsun."

The Proctors went to an organ recital at Ringmer given by Charles Macdonald. He told Charles that he had played CP's *Dedication* at Worthing and to the Proctor's delight, he played *Resurgam* in the recital they attended.

"We went to the Crematorium near Canterbury for Mary Manson's Funeral. Some years ago I had given them (Mary and her sister Jeannie) a pastel I had done which they much admired....of Rye Harbour from the East Bank. When Mary was so ill and unlikely to recover, Jeannie gave me some music and other things and returned the pastel picture. I decided to give the picture to the Harbour Master at Rye so I took it to him and he was delighted with it."

He had written to Lengnick's for permission for Kneller Hall to make the arrangement of the *Elegia*.

"I have got permission from Brunton for the Royal Marines to make an arrangement for single winds of the *Warden's Rondo*, which the Principal of the School hopes to arrange for their use. "

"You may recall a coloured girl 'cellist who played my Sonata for the Suggia prize...and I wrote something for her to play at ELY. She is on TV this week...".

In May 1991, he wrote: "My next task is to make chorus parts of my Ps 18 for Hastings Choir who are doing it in Sept." He went on : "We are sorry to say that Sir Ralph is rather poorly these days."

In June, he wrote that he had read Cecil Beaton's Diaries...."very interesting and witty."

"The Borderline Society is to have a talk on 'Christianity from a Scientific point of view' and a member is a Professor of Science and written great books etc. (Revd. Dr. John Polkinghorne FRS Pres. Queens' College, Cambridge)"

In July: "I was glad to get the report on the Alex concert via your Aunt...I fear that organisation will pack up ere long." Later in the month, he wrote: "Sir Ralph Millais is now always in bed...comfortable....and with no pain...but is obviously here for a limited time."

During July and August, Charles gave seven organ recitals in Rye Church. The one on August 22 included our Wedding March....*Marche Joyeuse*.

Later in August, he wrote:"I have a meeting with the Rector on Friday to try and sort out the Vidler Memorial Service...I hope by now he knows what is involved."

"I am fully aware that you...and some others...have much wished that I write my autobiography. I had even made a considerable start but found it not to be to my taste. Autobiography is obviously about SELF and I found it rather harrowing to dig up the past *per se* with all the trials and tribulations I endured of which very few, if anyone, know or could guess. I do know that maybe I have some history to relate which might be of interest and value. I hit on an idea which I approve of and it is that I write reminiscences about PEOPLE I knew and the times and conditions obviously thus related...and at the end you would find it in truth an autobiography for the nonce. To this end I have devised the title *Dear Jane and Howard*. This gives me the *raison d'être* and at the same time aims my words to a person and thus makes me have a target for my writing." I found this paragraph very interesting - but no chapters ever came to me.

On August 26 1991, Charles records that the Rector came for the monthly meeting. "Chiefly to sort out the Vidler Service. All really depends on what the Bp of Chichester rules, but we have sorted out what we can do in the meantime. Life is somewhat difficult at times. I was rather taken aback when *The Creation* was being considered for next DIY concert-Service at Rye as we did *Messiah* some time ago...when the Rector asked me the name of the composer!! I presume he knew the Author of the words. These little things knock one sideways at the time. Likewise the number of Memorial Services I have musically directed is not inconsiderable and he is not quite fully willing to encourage the offering of any ideas on the questions which arise. It makes life rather difficult to put it mildly." (Charles' maxim had always been "The Vicar is always right - even when he's wrong." He used to quote that to the Trinity College of Music students in the Organists' and Choirmasters' classes - as he knew, only too well, that the students might encounter 'local difficulties' with clergy once they became church organists.)

In September 1991 Charles wrote: "I am trying to get the *Russian Contakion* done for the Vidler and have made a simpler version......."

Charles' Schweitzer Lecture, which he gave to the Borderline Society, had been a "goodly success...one of the set called it superb". He wondered if the BBC would like it "for a talk - either music programme or Religious programme."

Later in September - Brian and Anne Hunter visited. "But the greatest thing for me was the ecstatic praise for the Schweitzer - copy I had sent them. They broached the idea of publication. Your remarks are interesting. Of course, THEOLOGY would be a fine venue and Vidler was the Editor of it for some 25 years."

"I am reading Lord Lichfield (photographer) autobiography."

A concert at Bexhill included Charles' *Diligam te, Domine* - a setting of verses from Psalm 18. "The reception the piece got was very good - and me personally - when I was invited by the Conductor to take a bow....quite something....to my great surprise!!"

A letter in early October read: "As you know the Vidler nightmare looms pretty large."

"At Evensong I played before the service the *Pastorale* and *Finale* of Guilmant *Sonata*....very loud and brilliant. This was the signal for those of the congregation seated in the choir stalls as close to the organ as possible to shout about 'tickets available' for the Harvest Lunch .....I stopped as required ffff suddenly...to their astonishment...but do you know the story...at a Concert at Queen's Hall the orchestra stopped suddenly and a lady was heard to say 'We fry ours in butter....' it nearly produced the same effect on Sunday."

At the end of October, Charles wrote: "RM was adamant that I have a time off to recover my equilibrium as I have really been quite terribly overwrought about the Vidler affair."

"Dr Murray Brown is leaving the (TCM) Corporation as Chairperson and they have appointed a JUDGE as Chairperson. (The Rt Hon Sir Peter Taylor.)"

In November 1991, in a letter which spanned a few days: "The Chairman of our Borderline Society [Canon Peter Harvey] is celebrating his 50th anniversary as Priest (at Rye Church) and is inviting Brownbill and the Rye Singers to provide the choral music...LAUS DEO. I am not involved, except to play the organ. He has asked me to play the *Great D Minor* before the service (presumably by JSB and I presume the *Toccata and Fugue* NOT the *Fantasia* or *Prelude* one, which is a possibility he doesn't know exists), then one of MY Compositions to blow them out. So I have already sketched out the same.......but it is not for discussion yet as it isn't finalised on paper but is completed in my mind. So I expect it will be 'paperised' by the end of the week." By the end of this letter, he wrote: "I finished my piece for Canon Harvey Jubilee Service and I am looking forward now to hearing it being played on the Rye organ by the Resident Organist there sometime....to see if it works."

On November 15: "I've got the first Vidler rehearsal tonight. Several people can't come all the time...once only....bad cold....can't sing....can't read etc.etc." Later he went on: "Canon Harvey piece to be called JUBILATION."

In early December 1991, "I go to the Densem choir rehearsal tomorrow as they are doing my two carols and they have invited me to help them with the ideas of my requirements." "I have a meeting with the Rector on Thursday so we shall hear further or less about the organ shiftings...."

It is interesting that Charles still referred to Mary as 'Densem' as, by now, she had married Knightley (Ken) Chetwood, though she did continue to use her former name for concerts on occasions.

The Memorial Service for Dr Vidler had taken place on November 23 and I had attended it. On December 7 1991, a very sad letter detailed the subsequent extremely unhappy events. Certain things in the Memorial Service had not gone 'according to plan' and Charles was blamed. The Proctors were extremely hurt but, in their usual private way, they 'kept their silence'. Charles wrote to the Rector, giving the three months' notice that was required of him and indicating that he would relinquish his position, with effect from March 5 1992. Confidentiality prohibits me from putting on record the details of this sad affair but, clearly, it was a source of heart-breaking unhappiness for them both. Luckily, Charles was very busy with many musical enterprises, immediately after this dreadful event, and this helped restore his shattered confidence.

The Canon Harvey fiftieth anniversary service had happened

and his letter of December 22 1991 read: "The Church was FULL. All went very well. RM and I agreed that NEVER have we had such a Catholic service in Rye since we have been here. We were refreshed and renewed in spirit beyond words." Consequently, the comment made the next day by the Rector was even harder to bear than it might have been. "Sunday service at Rye...the smallest congregation we have seen....Carol Service 6. pm. Choir not robed 'to keep it a family affair' and mediocre music. The exact opposite of the Sat. Service. The Rector expressed his delight and said how much nicer it was than the Sat service which was 'over the top'. TACET OMNES LUNGA PAUSA."

At the beginning of January 1992 -, he wrote: "Suffice it to say that my last Official Sunday is March 1 and that I have been able to 'stay on' at full salary until my successor is installed." Later that month he was to write: "There can be little if any doubt that St Mary's is not a happy place." The Proctors had been made aware of much unhappiness in the Church - in addition to their own particular situation. Things became even more unhappy when, in early February 1992, Bob Bowler - the Vicar's Warden - died suddenly.

Another disappointment was to follow. "The RSA have told me they cannot accommodate my Schweitzer lecture."

During February, the events leading up to the end of Charles' tenure as Organist and Choirmaster, and others events thereafter, proved a terrible strain for them both. The unrelia-bility of choir members only added to this.

On a brighter note, he wrote that he was reading the life of Burne-Jones.

Later in February: "RM had been 'researching' in the top attic studio....black hole cupboard...and found a lot of Henry Wood's letters to me. So I may show them to Jacobs (who is coming to tea soon) and the RAM in case they want to show them....after I have vetted them."

His letter of March 3 1992 contained a description of the presentation to him at the end of the morning service. He ended: "Not many....if ANY.....have any idea what this change in our lives can mean...after a lifetime with the C of E."

During this month, Charles was engaged to play the organ for the Schubert *Mass in E flat* at Winchelsea church and then at Fairlight. He was "reading the life of Eric Gill, the sculptor etc. who did the stations of the X at Westminster Cathedral. Most interesting....howbeit...so very immoral and immodest and utterly orful that one couldn't let anyone read it. Yet he was a renowned Roman Catholic, but as a psychological study, most interesting."

In April, he learned that a new organist had been appointed for Rye Church. He would start on November 1 so Charles' last Sunday would be October 25.

During a visit to him this month, we had a rather serious conversation about music and his place in the 'scheme of things'. He said that his job at Trinity was to start everyone off on their great voyage of discovery into music and hope they would take it on from there for the rest of their lives. I was reminded of a letter he wrote in 1972 after I had written to him, thanking him for all that the performance of the *Hiawatha Trilogy* had meant to me. (The Alexandra Choir had performed this at the Fairfield Halls in Croydon and it had been a completely new work to me - one which I had much enjoyed rehearsing and, subsequently, performing.) Charles wrote: "I am glad you of the 'new generation' can show appreciation of the real worth of music and poetic feeling once it has been presented to you. This is one of my missions in life........I feel from your letter my mission has in small part been successful. This is my reward - I ask no other."

By June 1992, Sir Ralph Millais had died.

"We have both arrived at the position of mind that we both agree that 15 years at Rye, under Three Rectors, coping with the demise of Sung Matins, Sung Evensong, destroying the Book of Common Prayer and the coping with the ASB...is quite enough and a CHANGE is due in any case. So we await wot possibilities if any present themselves."

During this month, he wrote: "The *Jubilation* at Bexhill earned for itself a very sudden burst of applause, and Warner introduced it by calling it 'this magnificent piece'. Also a nice letter from the Kent Organists' Association to whom I played the Winchelsea *St Thomas Liturgy* (Lengnick) and the *Dedication* (Oecumuse) and the President wrote thanks for the outing...and 'pieces ...showing that attractive, accessible and effective music is still being written'!"

Later in June: "Reading wonderful book - life of Ludwig II of Bavaria. New organist now starting Sept 1. 5 organ recitals on July 25, Aug 1, 8, 15 and 22."

In early July 1992: "Went to RSCM meeting....and I told them of our impending resignation and that the org. at Rye will be installed on Sept 1. The chairman made it abundantly clear to all...that I was not on the Committee as representing RYE but myself and that it would not be considered that the new organist was *ipso facto* member of the Committee and they hoped we would stay on. RM was originally co-opted as being the means of getting her included of course. Some of my friends asked Who is coming and Where from and all about him...which to their great surprise I could say....I don't know where he has come 'from' ie previous posts or what his musical qualifications were likely to be...to which they expressed some surprise and further SURMISE....so we left it at that."

Later in July, at the Fair on the Salts in Rye, they bought a record/tape machine - replacing the Millaisgram that had gone wrong and could not be fixed. (Sir Ralph Millais had given them some equipment that he no longer needed and they had christened it their 'Millaisgram'.) Also at this time, he told me that he was "working on a big piece - nearly finished" and that he was "counting the days until Sept 1."

In late July 1992, he wrote: "Last Friday was the final choir practice I take at Rye and as RM was not included in my farewell presentation in March, the Choir noted her work for them for 15 years....repeat FIFTEEN YEARS attending every service and practice with me....so they gave her a floral offering which now graces the Music Room. The Stowmarket Band gave a concert in Church last night....we didn't attend....as they were not invited to join us in the Sunday Service as has been their custom ever since I have been at Rye. It was too much for the Rector to cope with - he told me."

"The copying out (neatly) of latest piece is going well tho' a slow job. Things have to be sorted out.....I have to decide of the SATB who sings wot."

In August, the Proctors visited Lincolnshire. "The Lincs visit was an unparalleled success and also of unparalleled horrors of car driving....particularly along the M somethings. We 'phoned our solicitor friend and said we would like to visit him. He is much confined to a wheel chair and his wife was a pupil at the RAM so all knew my musical family friends. We then decided to alter our route via my grandfather's farm house where I spent most of my childish holidays... and then on to Fleet and saw my parents' house there where they lived since leaving London, then on to Gedney Church where I played my first Service on the organ there which was a converted Barrel Organ with the programme printed inside...now a posh 2-manual affair made by a good firm from Lincoln. Then called on our Solicitors who had invited my accountant to meet us. Then on to Bay Tree Farm which I inherited before we came here and sold to the resident Proctors....I had known all my life...and called on a John Proctor who was the only one left...and his crippled wife. They were delighted to see us. Then on to Spalding, the town my father was born in and went to the Grammar School there...as we drove along the river bank up stream."

"When in Lincs, we went to Spalding and cleaned up the Proctor graves. The stone was for Charles and Bettsie, my grandparents, and Alfred and Pamela, my parents. RM had taken the proper suds for the cleaning of and a bread knife to scratch off the green grime...so after that all the names were readable."

Charles visited Eric Wayman, an organist, who had been a student at Trinity College of Music and who was, by then, music master at Spalding Grammar School. Charles gave him the *Jubilation* piece.

On return to Sussex: "I finished the new piece at noon today - some 50 pages of neat copying - so I can get on to my next job...doing the 2 lectures on Gilbert and Sullivan."

"I am to play (on the last day of the Flower Fest) for Brownbill who has asked me to play the piano for *Magic Flute* - concert version I believe - in church. I am trying to book people for their hourly recitals during the daytime for the Flower Fest. You won't see me about Rye on Sept 1."

On August 8 1992: "I played through the new piece. It is in effect, over all, all things being equal, as the crow flies, without let or hindrance, at the end of the day, when all is said and done... The Passion according to St Luke. The Narrator is NOT a Tenor ...but the Choir. The solos are Cleopas, Jesus, Peter and small parts from the chorus. The CHORALES are words from the Litanies in EH with original music, CP, for congregational singing, participation etc. The accompaniments are organ and cembalo, the latter if possible and harpsichord, or synthetic harpsichord electric affair when it only plays for Jesus."

"I am now trying to tie up the organists for the Flower Show at Rye, playing as RM calls it 'music from wall to wall' from 10.30 am to 6. pm. It is not how I would have arranged it. I think half an hour every two hours would have been enough........but now-a-days of course we must have music while we work, eat, walk around.......To my ears, the BACKGROUND music one hears on TV incessantly is a nightmare only comparable with the M25."

Later that month, he had finished the PROBUS lecture and sent it to me to type. He was also doing another one for the Borderline Society. The workload that he continued to impose on himself during these years was immense and would have floored a much younger man. (He was now eighty-six).

He wrote about playing the piano for a concert performance of *Magic Flute*. "As you know, the music isn't easy - there are CUTS - the SCRIPT is being said in English but my pf music vocal score is in GERMAN and some of the other singers have differing editions...."

Later in August, he wrote that he had a rehearsal with Jan [Reeve] and [Mary Densem] - Jan was singing his *Come Live with me* and *King David* in a concert and Charles was to play his *Duo*

Concertante No 2 with Mary. The concert was due to take place on September 18.

"Next week, Josie Kane of the Alex is coming to discuss the future, if any, of the Alex. It seems they are in a bad way, though, thank God, they are not in debt. I give the PROBUS lecture at the George, Rye, on Wed. and *Magic Flute* in Church, rehearsal 7.30. *Magic Flute* rehearsal on Friday and the Organ Beano Flower Fest on Sat with *Magic Flute* at the end of the day."

In early September, he played for an 'amazing' wedding at Winchelsea... Someone asked him "Who was the Pachelbel by?"......

They went to Ascot for big lunch party in a marquee for the Ruby Wedding celebrations of Peter and Valerie. "RM couldn't get on the way home quick enough." Those kinds of events were not something which the Proctors coped with easily. On the same day, Brownbill and the Madrigalia were to do Howells' Mass in the service at Rye....but, in the words of someone in the know, as my successor 'couldn't cope, and was HOPELESS', Brownbill had to get an organist from London!"

"Re. the Alex: Most of the officials of the Alex, including the Secretary, have resigned and I have made it abundantly clear to all and sundry, 'I see from the Constitution I have no powers at all in the running of the choir and the Management is entirely in the hands of the Chairman and Committee'. Personally I think the whole thing will fold up and disappear........I hope so. The situation with the Chairman and Conductor with no money and a very impoverished membership makes it to my mind an automatic consequence."

"It is a real relief now that the Alex is out of my ken, and all other things, like organ recitals and 'Ascotations' and farewells...which didn't materialise anyway...are out of the way. So will now close and ready to begin a clean sweep with no aggro at *** to cope with...IT and HIM don't exist."

I want to insert a personal vignette. Up to this point, neither Howard nor I had ever addressed the Proctors as anything but Mr and Mrs Proctor. Interestingly, a number of letters I received from his former students referred to this very point. "We would never *dream* of calling him anything other than Mr Proctor." Again, this was consistent with the era from which he came and none of us would ever have considered doing other. On September 21 1992, on a tour of East Sussex with Howard's aunt, Lorraine, we all met for lunch with the Proctors at the Mermaid Inn at Rye. (September 21 was not only Rosemary's birthday but also Lorraine's wedding anniversary, though she had been a widow for some years. This lunch party was to be a celebration of both these events.) When we introduced Lorraine to the Proctors, she was unsure how to address them and enquired what she should call them. At that point, we were invited to use their Christian names - and did so from that time. Many people have found this rather strange since, by this time, we had known them well and had been close friends for a number of years. But I feel that that particular incident adds to the picture of Charles' life that this book presents.

By October, Charles had written two new carols for Winchelsea - *Deux Aubades: Mon Petit Jesu* and *Chanson Noël*. Later that month: "Jan wants to do 4 CP songs at Hastings Carol Concert. Doing the Brownbill *Magic Flute* again in Hastings in Nov."

November 1992: "I was much cheered today. On Secombe's Sunday show..they visited Boston Church.......I know from childhood days.......and by a miracle they showed the whole of the organist in person playing the *D Minor Tocc and Fugue*. I was so impressed by the playing, the modesty of the organist and the sounds and sights of Boston again........I wrote to him and sent my *Choral Preludes* with the hope that I might perhaps know the sounds of my music might be heard within the walls of the Church. I heard nothing for 14 days......and felt.......it was again 'one of those things'......but today had a tape from him of his playing there and a wonderful letter telling me he has played already many of my stuffs in the church and speaking in terms of considerable appreciation. The tape he sent is one of the finest I have ever heard.....as the resonance of the church and the organ is absolutely first class."

Charles was thrilled that Barry Brunton accepted for publication by Oecumuse his 'big new piece', *Pax Vobiscum*.

In mid-November, Charles was informed that the second performance of the *Magic Flute* was not now at Hastings but at Westfield Village Church. The Church was very small and everything about the evening was very difficult...no lights, cold etc.

In December 1992: "Nice letter from Boston organist thanking me for the tape and copy of the *Ten Occasional Pieces*. (This was the new title of what had started life as *Fêtes des Jours*.) All highly appreciated and he thinks the *Chartres Carillon* very intriguing. He obviously understands and appreciates my music ....and PLAYS it."

"We saw a most interesting TV on John Tavener...you may recall was a Prof at Trinity with me and we adjudicated a students' composition competition together."

On December 16 1992, at a concert in Hastings, Jan Reeve did four of Charles' songs - *Come live with me and be my love, King*

David, Children's Carol, Little Lamb. Jan made a special point of announcing that Charles had written them and that he was present and inviting him from the audience for separate applause - which afforded him great pleasure.

On December 15 the Winchelsea Carol Concert had taken place and they had done two new Carols written by Charles - *Mon Petit Jesu* and *Chanson Noël*.

January 1993: "We had a Borderline meeting last week but some of us are rather opposed to the Comparative Religion outlook which is creeping into our meetings from LAYMEN who want a BROADER basis for thought than the Christian ethic seems to supply."

"The Rye weekly leaflet indicates that a Working Party of active members of the congregation had suggested 'improvements' to the Family Communion service - among them: (1) using alternative and somewhat more cheerful and upbeat musical settings for both the Credal Hymn and the *Gloria*. (2) taking out the *Agnus Dei* in order to keep the service at its current length (3) making occasional use of keyboard and wind instruments to accompany those hymns for which the organ is not necessarily so ideal." I can well imagine the huge sigh of relief that Charles would have breathed, knowing that he would not be involved in all that!

When Charles had finished *Pax Vobiscum*, he had asked me if I would be prepared to copy it. I had to give a very honest answer that, while I was happy to undertake the task, it was such a massive one that it would take me some years to complete - and I knew that would not be something he would like to contemplate, given that he was now aged eighty-six. However, a friend who lived in the same block of flats as Howard and I, David Griffin, was an expert with computers and had a music programme on his machine. He agreed to prepare the score using his computer. It was a heaven-sent gift!! The score was prepared this way in a very short time. That was not the only problem concerning the production of the *Pax Vobiscum*. There were a number of considerations to be taken into account - some of possibly major significance - and I wrote a five-page letter to Charles - and Rosemary - about this. My letter took a vey long time to write, setting out, as it did, all situations as I saw them - some of which were unknown to Charles. His letter dated November 30 1982 began: "I will begin the reply to your fine letter para. by para." It went on "....we are both very conscious of your great concern about our affairs and most deeply appreciate this." I knew *Pax Vobiscum* meant a great deal to both of them - possibly more than any other composition Charles had ever produced. The difficulties which I predicted (and with which he wholeheartedly agreed) could have become insurmountable problems and I knew that every possible facet of production needed to be thought through and a 'way round every one' found. This we successfully accomplished. His letter concluded: "You will know that the FIRST Book of my Autobiography will be entitled *There is Always Something*. Volume TWO will be titled *You Never Know.......* Oh how often have I said this to myself and RM about things, situations and people."

In February 1993, Charles wrote: "You will be glad to know that my friend Charles Macdonald is playing my *Duo Concertante No 1* at the lunch time recital at Brighton Parish Church...this time playing the PIANO part I gather and a friend doing the organ part....in the Brighton Festival. This is promising news . I hope to get him interested in the PV (when it comes out) for Steyning."

Later that month: "I have just finished my NEW PIECE. It is

MISSA SINE NOMINE. It is an ORGAN MASS ie not a sung mass but a 'played mass'....without any words."

In March he wrote: "I go to Densem's today to have a rehearsal with Hallé (Leo) on two pianos of the Liszt *Concerto*. I recall that I played it at Buxton with their orchestra once...and on successive seasons, Beethoven G, Grieg, and my own. Those are far off days!" (Charles was to conduct one of the Liszt Piano Concerti in a concert in Winchelsea Church.)

Next month, he received more gloomy news of what was left of the Alexandra Choir - now the Alexandra Singers. "I had a distressing letter from Josie Kane...she is personally in a very poor way herself but running the new ALEX SINGERS from off the rump of the Choir. She personally was responsible for the CAROL concert at the RAH and they made a good amount for the fund." At this point, Josie's health was giving much cause for concern.

"It is interesting that VW always looked upon himself as an Amateur.....I always say so of Beethoven.........these two as they write are never sure of themselves....not knowing 'what is likely to come'..... different from Lovelock who knew EXACTLY what was coming and how....Kitson and all the other academics....where there is no room left for them to open their minds. DO look at Beethoven, and you will see towards the final page of each composition there is a place where something happens, you couldn't have guessed...nor probably did he. *Piano Sonata Op 10 No3 in D*. Look at the final *Rondo*. Not far from the end...some bars of tied syncopation WHICH SEEM TO HAVE NO CONNECTION WITH THE PAST....this passage always moves me to tears, it is so wonderful. THAT PAGE, to my mind, puts Beethoven into the Immortal realms." It is interesting that this is the same Sonata that had so affected the young Malcolm Sargent - though he had referred to the second movement.

In May, Barry Brunton of Oecumuse wrote "I would be happy to take both the pieces entitled *Duo Concertante* providing Jane is able to take care of the origination as usual. There's no need to send copies of the scores, meanwhile". Charles wrote to me: "How many composers' music is agreed to be published by the publisher - WITHOUT EVEN HAVING SEEN THE WORK????"

"[Geoffrey] Hanson rang up and asked if I would approve of a performance (of *Pax Vobiscum*) by his Ripieno at All Saints E Finchley."

"I wrote earlier to several friends...enclosing the Synopsis (of *Pax Vobisum*) AND a stamp for their reply. They have only got to say....'please send V. Score for perusal' OR 'no thank you....I am not amused'...but they haven't done either." This upset Charles tremendously - particularly as *Pax Vobiscum* was a work which meant more to him than other things he had written. The words of the text had been selected by Rosemary from the Gospel according to Saint Luke so he felt it was very much a 'joint production'. A few weeks later, he was to write: "I am still trying to get people interested in PAX....which I think is 'the best of me'."

In July he wrote that "Lesley Brownbill is coming tomorrow to go through the PAX in the hope that she might do it with her Madrigalia."

"My first *Organ Sonata* was inspired by a visit to the organ loft (St Albans) by Dr Tysoe - the then organist. It is interesting to recall the circumstances of one's inspiration for composing."

In August, the Proctors attended Josie Kane's funeral at Gravesend.

Earlier in the year, I had sent him a quotation from Plato - about music . This had been given to me by Peter Gellhorn at a music summer school which I had attended. I thought Charles would be interested to read it. His reaction, in a letter dated August 14 1993, was: "We were interested in the Plato definition of Music. Coming from the pre-Christian era...it makes strange reading....I wonder exactly what experiences of music were available in those days." The quotation read:

> Music is a moral law. It gives a soul to the universe,
> wings to the mind, flight to the imagination, a charm to
> sadness - gaiety and life to everything.
>
> It is the essence of order, and leads to all that is good,
> just and beautiful, of which it is the invisible, but
> nevertheless dazzling, passionate and eternal form.
> Plato 429 - 347BC

To my great surprise and joy, the next time Howard and I visited the Proctors, Charles presented us with a four-part setting of these words which he had written, with an inscription reading "Dedicated to Jane and Howard Spurr, Winchelsea July 13 1993" . Not only was this a lovely surprise, but he had not mentioned to me in any of his letters that he was working on this piece.

"It is a week since we went to Josie's funeral. I am afraid it rather upset me more than I had counted on....not so much her death which was welcome in the circs. but the opening up of remembrances of the ALEX....likewise Trinity."

In September 1993, he wrote: "Neither of us has set foot in St

Mary's, Rye since Sept I last year. You can guess what we both have felt."

On October 16, Charles was to play the organ for the Fauré *Requiem* and Vivaldi *Gloria* with Leo Hallé and the Winchelsea Singers.

On a visit to Rye, the Proctors ran into the Rector. He told them that he was resigning from Rye Church in June "as I have got things in good order for a younger man...I will be 61 and it now needs a young man of about 40....as I have put the finances of the church in apple pie order..the congregations are growing...."

"Winchelsea Singers concert went well. Good house...Choir did splendidly."

In November 1993, Charles told us that Lady Batsford was moving to London. This was another sadness for the Proctors as yet another friend moved away.

"I have read the life of Rutland Boughton whom I worked with...one of the most interesting musical characters I have ever met....and you know that the Bach book has my unqualified admiration."

At the beginning of December, he wrote that he had played for a "big funeral at Winchelsea, Winchelsea Carol Service/Concert ditto at the Beach church." Charles enjoyed these opportunities to play the organ or piano and was very pleased to be invited to undertake them.

1994 opened with the news that "My cousin (Eileen) died before Xmas - leaving me the last of all the relations born in the same year...." Eileen had lived in London and, after the

Proctors moved to Winchelsea, Charles would stay with her on those occasions when he needed overnight accommodation in the capital.

Later that month, it was clear that he was 'In Painting' once more. "I finished my Triptych...ie the three pictures 20 X 16 of the Nativity, Visit of the Three Wise Men and the Flight into Egypt. You may recall I told you that RM wanted this as her Xmas present. I couldn't finish them all before Xmas but I managed to finish them today. With her usual incredible discernment she termed them my *Heiligenstadt Testament*."

"We heard that much-thought-of Beethoven pianist Brendel, give a talk on Beethoven and played the *D minor Sonata*...which I heard Paderewski play at RAH in the presence of King George V and Queen Mary at the end of the World War I in aid of Earl Haigh's Fund which became the Royal British Legion later. I am sorry but no one can kill that wonderful performance after all these years...I studied it with Sauer......so I really find it hard to bear other people playing it."

"It seems to be 'in the air'"that some people hereabouts can't wait until June...when some change will take place" (This was a reference to the forthcoming departure of the Rector of Rye.) Later he wrote: "RM saw the Warden of Rye and it seems they await July with pleasurable anticipation....."

"RM decided that the three Nativity pictures shall be framed and hung in the Oratory where we are now satisfied." The Oratory was a small room in Bay Tree House which they used for prayer and meditation.

In February, when Rye was seeking a successor to the Rector, Charles had been told: "One person came to look around but when he knew his predecessor was going to live in the parish, he upped and went orff!"

"I have heard from the Heathfield Choral Soc who looked at *Pax Vobiscum* . Quite nice letter from the Conductor who thinks it might not be suitable for his Society........and they have planned up to Nov 1995. But he will keep it in his mind as the accompaniment is not too expensive etc."

Charles made reference to a sermon by Eric James printed in his book *The Voice Said, Cry* (SPCK 1994). The sermon was entitled *In Memoriam Edwin Land, Inventor of Polaroid.* "What is brought out so clearly is that the ARTIST - be he an Inventor, Musician, Poet - has a double life...the internal and the external, the solo and the member of the ensemble of mankind and the two must be lived at the same time without friction. I put it badly but Eric puts it well and truly wonderfully. This ought to be preached in schools of art. So many students...and full-grown artists too - have miserable lives as they cannot adjust or even know of the true situation. So much unhappiness is otherwise endured... and, as Eric points out, recourse to drugs and alcohol is resorted to out of sheer ignorance of the real cause of the unknowing adjustment that needs to be recognised. Think in terms of Van Gogh and similar artists and you will see the situation."

Later in February, Charles had seen an advertisement for an organist for what had been his first church, Holy Trinity, East Finchley. "Adv for organist at Holy Trinity E Finchley. My FIRST JOB 2 choir practices a week two Sunday services for £40 pa."

In March, a letter read: "The Rector (Winchelsea) asked me on Friday at the concert to play last Sunday and went into finance....and the fact that there should perhaps be an on-going engagement while the organist is away." (The current organist was away indefinitely due to illness in his family.)

"I understand Jan is singing my *Earth's Holiday* song at Hastings some lunch time concert or other. I am particularly fond of this song...as it's so racy and tears along....if properly played."

"I am very cross that having paid my car licence £130 recently, they have now sent me a DEMAND note. But we have the discs on the car to prove it has been paid. Also from my Investment Building Society, they are having Investors put on their computer system...some 4,000 names. Will I kindly fill in the enclosed form telling them what investments I have in their Society. I would have thought THEY would have been in a position to tell ME what the situation is!!!!!" Things like this made him despair and he found it hard to cope with the repercussions. It was not easy to deal with things on the telephone because of his deteriorating hearing - so he felt rather helpless when confronted with these all too frequent annoyances of everyday life.

"RM has gone to a Governors' meeting at Winchelsea School but after almost 20 years she will retire....and be relieved of this rather irksome business."

Charles' birthday was April 5, the same date as Louis Spohr, so this was always known as 'Spohr Day'. Around the time of his birthday, he would revert to calling himself 'Spohr' - just for fun and to perpetuate a long-standing joke. The Proctors did not like mention being made of their birthdays but because Charles' birthday was not being celebrated - we were merely celebrating Spohr's birthday - that was acceptable! On a visit to Bay Tree House, Charles had taken me into the Oratory in their house to show me the Triptych. This had been a great honour as no women (other than Rosemary) were admitted to this room. "As custodian of his work, I must tell you that only very few people are allowed in the Spohr Chapel in fact generally speaking only priests of the male order are permitted. So I was glad you saw the Triptych and found it of interest." Of great significance was that, included in the paintings were Rosemary's late father, Father Rennie, and the late Father Hill of Brede - two priests who had been central to the lives of both Charles and Rosemary.

In May 1994, another close friend, Lady Millais, moved to London. "Lady M came for tea the other day before she left for London. We didn't have tears of farewell but as she went out I felt very sad as it was the end of an epoch for us with Sir R and she, no longer hereabouts."

Charles had some medical problems involving swelling of ankles and legs. "Locals are aware that something going on as District Nurse has to come and take blood samples and Dr has to come and see me *in situ*." They were not happy that anyone knew of any problems that there might be but, of course, it was difficult to conceal them when the District Nurse was seen to visit.

"I am re-reading the lives of the Millais and Holman-Hunts who, of course, lived at Greyfriars here."

By the end of May, Charles was in hospital.

On June 8 1994, I gave a talk to the Borderline Society on *The History of Christian Action*. Charles was still in hospital but no mention was made of this at the meeting. The Society was told that he was 'not available'. When the talk and lunch were over, Rosemary took me to the hospital to visit Charles. I felt very honoured - as, generally, the only person who would have been allowed to visit would have been Rosemary. A similar thing was to apply later when Rosemary was in hospital.

David Griffin, having completed his work on *Pax Vobiscum*, was working on Charles' *Duo Concertante No 2*.

A further example of the Proctor's desire for absolute privacy was contained in a letter from Rosemary after Charles had been discharged from hospital: "........keeping the news from neighbours, gossip being the currency....being the most difficult! We two being the most private people imaginable when it comes to privacy....."

On June 21 in Winchelsea Church, the Madrigalia, conducted by Lesley Brownbill, had given the first performance of *Pax Vobiscum*. Thankfully, Charles was able to be there. There had been some doubt about this because of his health, but in his letter of July 3 he wrote: "I managed to put on a 'good show' for PAX...but shortly I hope to be on a well-being path." The evening must have been a strain for him, having only recently returned from hospital.

"We hope to go to TCM on Friday for the Farewell concert and reception of Jones...the Principal....We mayhap be able to visit the RSA to see RM's bust of Sir Brian Batsford, who was one-time Chairman of RSA."

At the end of July, he wrote: "I had a good interview with my Consultant at the Hospital and it seems that I shall be given treatment under the supervision of the Dr as a lasting benefit!! as there is no final cure for the condition in which I find myself. Suffice it to say I am now pretty well in myself and able to cope with most things..........although to get over-tired should be avoided." We were never told what the 'condition' was.

At the beginning of August: "Yesterday I had that good pianist to give a lesson to." This was David Meacock whom he had first met in 1985 when he heard him play the Liszt *Piano Concerto in E flat* in the main Concerto Class of the Hastings Music Festival. David subsequently played to him on several occasions and, on a visit to Bay Tree House, Charles played me a tape recording of him working with David on the Liszt *Sonata in B Minor*. It was, in effect, a master class on the work. It was the only time I had ever heard him 'expound' on a piano work and it was absolutely fascinating - especially when he, himself, played sections of the work to demonstrate his point.

An excerpt from one of the many similar letters he wrote around this time: "I have no further news about PAX performances. Although I sent a nice letter to a FRIEND with an sae for reply....NOT AN SQUEAK."

In August 1994, they had a holiday at the New Wilmington Hotel in Eastbourne. "All arrangements were made by our Music Society." It proved to be a restful time for them both - a much-needed break.

"We heard Jan sing the *Sea Pictures* and my *Earth's Holiday* at Hastings on Wed. lunch hour."

Later that month: "I am reading the book I bought at Brede - *Space, Time and Incarnation* by Thomas F Torrance, professor in Edinburgh. It is quite the most mind-boggling thing I have ever read in the style that I very much approve of. It is exciting to read........yet profound in its implications." But another sign of his rapidly deteriorating hearing was to appear: "At church we could hear nothing as no loudspeakers...."

In September: "This week sees the installation of the new Rector at RYE (Shepherd??)"

"RM has ceased to be a Governor of the School here after some 17 years...and is being succeeded by Mrs Peter Harvey who will see to it that the Anglo-Catholic tradition is being kept.........as RM was invited by the then Rector to be a Governor for that very purpose." Mrs Harvey was the wife of Canon Peter Harvey whose 50th Anniversary of Ordination service had taken place in December 1991.

In October, he received the news that "Brunton is issuing a new edition of CP Purcell arrangements. I am pleased he is taking all this trouble, bearing in mind that PAX has no future as far as I can see."

"We went to the thanksgiving for Dorothy Wood, mother of the tenor you know, and the sub-organist from Winchester played the service and accp. IT IS THE FIRST TIME WE HAVE BEEN TO RYE CHURCH SINCE WE LEFT. We found the atmosphere cleansed and quite peaceful. Many people greeted RM and said how much they had missed her."

"I can see no future for my compositions with Brunton unless they are produced for him in the PAX format." (ie computer set)

By November, he had yet another new piece on the stocks. "My new piece....64 bars. I have decided with RM's insistence that it be played at the Carol Concert/Service here to blow out the faithful."

"I am having my new piece photoed and will send a copy to Brunton really by way of a celebration as being the first exercise done since my recent illness." (This turned out to be the *Winchelsea Carillon*.)

In December he wrote: "Winches Carol Concert/Service was

a great success. Then had to do the School Carol Service." Carol services and carol concerts can be extremely taxing - as anyone who has been involved with them will know. These two events, coming close together, proved very demanding for Charles.

On December 28, the Proctors gave their annual Christmas Tea Party at Bay Tree House. "RM played the Winches 'For unto us' from MESSIAH we did last week and then as the mood was set thereby...delivered a short talk on Handel and the *Messiah* work. This proved interesting and I supplemented it with stories of the 1,000 choir I did for the Henry Wood Soc. at their final concert. Also when I did *Messiah* in its entirety for the Good Friday perf. with the Royal Choral Soc. after Sargent had died in the previous Dec. This and stories of the Crystal Palace Handel Festival I attended made good listening for them as were interested."

At the beginning of 1995, another rare glimpse into Charles's personality: "Personally I would find it quite impossible to read the Litany without a flood of tears........the beauty and comprehension of its contents and the poetry of the words I find moving beyond endurance."

A letter in this same month caused me some concern. He had heard from Oecumuse and the situation there seemed to have changed somewhat - to the extent that the question of Oecumuse publishing Charles' work in the future was in some doubt. "It's not much good composing when it will not be published as nobody is interesting in playing it." I was well aware that his composing and painting activities really 'kept him going' and should he give up either of these, his life would not be the same. I also knew just how much composing meant to him. This, combined with his somewhat deteriorating health, led me to write to him on January 24 1995: "You *can't* say 'It's not much good composing when it will not be published.....' because history alone must be the judge of your compositions. And who knows what the future holds for such compositions? None of us....but we *do* know what it holds if there are no compositions for history to judge." To my delight, his reply read: "I quite agree with you....one must go on....but I fear that one or two circumstances made me lose my grip of things as I know ought to be. Since seeing my Consultant, I have not been so very 'on top' as I had hoped." This was a most unusual letter from Charles as he rarely put such thoughts into words. His Consultant subsequently changed his medication and his health showed a marked improvement.

In his work at the Foreign office, Howard was engaged in making detailed preparations to commemorate the fiftieth anniverary of VE Day. "We hope H gets on well with the 50th anniversary of the emancipation of Europe with the FO and that he will make Royalty feel at ease when he interviews them...As my mother always said after I was presented to Queen Mary that 'she hoped I made her feel at ease'....as Fairbairn told me I was not to be shy...for the Queen was rather awkward at meeting people and blinked and stuttered a good deal.....and I was not able to 'grip her hand' only admit it into my grasp which I did and felt her knuckles gyrate...in her net gloves."

By February, I was convinced that Charles was 'back on an even keel' as this letter demonstrated: "At the moment I have finished 2 pieces and another two are on the stocks. My method at present is to write a *Prelude* and *Postlude* for myself to play at Winches at the monthly School Mass applicable to the Day. Last Monday was the Anniversary of the Queen's Accession so I did two such pieces, which RM approved of.....Next Service is Ash Wed. and I am writing for that now. It gives me something to do and a *raison d'être*....so I feel I am not wasting time."

"We have the Borderline Soc. tomorrow...and we may go although the people there are somewhat now unorganised... they seem to be our only friends hereabouts."

Charles sent me an article about the late Dr William Lloyd Webber, written by his sons. Excerpts included: "William had a horror of self-promotion. He never talked about his music." "William was a private man, retiring and modest." "In his final years he began unexpectedly to write again. There was a particular stimulus for this, though that should remain private. I think he felt he had to compose again." I found this an interesting article as the things written about Lloyd Webber were very similar to those that might have been written about Charles.

"Recently I have completed the next *Prelude* and *Postlude* for our next School Mass on Ash Wed. The *Prelude* is a Trio on a ground bass with the two upper voices written in Invertible Counterpoint so that the tune comes on the top then is translated...like Bottom....to the lower voice while the original lower one is played above now."

By mid-March, his compositions were progressing. "Today completed my two pieces *Prelude* and *Postlude*. This one next week is the BVM Annunciation...... Also I have now adopted Bach's way of writing, long lines of quavers....it is easier to draw as being a natural shape not a straight line and makes things plainer for the reader."

At the Winchelsea PCC meeting in March, a letter was read out from from the Rector (who was absent due to illness) advising the meeting that he was to retire in September for health reasons.

Out of the blue, a letter told us: "I have written a Testimonial concerning you....and including Howard.... and am putting it in my desk here with my other PRIVATE PAPERS eg Will etc. This Testimonial is sealed and is written TO WHOM IT MAY CONCERN. In the event of 'not being available' when you might need such a Testimonial." We did not see this until after Charles' death - but we felt it was an extremely thoughtful thing to have done for us.

Charles sent me a copy of an Order of Service. "As the Parish Magazine had it....yesterday pm was to be the HC for the Annunciation.....but as the Rector is unwell It turned into the enclosed DIY affair. So I did NOT play on the organ my *Prelude* and *Postlude* I had composed for this Occasion. BUT ANYWAY I HAVE THE CONSOLATION THAT I HAVE COMPOSED THE PIECE....AND THAT ANYWAY IS ITS VALUE."

A letter dated March 30 included this telling sentence. "I find modern ways of thinking now prevalent so far away from my own set of values which belong to another age, I cannot judge present day standards of thought except in those terms...in effect OUT OF DATE."

By April, composition is very much *in* again. "On Thursday, the Administrator (at Winchelsea) rang up and asked me to play the final hymn for the flock at 8. am on Easter Day. I was a bit vague as to which hymn it might be....as it happened "The Day of Resurrection"......a tune I do not like. So on the strength of this I thought it a good opportunity to write a *Postlude* to blow out the Faithful so did an one on 'Jesus Christ is Risen Today...Alleluya'. I started it off in my head with promising results and by Sat. night I'd finished it. It can go into my collection. It is something to DO. I've begun an Ascension one...which promises well." Then in May: "I am busy composing and am on page 9 at the moment so it promises well. A Prelude on *Veni Creator*...in canon in 4 parts." "As you know I am composing a *Prelude* and *Postlude* for the school services as nobody wants them for the regular services...so I have done Whit, Ascension and now Trinity. I took a hymn from EH for Trinity and in my version it comes three times - 1) the Father 2) canon to represent Father & Son, the third time in Triple Canon to represent the Trinity."

Later in May, I was very pleased to receive the following news: "You will be pleased to know that the RAM have accepted for their Library the whole ARCHIVES of the ALEXANDRA CHOIR, some three volumes of programmes etc., all due to the work of Baldwin and Edna Norton. This is most gratifying. I have the photocopies of the Agreement etc. ...so all is in order and official." (Both Marjorie Baldwin and Edna Norton had been long-standing members of the Alexandra Choir.)

In June: "On Whit Sunday we went to Christ Church St Leonards as a special treat of MASS. The organ there is quite wonderful Willis and a very good resonant church, singing of the choir good and of course the ritual and vestments etc. are quite splendid. I've known the church most of my life and it was good to renew acquaintance with it. When I got out after the service.........I felt I had been in another world and said to RM 'I haven't taken part in a church worship service.........for YEARS'. Here things meant something and the reverence of the clergy etc. was quite moving. None of the DIY nonsense."

Later that month, he received some news which pleased him: "I have just had a letter from Winchelsea Singers asking me to accept the nomination as an Honorary Member, which is kind and delightful of them."

June 13 brought a letter from Rosemary telling us she was going into the Horder Centre for a hip replacement operation.

Meanwhile, Charles wrote that he was reading Gerald Moore's Autobiography *Am I Too Loud?* and that he had played for a big concert (June 27) with Hallé and Winchelsea Singers to commemorate 'the 700th anniversary of the 1st recorded Mayoring and the Beating Retreat.'

In July, the Proctors heard via Edna Norton that Marjorie Baldwin has died. They also heard that H A Bate had died.

Happily, Charles was still composing. "I have completed the arrangement of *The Holly and the Ivy* (for Winchelsea Christmas)."

On July 18, Charles told us that he had had " an appreciative letter from the Librarian of the RAM about the Henry Wood/Alex Archives....as they would provide history of music in the war years...I am glad about this as NOBODY knows what was achieved during those years."

Rosemary was back from hospital when he wrote: "The lady NEXT DOOR was taken to Conquest Hospital while RM was away. She is in a bad way for reasons that can best be left to the imagination...now she is at the Psychological Dept to try to sort things out mentally. We have rejoiced that we have had no neighbour while RM is getting better." Because of their extremely private life-style, during Rosemary's convalescence, they maintained a very 'low profile'.

"The man from Jamaica next door but one has returned here. He finds my *Sonata* somewhat difficult for amateur pianists in Jamaica to cope with the time signatures that change every so often....moreover he has not brought his violin with him......"

Charles has bought the music and posted it to his neighbour, who was then in Jamaica - but this now seemed to be the end of yet another possibility of a performance of one of Charles' works.

"RM continues to make good progress, We are not allowing anyone into the house for the time being as RM is not really in a fit state enough to cope with visitors in any shape or form.....at the moment." At the end of July, a letter told us that "RM given clean sheet of health by surgeon at Horder."

In August, a letter told us: "The BIG KNEWS is that there has been a big bust up in the Winchelsea Singers...and Leo Hallé is OFF. I won't give details etc....but they have appointed a lady conductress...FRCO...who plays at Icklesham and obviously is glad to get in with the Winches Set. I don't know her...but have only heard her play here once or twice. I shall be interested to see how the lady gets on with the local singers.....Densem is very keen on her....so all is set fair in that direction. I have been asked to play at the Xmas Carol Concert and as they have promised to do my *Holly and Ivy* I am pleased."

Charles wrote some news which might not have seemed important - but was significant to Winchelsea residents: "The local shop in Winchelsea has been taken over by a new proprietor." Such things can be of great concern, especially to the older generation, who have relied on such people for some time - and until news of a new proprietor was known, things were rather unsettling.

On August 29, Rosemary died - very suddenly - of a heart attack. Apparently, feeling unwell and being upstairs in the house, she summoned Charles by knocking on the floor and instructed him to call the doctor - but she died while the doctor was in attendance. The night before the funeral,

Rosemary's coffin rested in the Oratory in Bay Tree House - surrounded by so many of the things that had meant so much to her during her life. She was buried in Winchelsea churchyard on September 1. Charles' life was never the same again. All his friends were extremely concerned for him and could not contemplate how he would manage without Rosemary. In the event, after the initial shock and when the funeral was over, he 'set to' to organise everything in a business-like way. His sole aim was to ensure that all her wishes, contained in her Will, were honoured.

At the time of Rosemary's death, we said very little to Charles about it. He knew not only how *we* felt, but he also knew what we were feeling for him and how our thoughts did not need to be put into words. Knowing him as we did, we knew that this was the only way to deal with the situation, if we were to be of help to him. On September 1 - the day of Rosemary's funeral which, of course, we had attended - he wrote to us: "I appreciate your reticence to say so little in these present cir- cumstances. Your reticence has been just a wonderful help. Thank you."

A new file was opened for business letters connected with helping Charles sort out things to do with Rosemary's death. Howard and I accepted their car from him on a loan basis initially, as Charles did not drive. Eventually, we purchased it from him though we did not keep it for long as, living in Central London, it was an unnecessary and expensive encumbrance. Removing it from Winchelsea, however, had been a great help to him.

In addition to the personal letters from which I have quoted at length, more correspondence was now produced in connection with the work involved with sorting out

Rosemary's Estate. This is of no concern to this book as it dealt with merely administrative and practical matters.

Charles' brother-in-law, Peter Rennie visited him. "When Peter arrived, I read to him a report about things done and things to be done....so that he could be up-to-date...and he took the copy away with him. I also made the point of telling him in the report of J and H in full so that he should know your position in our esteem.......Likewise a full report about Ken [Chetwood] and his connection with our business......Also about the loan of the car with the possibility of eventual ownership. I am happy to say all this was received with interest and complete satisfaction."

In November: "I am re-reading Hawkins book on *Time* etc. and I find it helpful dealing with things too big to understand...and too immense to comprehend."

In time, and with Ken Chetwood's invaluable help, all the business things were sorted out.

In December, he wrote: "I've had a note from the CBS Soc (Confraternity of the Blessed Sacrament) which Rosemary belonged to." Later that month: "Played for Celebration of Christmas Music by the Winchelsea Singers in Winchelsea Church. Conductor Jean Taverner CP organ and Mary Chetwood Piano. Performed CP arrangement of *Holly and Ivy* and at the end played the *Winchelsea Carillon*." He told us that he had made a new Will and arranged for people to come and witness his signature. We knew nothing of its content.

As he had done for some years, he played for the Children's School Carol Service at Winchelsea School.

On December 27, he wrote: "It is rather strange that I am deep down quite happy...as I was when Peter joined me in the Oratory before the Funeral. I think there was in a way an AURA of HAPPINESS in the air which I could not account for...and I expected to be devastated...and *was* later on of course....but again now....I am happy on things I have worked out in clear minded thought. I am thankful for Rosemary, I pray she may be cared for and she had no long illness to bear..and she was not called upon to look after me in the event of illness...and that she was not called upon to live here alone. Having always been a 'loner' as an only child...and having had my own flat in London at Warwick Avenue before my parents went back to Lincs....I am capable of looking after myself on the whole....I am quite happy to be alone here with its redolent memories and joys. Also.....I have come to think in terms of my own decease.......we do not know what is in store for anyone...We live in some sort of Hope...but anyway I shall be in the same state...whatever it is, as Rosemary....that is as far as I can go...."

In January 1996, he wrote about his *Piano Concerto*, which he had composed many years previously. "My pf Concerto was done at one of our Alex concerts with the LSO and went superbly at rehearsal in the studio....but the soloist lost it at the performance when it didn't come through."

He continued to send his compositions to me for critical comment. "Please look at the *Wachet Auf* piece with *musical* criticism as well as copying shortcomings. I would like you to approve of the musical content as well."

When I returned this composition to him, he wrote: "Thank you for the critique of *Wachet Auf.* I got this on Monday morn and it cheered me up no end. First because you approve, and too that you saw through the whole thing and READ what was in it without any 'programme notes' - but through the music itself. In short.......you got the message and it came to you loud and clear. Even to the point of appreciating the chords MERELY in D major.....You see my musical philosophy is grounded in LVB who appreciated these very things. The *Finale* of the *Fifth Symphony*, when the burst of C major comes, is only obtained by the "what is he up to?" in the preceding bars...so you could say "I appreciated the *merely* C chords at the beginning of the *Finale* of the *Fifth Symphony* with equal truth. So thank you for being so far seeing as regards my own little works."

"I must say things are sometimes a bit hard here alone then I console myself that I am truly thankful that *I* am left alone rather than RM for I feel I can stand up to things probably better than she would have been able...for so much of my own life earlier was alone in my own flat at Warwick Avenue...my parents going back to Lincs."

By mid-January, he had received confirmation that probate had been granted for Rosemary's Will.

"I am really happy here....strange as it may seem.... only too glad to endure the loneliness and difficulties...that RM has not been called upon to undergo. I feel I am really doing it for her and this makes me content to do so."

"I have being going into BRUCKNER and think that he is perhaps a better composer than I had imagined...if you take it as you should...that his one object in Life was to be orientated into the Christian belief."

"I've been reading again the life of WIDOR...and all the intrigues about the Head of the Conservatoire."

"I am wrestling with another Introit for Candlemas as I have, as you know, done the blow-out piece."

In late January: "I am getting on with the *Prelude on ALBANO* for the Feb Service as Canon Harvey likes it and will be there."

"The Rector, Scott, is calling for me at 12 today to take me to his retirement home at Peasmarsh for LUNCH....it is the FIRST TIME either of us has had a meal with them in 17 years!!!!!"

He had a visit from Rosemary's godchild and husband "to collect necklace and china tea set left in RM's Will."

His hearing was now very bad. He played for a Memorial Service. "It went well and Mary D turned over for me in the Widor and was very impressed.....NOT A SINGLE WORD of the human voice could I hear but Mary D gave me the signal WHEN to start up the hymns...as I did just recognise the words of the announcement."

"I had got the Candlemas piece on my mind but as David is away, I shall not hurry this affair."

"It is now 5 months since Rosemary died...but in my mind it seems but 5 weeks. I just don't understand my own reactions...but I do not worry, only every day thank God that she is not here alone....I feel I can, must and will cope."

In February 1996, Charles sent me a letter from Stanley Sackett (an eighty year old organist in Jersey) which he had sent to 'Basil and Joyce' - mutual friends: "Please tell Mr Charles Proctor that I like his *Winchelsea Carillon* very much as I enjoy the 'French toccata' style. It will make a good recital item and it will be useful as a lively voluntary. I think the final section with the pedal 5ths is very effective and most exciting."

"I am reading *César Franck* again....it is wonderful that one's mind is broadened with experience so that as one gets older, one's understanding becomes deeper. The intrigues in the Academic worlds of music were rampant in those days....and still are...."

In February 1996, he sent me new pieces - *Plaistow* (EH 69) and *Albano* had been done, and a new edition of *Lucis Creator* - a version of which he had previously sent to me - with new key signature so accidentals amended.

"I want you to QUESTION any music I compose....as now my Physical hearing is not good but my mental hearing of music is I think OK but I don't want for this reason to perhaps make 'BOBOS' as the President of the USA used to say."

"Am re-reading *Franck* by d'Indy. I can appreciate so much more now living as I do outside the Profession.....the Curé d'Ars means so much more even than he did before RM died."

Later: "Am composing another *Chorale Prelude.*"

"All this recent fuss about opera at RAH.......when I conducted *Faust* for 14 performances there some 60 years ago."

Another rather revealing letter, written after I had visited him the previous day and had a long talk. "I think this was the first really DEEP talk we have had. I mean in depth of spiritual resources...You saw at first hand the 'level' of RM's and my life at which we lived for 50 years together. One of these days you will be able to read, if you so wish, the great bulk of her literary work. I am of the opinion that one day, when people may wish to assess our respective artistic worth...they will find, as I firmly believe, that RM's work far transcends my own. Personally I find her work in the literary sense of the same stuffs as the great poets in the English language. I could not bear to read a lot of her stuffs as it had and has the same QUALITY as Shakespeare.

I find that, for example, I cannot quote Shakespeare without tears...so I don't quote 'I know a bank'......Shakespeare is quite impossible to say aloud! And the same QUALITY exists in RM's work for me. She had to tell me when she started to quote something of her own....... "It's alright...it won't make you cry" So posterity is in for a great awakening in this direction." Sadly this did not prove to be the case.

"I hear that Canon Harvey died yesterday...so I think that will be the end of the Borderline Soc. It fulfilled its purpose and now is really extinct."

"I had a rather restless night after you had gone...The whole visit was, of course, rather disturbing bringing back so many connotations...but I feel this was but a mechanical repercussion on the mind..and one can't expect other results....."

"I sits and awaits people who promise to come and don't.....who promise to *foam* and don't...who have answer-*foams* and don't put them on to see wot the message is...if any...."

"I have fixed up to see my Dr. this week as my 6 months appointment is not until the end of April. I don't want things to get out of hand....my present difficulty is being somewhat short of breath...and this is one of the items he asked me about some time ago. Generally speaking I am pretty fit but sometime the Situation tries to get the upper hand and I have to control my emotions and thoughts...... which is not always an easy thing to do."

"MY BUTLER has arrived and is going to do me for 2 hours. He is a reasonable sort of person who seems in my eyes to promise well. " (Mary Chetwood had organised this gentleman to come and help with some housework in Bay Tree House.)

In March, Eric Wayman from Lincolnshire visited Charles. "WAYMAN DAY. All went *very* well and he was quite delightful. He took away the things for the Solicitor in Holbeach and for the Gentlemen's Soc, [in Spalding] so all that is completed. His visit was, of course, somewhat harrowing as these things can be of RM's possessions......but more so as he comes from Spalding where I spent so much of my childish holidays with my Grandmother....redolent with memories...I found this more disturbing than I had imagined...but one has to face up to things."

"I am on the whole quite well but I think these emotional upsets give me some physical reactions of the which he [his Doctor] is not quite capable of understanding. As you know, I am FEELINGS only, in a very very thin skin and it takes all my time and energy to keep an EVEN KEEL, which I must do, try and keep...but it is not always as easy as people may imagine."

When clearing Rosemary's room: "I found the Volumes of photos...of her Sculptures, Fr. Rennie and Stuart Bedford, and others."

"I understand a new RECTOR [for Winchelsea] has been chosen...but no announcement will be made for 2 weeks."

"I am trying to get an EASTER CHORALE to go in triple canon and it's not that easy!!!"

Later in March: "Have heard from Mrs Mossop that J has had a stroke but she now has the Roman pots from Wayman." [John Mossop had been Charles' solicitor in Lincolnshire for many years.]

He heard that the new Rector of Winchelsea was to be Keith Wood. Charles was still playing for Winchelsea School Services.

"Peter [Charles' brother-in-law] is coming in April to take away all the Rennie Memorabilia......plus all the unwanted by me JEWELLERY and has adopted my suggestion that the Rennie LADIES have a choice free......ie nothing to do with the WILL and the rest he will dispose of and give me all the proceeds."

"I have just finished the EASTER PRELUDE on *Rex Gloriose* (EH) ending up in Triple Canon."

"The resident organist here (Calladine) has resigned...to finish in July. The Conductress of the Singers (Jean Taverner) has applied."

Jean Taverner was appointed as Organist at Winchelsea Church but Charles had been invited to 'blow out' the congregation at the end of the Installation of the new Rector, with both his and the newly appointed organist's permission.

"I am composing a piece for the Rector's Installation Service to blow them out."

In April, he wrote: "Fr Rennie [his father-in-law] made the point 'All things should be made to act as a service and honour to the MASS. Therefore music, ceremonial, colour, lights, incense - ALL to that end.' NOT 'What the people like' - a fact that is of no consequence. It is for the Mass we do these things."

I had written to Charles reminding him what a lot he had given to a large number of people through his musical abilities/skills etc., to which he replied "....trying to give people the 'experience' of music which I feel is so completely lacking these days. After hearing Paderewski, I have never BEEN the same person....likewise after Toscanini...and of course Sauer......but I am so sad that so few people seem to have the 'experience' of great Art - whether music or any other Art."

"My chief engagement to look forward to is the great OBE Service at St Paul's on Wed May 8 at 11.30 am."

An Exhibition of Rosemary's artistic works was proposed. This met with Charles' complete approval. The Exhibition took place in the Rye Adult Education Centre on July 20 and 21 1996.

In May, his health was troubling him again. His pills were changed and had more iron in them. "I have felt rather orful lately and am sure this is the reason for NOW I feel so much better although with but one day's treatment."

Charles stayed with us overnight in our flat in London before he attended the OBE Service at St Paul's Cathedral. He wrote: "Thank you for your kind and thoughtful hospitality over the OBE visit. I feel it was worth the effort on my part as I fulfilled something I can't exactly say what by attending. To have the Decoration and NOT live up to all it signifies would be quite unforgivable. I felt that my visit was in some measure a thanksgiving to so many of my friends who had contributed to my professional work which has found its reward in the Service at St Paul's."

Eric James had sent Charles the first verse (of a much longer poem) by John Donne. It was one of his 'Divine Poems', written 'in 1623 or thereabouts', entitled *Hymne to God my God, in my sicknesse*, and the lines Eric sent read:

Since I am comming to that Holy roome,
    Where, with thy Quire of Saints for evermore,
I shall be made thy Musique; As I come
      I tune the Instrument here at the dore,
    And what I must doe then, thinke here before.

Charles sent his four-part setting of these words to Eric who sent him a 'generous critique of it'. I have a copy here and each time I play it, I cannot help but feel it was an entirely appropriate piece to have written, so close to the time of his own death.

"I am enjoying the Curé d'Ars - as the print is large and well set out and I find it good bedtime reading."

In July, he wrote: "The Rector came here to tell me that he wants things as per to go on at the school...ALSO asked if I would be available if the Resident organist was ever unavailable. I was relieved about this from a Financial point of view anyway."

"I am re-reading Boughton's book on Bach and I think it is the toughest reading I have encountered for many years...but I now understand more about things than when I first read it."

By August, the headstone on Rosemary's grave was in place.

"I am composing a carol as requested by the Conductor of the Winchelsea Singers for MEN only."

In October, Deena Oetting and her daughter, Pat, had visited from America. Rosemary had met Deena when they were both nursing during the war and they had kept in touch. Charles wrote that he had rested after their visit "to get over the draining emotions I had suffered from the visit of Deena".

By now, Charles' health was giving great cause for concern. November 6 1996 was his last letter to me. "I saw on TV students with tutors from Cambs, as well as at table....one or two WEARING caps indoors in the Tutor's study!!!! I've never seen such a lack of manners."

"The Winches Singers concert is Sunday evening. Mary isn't playing as they have an organist from Bexhill... I may not go to the party as I find conversation so difficult. I shall have to...next Carol Concert, when they do my piece."

He died during the morning of November 26 1996, alone in his music room. At the time of his death, he was still very much 'In Music'. His latest composition was in a letter to me, lying on his piano. He had not managed to walk to the postbox.

Chapter 5

IN THE END

Charles Proctor died on November 26 1996.

My husband and I had spent the weekend with him just three weeks earlier and he had prepared a cooked meal for us. (Before Rosemary's death, whenever we visited, the meals would be prepared and served by her - but Charles always made a jelly as he knew I was very fond of it. He went to great lengths to tell us how he had had to rise at an extraordinarily early hour to prepare this dish. We never failed to show our deep appreciation of this sacrifice!) On this last visit, and with his particular brand of humour, he had appeared at the kitchen door looking very anxious - only to tell us that he had put the jelly in the oven and it had melted. Was this to be our first indication that he was 'losing his grip'? Before we could utter, he re-appeared bearing a beautifully cooked bread and butter pudding - something that was a favourite of us all. We were very touched that he should have gone to all this trouble when he was not feeling well.

His health had been giving cause for concern for a while and he was waiting to go into the Conquest Hospital at Hastings. I am not sure what treatment or surgery was to be carried out but it might have been to do with his heart. He had a small suitcase, packed and waiting in his hallway - ready to leave at a moment's notice. In the last two weeks of his life, he had taken to telephoning me three times a day. This was extraordinary as he was not a person who enjoyed talking on the telephone, primarily because his hearing had deteriorated considerably. But even before this, he was not someone you would ring 'for a chat'. Small talk was not something that interested him! I knew he was very concerned about his forthcoming hospital visit, but at the same time, he was anxious for it to be as soon as possible as he felt very unwell. He was finding it increasingly difficult to walk, even relatively short distances - to the local pub (where, occasionally, he would have his lunch and which was but a few yards from Bay Tree House) and to the local Post Office. Each time we spoke on the telephone, (I was still living in London at this time), we arranged a time for the next call. On Tuesday November 26 1996, he was due to ring me at 12.30 pm When no call came, I waited a while and then rang him. I repeated the exercise a number of times without success. By now, my possible explanations of where he might have been had 'worn thin'. I telephoned the pub, who had not seen him. I telephoned the local Cottage Hospital in Rye - but he had not been admitted. Finally, I telephoned the Conquest Hospital, in case there had been a sudden cancellation and he had been 'slotted in'. To my horror, the relevant department of the hospital told me that not only was he not there but he was unlikely to be called for his appointment before February the following year! Eventually, at about 2.30 pm, I took the only course of action left to me and telephoned the police. When they got to Bay Tree House and looked through the window of his music room, they saw him sitting in his chair. They forced an entry into the house and found him dead. The doctor who attended estimated that he had died at about 10.30 that morning. He was fully dressed and a cup of soup sat beside him on the table. The telephone message from the policeman did not come as a shock to me. I was glad that he had died in that way - in his music room, surrounded by his familiar things, preparing to send me his latest composition, in expectation of finalising it when he had received my comments on it.

He was active to the very end, and I feel he would have been quite content with the 'manner of his passing'.

Rosemary had died just over a year earlier - on August 29 2005. Her Will had contained numerous small bequests. As anyone who has ever had to deal with such matters will appreciate, much work is involved in tracking down the items listed, locating the beneficiary and finally sending the item or arranging for its collection. Added to this was the huge and unenviable task of dealing with her clothes - surely one of the hardest parts of the aftermath of someone's death. All this Charles did - with minimal help from others. This was not for lack of offers of help. It was something he felt he must do himself - for Rosemary. It was not easy for him but, with his usual single-mindedness, he dealt with everything in an orderly and efficient way. By November 1996, almost everything was done. One thing was outstanding. He awaited one cheque. He knew that when that arrived, he would be able to 'draw a line' under the business side of Rosemary's death. On the morning of November 26 1996, that cheque arrived and he put it into his jacket pocket - where it was found when he died. I believe that, with the final piece of the jigsaw in place, he could say of his own life, "All is fulfilled", and, willingly and peacefully 'go to meet his Maker, in sure and certain hope of the resurrection to eternal life, through our Lord and Saviour Jesus Christ'.

Charles and Rosemary lie buried together in Winchelsea churchyard. Their tombstone reads:

Jane Spurr

CREDO
ROSEMARY PROCTOR
29 8 1995
AMOR VINCIT OMNIA
CHARLES PROCTOR
26 11 1996

The words I have chosen to end my small tribute to Charles are those of the Angel's Farewell from Elgar's *The Dream of Gerontius* - a work so dear to the heart of both Charles and Rosemary:

> *"Softly and gently, dearly ransomed soul,*
> *in my most loving arms I now enfold thee.....*
>
> *Farewell, but not for ever! brother dear........*

May they both rest in peace.

Emil von Sauer

Charles Proctor in the 1930s

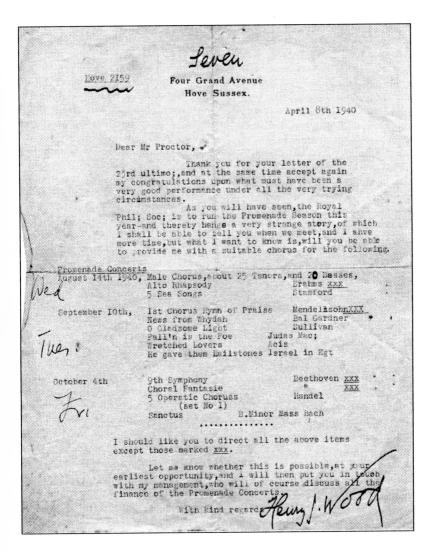

Facsimile of letter from Sir Henry Wood asking Charles Proctor to form a choir for the Promenade Concerts.

Charles and Rosemary Proctor on their wedding day July 21 1945

At the organ of St Jude-on-the-Hill, Hampstead Garden Suburb

The author and Charles Proctor at the party to mark his retirement as Conductor of the Alexandra Choir in December 1978

At home with his beloved Pansy

Charles Proctor in the 1980s

One of the the last photographs of Charles and Rosemary
shortly before her death in 1995

The Proctors' grave in Winchelsea churchyard

Chapter 6

RECOLLECTIONS AND APPRECIATIONS

I am most grateful to those people who wrote to me about Charles Proctor. I am happy to say that, without exception, their recollections and appreciations echo my own sentiments entirely. I have quoted from a selection of the letters, arranged as relevant to the different areas of his life and work.

* * * * * * * * * *

Alexandra Choir

"Little did I know, when I joined the Choir, how many marvellous years of music-making were ahead of me. I have such cherished memories of the many concerts in which I felt privileged to sing and all the friends I made along the way. I am so grateful to Charles Proctor for all those things."

"He was a kind and understanding man. He was so happy and patient."

"When he conducted, he had a magnetism that drew all eyes to him and he willed his musicians, singers in particular, to heights they would not have dreamt they could attain. He was truly inspirational."

Incorporated Society of Musicians

"When Charles was Treasurer of the ISM, he was a great success at the Annual General Meetings, presenting the accounts with aplomb and authority. Later we met less often but I used to get news of him from a friend who had a grand-daughter in the choir at Rye Parish Church and I received reports of the 'kindly but rather overwhelming organist'. I think I last saw Charles when he was about eighty-five and still in full sail when he attended an inaugural meeting at the RAM to discuss the formation of a Guild of Fellows and Hon RAMs. At the appropriate moment, he got to his feet and spoke something like this: 'When the postman recently handed me an envelope embossed with the words Royal Academy of Music, I said to myself "Why are they writing to me after all this time? They must be after my money." I now know that was right.' Charles had certainly not lost his touch."

Royal College of Organists

"Charles Proctor was a Member of the Council and Examiner. I remember most clearly his most unswerving support and invaluable help as I struggled to implement the Council's policy to promote the art of organ-playing and choir-training. He and his wife, Rosemary, rarely missed an evening educational event at the College and their commitment remained steadfast even after they had moved from London down to Rye. I remember them both with admiration and affection."

Rye Church

"I remember his fantastic renditions of all the Rheinberger

Organ Sonatas whilst he was at St Mary's Rye. They were inspirational. He was quite a character, even formidable at times! He certainly didn't suffer fools gladly! I liked him and respected him highly. I still have a copy of his book *The Class Music Teacher*. He wrote very clearly and I found his writings very readable and helpful."

Schools

"At the time of my meeting with Mr Proctor (as I find it much easier to think of him), I was an 11 to 13 year old pupil at Woodhouse Grammar School in Friern Barnet, North London. To a young and somewhat awe-struck school pupil, Mr. Proctor seemed a very distant and imposing figure. The feelings that come back from that time are of a very imposing man who was after a particular and very specific result in the music he was producing. He was most specific in his direction and very unforgiving - result was what mattered, it seemed, and it was up to us to deliver. There was never any question of us being unable - we were expected to rise to his level. It was a much less egalitarian time of course and that had a part to play in this feeling, but he carried an absolute assurance about him, that it was up to us to rise up, rather than him to descend to our level. However, these high expectations were matched by a close attention to detail and a care in rehearsal.

We had been coached in our music lessons by Mr Roberts (known to us all as 'Uncle Bob' - how different from 'Mr Proctor' and significantly so) and only met Mr Proctor for the final rehearsals in the church. I remember him as being totally in command over all of us, and over Mr. Roberts at the organ - and effortlessly so. Not once do I remember the petulant temperamental outbursts that sometimes mark the unsure and incompetent director (of both music and stage) - only a focussed, calm approach of someone determined to achieve a creditable result. So what did Mr. Proctor leave me? A love of music, undoubtedly. A confidence in myself as someone who could actually hold a tune - and a part. Later, I joined the Parish Church choir and have discovered a love of this particular musical form for which I think that Mr. Proctor was the original inspiration."

"At Woodhouse School, from age 11 - 16, Mr Proctor (I still can't call him Charles, even at age 57) selected me to sing all the soprano solos for the *Messiah*. He privately tutored me during the lunch time and he petrified the life out of me. To a very small 11 year old he looked enormous, but he would give me a smile over his half-moon reading glasses and I would feel fine and enjoyed singing for him. He always managed to get the best from everyone. He never called me by my name. I was always 'noodle face' - which I didn't take too readily to! I remember him driving away from school on his Lambretta scooter. He looked rather comical - this huge man, wearing a big coat and a dark beret, weighing down this little bike with his music case strapped on the back, disappearing down the school drive. I know that I owe my musical career to Charles Proctor. I was a very shy little girl but he awoke in me the talent that I have used and loved all my life and I shall always be grateful to him for that."

Trinity College of Music

Students

"I was lucky enough to receive harmony lessons I shall never forget. Full of encouragement with my very average exercises - he would say 'Beautiful, beautiful'....He made me compose by dint of his sheer enthusiasm and also taught me some keyboard harmony (I was a string player) which of course has always been useful in my teaching. He was always very kind, and interested in all my musical projects. I have always been very grateful to have had such an inspiring teacher."

"I had a high opinion of CP. His teaching was vibrant and I loved him as a person. He had a very sharp wit."

"Charles Proctor is one person who stands out in my memory from my student days and someone I remember with great affection. I do think he was a great gentleman and teacher who always gave us encouragement to improve our musical abilities. I learned a great deal from him which has helped me in my musical career. I am sure there are many hundreds of students to whom CP gave encouragement in their musical education and I am sure his ideas and teaching methods will be passed down through the generations to come. We loved to hear his stories and anecdotes of his early musical career and his very descriptive criticisms of our conducting - such as 'You are not making omelettes!' or 'You are not hanging out the washing!'. He was truly a great musician who was able to inspire others. I count myself very fortunate that I was one of his students."

"I have very fond memories of 'Charlie'. A larger-than-life character of the old school, he was the first member of staff to make an impression on me on my arrival at Mandeville Place. I remember choir practices being enormous fun with his sharp and dry wit invariably enlivening proceedings. 'Charlie' taught me a number of things that have stayed with me throughout my professional career as a conductor: 'Whatever piece you're conducting must be, to you, the greatest piece of music in the world - at least while you're conducting it. If you don't believe this yourself, how can you hope to convince your performers and audience.' 'As a conductor *always* be decisive and ready to make a decision. There's nothing worse for a singer/player to have a question answered by the conductor with a wet 'Oh, I don't know'. That suggests a lack of preparation and they'll quickly lose confidence in you. Having made a decision, stick with it, making changes of mind very much the exception and give the reason for the change ie "We *will* have to take this more slowly after all simply because of the acoustics.'" 'Conductors are *always* right!!!'"

"I played through several of the accompaniments for the forthcoming concert. I couldn't seem to please him. Finally I played him the introduction to Parry's *I Was Glad*. To my relief and delight, he remarked 'That's good enough for *any* coronation!'

At a rehearsal of Mahler's *Eighth Symphony* with the TCM choir, CP was dissatisfied with the student accompanist's attempt at the orchestral reduction of a certain passage. CP turned him off the stool and demonstrated the passage himself. The most amazing welter of sound burst forth from the old Hinde Street grand piano, eliciting enthusiastic and spontaneous applause from all of us. Clearly pleased, and touched by this response, CP said 'Well, I did learn once, you know!'

To a class at TCM: 'My new book, *The Class Music Teacher*, has just been published. On passing the London Music Shop this morning, I noticed there were three copies in the window. I hope to goodness they're gone by lunchtime!'".

"I well remember CP's Choral Repertoire and Choral Conducting classes when we all sat in the Lecture Hall nervously waiting to make a fool of ourselves by rehearsing a song from the National Song Book. I recall working out (as we all did) that if I sat in such and such a chair each week, when it came to my turn it would be *Cherry Ripe* which had a very easy accompaniment. Imagine my terror when I turned up confidently to the lecture, ready after days of practice, to take my fellow students through *Cherry Ripe*, only to find that the seat next to me was empty that week and I had to struggle through a piece I had not even glanced at!. CP filled me with fear, but also tremendous respect. He really instilled in me a love for Elgar's music. Despite the terror he instilled in me, which was, I am sure, mainly due to my own inadequacies, he enhanced my love of the choral masterpieces and underneath that 'hard' exterior beat the heart of a very kind and generous old softie."

"If 'Charlie' took no prisoners and could be quite fearsome at times, it was because he brooked no compromise in musical or professional standards.

Because of a shortage of altos, I became an honorary member of the Organists' and Choirmasters' class. To me 'Charlie' appeared to be in his real element here, being both inspired and inspiring in teaching this branch of music. These classes became the highlight of my week. Although, obviously, playing the organ never entered the picture so far as I was concerned, I nonetheless learnt a good deal through listening to his advice and comments to the organ students.

I am convinced it was what I was learning from 'Charlie' that was making the prospect of a multifarious musical career very attractive. That I had such a varied and fascinating career, doing something of just about everything, was almost entirely due to 'Charlie' and I have never ceased to be grateful to him. What other teachers gave was instrumental and paperwork techniques: what Charlie gave was the same *plus* survival techniques.

Dear old 'Charlie' - who can forget him? A larger-than-life general musical practitioner *par excellence* - no wonder we were all in awe of him, and a truly human person of warmth, humour and utmost integrity - no wonder we all loved him."

"I was in a conducting class taken by Charles Proctor. I suppose my memory of these was the sheer terror of conducting in front of my whole year group. However it did teach me the basics of conducting technique which I have found invaluable in later years when I conducted various groups, including orchestras, brass bands and choirs. The most memorable experience I have is singing in the choir, which was taken by Charles, and performing with the TCM orchestra such fantastic works as Elgar's *The Kingdom* and *The Music Makers* and Bliss' *Morning Heroes*. Charles seemed to have a real affinity with English choral music which left me wanting to know and sing more of these great works."

"Charles' courses were always very practical. He was always aware of what would be required of us in our professional musical careers, and for that I have been most grateful."

"Charles had a profound effect on many aspects of my musical career and I feel proud to have been a pupil."

"As a teacher and musician, Charles was excellent. One comment he made during a lesson has stuck in my mind 'The amateur musician will practise a piece until he can play it correctly while the professional will practise until he cannot play it incorrectly.' To students, Charles Proctor could often appear somewhat gruff and forbidding, but inside there was a warm, caring person with a sense of humour."

"When I played the piano (which was not my first study) Charles would always manage to say something nice, like 'musical' or something to that effect. I loved that man so much! I still think of him often. He really touched me somehow and I always cherish those memories. In 2001 I visited his grave and was immediately moved to tears. What a wonderful, wonderful inscription."

"I shall always value his sound teaching of conducting technique, which has stood me in good stead over the years. I have done a great deal of choral and orchestral conducting and I still hear him in the background, picking me up on things: 'Keep the bottom of the beat level' 'Have the score in your head, not your head in the score.' And in an attempt to obtain better diction from singers - be they soloists or choir members - 'Never forget that your audience is a bit hard of hearing and a little slow on the up-take.' And, of course, his great command cf the music of Elgar. Who can forget such magisterial authority as he put down the first beat of *The Kingdom* as the low strings, bassoons, and 32' on the St Sepulchre's organ thundered out that sonorous low E flat. And the great performance of Beethoven's *Missa Solemnis*. How much we all learned about Beethoven from that experience! Charles' opinions and views were always valued. He had that charisma."

"About ten years after leaving Trinity, I was sitting one evening in the front room of our home in Cley Hall Drive. My attention was suddenly drawn to a grey-haired elderly gentleman pottering about across the road looking lost. What was most odd was that he was wearing carpet slippers. Suddenly he veered across the road in the direction of our house and knocked on the front door. 'Mr Spalding (another name he had for me), at last I've found you.' It was Charles Proctor. He was in the area to see his solicitor and was staying at the Cley Hall Hotel. He had remembered that I lived in Cley Hall Drive and had popped out (not bothering to put his shoes on) assuming we must live just round the corner, when in fact he had to walk for nearly a mile. I was tremendously touched that he had not only remembered me but had made the effort to look me up. I drove him back to his hotel after a long chat about the good old days.

One week I had not done any harmony for my lesson. I thought to myself: He likes to chat about so many aspects of music. I will ask him about his favourite music. I naively posed the question "Mr Proctor, I wonder what your favourite music is?" He paused for a moment then looked me in the eye and replied: 'My boy, my favourite piece of music is the one I happen to be performing at the time! Now where's your harmony?' This somewhat profound statement has stayed with me ever since and has often helped me through some difficult musical experiences.

Charles Proctor has probably had a greater influence on my musical career than any other person. I learned so much about conducting and rehearsing in both our classes and in the individual lessons I had with him, and indeed, from just witnessing him on the podium. The opportunities and experiences he gave me have left me with some wonderful memories."

Fellow members of staff

"When Charles was Conductor of the College Choir, succeeding students were greatly influenced by him; he was held in great affection. I examined with him on several occasions; he was always very fair to both the College and the student. His humour was wonderfully dry, but always after the student had left the room. Charles was greatly admired by staff and students alike and my personal memory is that of a splendid and lovable musician who was completely dedicated to his art."

"I was amused to see that he [a former student], like us all, refers to him as 'Mr Proctor'. I think the heavens would have fallen in had we dared to call him 'Charles'."

A pianist who Charles met at the Hastings Concerto Competition

"My piano teacher had stopped teaching and I was wondering to whom I should go who would be sympathetic to my continental technique. I remembered meeting Charles and so rang him up. Thinking of him as a 'grand-pupil' of Liszt, I wanted to play some Liszt to him. He invited me to see him, and we duly went through the big pieces I had played, including the Liszt *Sonata in B Minor*, the *E flat Concerto*, the Transcendental étude *Mazeppa*, *Les jeux d'eau a la Villa d'Este* and some Schubert Song Transcriptions. We also went through Schumann's *Toccata*. My parents had been away on holiday, and on hearing me practising the day after seeing Charles, asked me what had happened as they thought my playing had improved beyond all recognition: in just one lesson, Charles had completely changed my playing, bringing together everything the other teachers had given me and adding more. The biggest thing he taught me was the art of Rubato, especially when applied to Liszt's cadenzas. On a subsequent visit, he gave me a piece of his birthday cake, He had made it himself and because he liked white icing, he said that he had tripled the thickness of the icing. There was probably as much white icing as cake - terrifically decadent, a bit like eating rock-hard sweet snowballs".

A family member - writing of Charles and Rosemary

"I know of no two people who were more dedicated to each other, so supportive of each other and who had so many interests in common."

A former Rector of Winchelsea Church

"Charles was for many years in charge of the School Choir at

Winchelsea, as well as Organist at Rye, and he played for our regular School Eucharists at Winchelsea Church. We felt very privileged to have such a distinguished musician in this relatively humble capacity in a small primary school. Of course, it enabled us to keep a higher standard of music in these services then would otherwise have been possible. He also arranged the *Angelus* for the children. We very much appreciated his loyalty, commitment and dry wit, both in the Church fellowship and in the wider Town community."

* * * * * * * * *

To my great delight, just as I was completing this section of the book, a letter arrived from Lady Millais. Sir Ralph and Lady Millais were great friends of the Proctors when they lived in Winchelsea. Immediately, I felt there could be no more fitting conclusion to this section of the book that Lady Millais' letter - summing up, as it does, the life of Charles in his latter years, and painting a most evocative and nostalgic picture of the Proctors and their life in Winchelsea at that time.

Memories of Charles Proctor are very dear to me. My husband and I lived only a short distance down the same road from Charles and Rosemary. But it was always Charles on his own who would walk down the street for a chat and a cup of tea. And how I did enjoy these afternoons. He would sit and talk for hours about his music and his early life in Vienna where he was studying and finding his talent - working so hard and playing his piano for hours and hours every day. He was also a born teacher and would tell me stories of all the famous composers. Much as I love music I am very ignorant on the subject and dear Charles filled in so many blanks - all of which I found absolutely absorbing.

I also try to play the piano (very badly) and give pleasure to no one except myself! Charles would write charming simple tunes for me to play named 'My Ladye Millais' Note-Book' which consisted of 6 or 7 little tunes composed and written by him for me. I found this very touching - that such an expert would bother with such a goose as myself!

Rosemary made him take up painting which was quite wonderful as it gave him great pleasure in his retirement. They would go for picnics, either down to the beach or on the banks of the Rother or down the beautiful country lanes round Winchelsea - complete with their hamper of food and drink plus all their painting gear. It was a wonderful sight to see them completely lost in a world of their own - blissful in comfortable old clothes and splendid shaggy straw hats. Sometimes we would join them for a quick drink!

Summer time and Rosemary decided to give a tea party in her delightfully artistic rambling colourful garden where flowers were allowed to rampage at will everywhere. Many guests were seated all over the various nooks in this garden and were fed with scones and home-made jams and cups of tea and biscuits. The door to the Music Room was left open and Charles was seated at his piano playing glorious music. I went in and begged to be allowed to sit beside him to listen. He agreed. "BUT if you open your mouth or say one word OUT you go." So I then knew where I was and sat as still as a mouse beside the Maestro, revelling in every note played.

Christmas also was a time for tea and carols in the Drawing Room. This was again something I remember. The room was absolutely crammed with treasures of every sort - China decorations, feathers, beads, cushions - cards and of course pictures, pictures and more pictures. They were everywhere and covered the walls of the house from top to bottom.

Charles painted landscapes and Rosemary loved her huge brightly coloured flowers. It was an education to be asked to their house and Ralph and I spent many happy hours with them both. It was a dwelling of ART in the truest form. Music, Painting and Poetry, blessed by deep religious devotion. Then there would be silence - and one would know that Charles was in his world of Music - composing. Indeed, he was a very great man.

Chapter 7

QUOTABLE QUOTES FROM LETTERS

The following is but a small selection of what I call 'Quotable Quotes' from Charles' letters - some of which were to other people. They were often accompanied by a relevant illustration, drawn by Charles, which might occupy a whole page. I hesitate to describe them as *Hoffnung-esque* - so will merely call them *Proctor-esque*.

* * * * * * * * *

From a letter to a fellow organist on how to play a particular Proctor composition: "I suggest it should be boiled for 10 hours and put into a jelly mould to cool for 3 weeks then, when it has matured, it can be turned out and re-heated according to taste and served with yogurt!"

Description of a meal at a hotel in Eastbourne: "We got cracking on the tomato soup. You know that red polish they do tiles with.....the boiling of this red stuff was the tomato soup. I had steak of beef.....I have written *Vocalises*....songs without words...This was steak without taste. The potatoes were fried which I can't eat so had to do without as there were no other. The cauliflower was like boiled woollen underwear with a dab of butter on the top (this last I had to turn over to madam)...the greens were undistinguishable...either peas or cabbage...I know not. The FRESH fruit salad was without blemish...it was truly FRESHLY turned out of tins. We did not stay for the coffee."

"I took the boys the other day at rehearsal. They were not making the words dramatic enough in the Psalms - so I read, in my inimitable way 'He stilleth the RAGING of the SEA'. Can't you just hear me terrifying the little boys? When I added 'If HE didn't do it, who DID?' - one little boy piped up 'Please sir, I didn't!'"

Description of an organ he had to play for a funeral. "The great organ is filletted and the bones are about the place so I may have to play on a little electronic thing the size of a toothbrush!!"

"The TURKEY was wonderful...but we found out afterwards it was PORK."

"My cold is still bad and my chest inside feels like a room full of Xmas decorations with festoons of streamers of coloured paper. My cough is equal to a Bombard on the Solo Organ (Harrison)."

"During my soul-searching playing of a Chorale Prelude to prepare the faithful for the oncoming service, the undertaker came and whispered...but I barked back at him 'Wot yer say?' - as I can't hear a conversation, play with two hands and two feet and read music at the same time unless I have SOME idea of the subject of the conversation. He brandished some notes ie MONET by the keys and said 'How much do you want?'. I told him but then remembered that I had been given a 'raise' so I gave him the relevant price with VAT - all this and me playing my Chorale Prelude by Wallbank, a lovely but tricky piece as it has lots of vinegar in its harmonies."

"One item was for solo flute. There were only about 35 people there and a solo flute sounded like smoked salmon without lemon or bread and butter."

"In all my life, I have never heard such dry, boring, silly music. I don't know whose....sort of Elgar dehydrated, put in powder form and warm water poured over it - and NOT stirred."

"The Good Friday Procession of Witness will probably look like a miners' strike demonstration - without banners."

"Our toaster does its stuff on the slant - so one can never get a good set of toasted pieces, evenly cooked, and the burners are such that they only see out of one eye."

Charles had sent one of his compositions to me for my comments and I had duly responded. His reply: "The Agnus Dei. Had a student written wot I wrote...I would have suggested your version....HOWEVER to my small mind..my AMEN is related to previous JESUS CHRIST so must stand. Your version is 'pretty and *crêpe de sheen*'. I prefer my Walls sausage idea."

After an excellent meal in the Smugglers' Inn, Pett: "It was so good that on the way out I went to the counter and spoke to the manageress. 'Excuse me, are you the person to whom one can make complaints?' - looking into her eyes as tho she had consecutive fifths between the extreme parts and had doubled her major thirds and got false relation as well....to which with terror in her eyes she says 'YES'... 'Good' says I 'I haven't got any...it was a most excellent lunch....thank you'.....Smiles all round."

"The organ had had a complete nervous collapse (due to changes in temperature etc.) The tuner came and put things to right. The next day the organ had a complete epileptic fit, throwing its arms up into the air...rolling on the ground and making such moans and groans and shrieks and screams that it made people in the Square think that the entire congregation had taken to *delirium tremens*."

The Proctors went to a very posh house in Winchelsea. "The house is perfection on the *Homes and Gardens* style....not ours....one daren't drop an H in case it leaves a mark on the pink carpet."

"The clergyman was about as inspiring as a piece of spaggetti that had fallen into the washing up water...."

Charles said he would send me the Schumann Funeral March music for me to copy out for Brunton. "The work for you is very straightforward as all the bars are of the same size and the music is obviously diatonic so if an F sharp appears in a tonic chord of C major, you can well bet it is a squashed fly and not a piece of Schumann's masterpiece."

After reading a sermon which he had really appreciated: "It was the very Oxo cube of thought."

After a talk which he had attended. "I can best describe the talk as being 'without ceasing' so that a cigarette paper could not be inserted between words or sentences or even paragraphs."

APPENDIX A

CONCERTS IN WHICH THE ALEXANDRA CHOIR PARTICIPATED FROM 1943 UNTIL 1978

1943 A series of concerts was given at the Stoll Theatre, Kingsway entitled 'A Season of Music for the People' and included performances of Beethoven *Ninth Symphony*, Mendelssohn *Elijah* and Handel *Messiah* - with the LSO. The concerts were conducted by Charles Proctor.

June 3 - RAH - Dunkirk Memorial Concert . Parry *Blest Pair of Sirens, England*, Quilter *Non Nobis Domine* - conducted by Sir Adrian Boult.

July/August - participation in Proms. Handel - *Plague Choruses from Israel in Egypt*, Brahms *Liebeslieder Waltzer, Song of Destiny*, Delius *Sea Drift* and Beethoven *Ninth Symphony*.

September - Festival of Russian Music. Khachaturian *Ode to Stalin.*

December - Debussy *Three Nocturnes*. LPO conducted by Basil Cameron.

Also in December - Beethoven *Ninth Symphony*. LSO conducted by George Weldon.

Also in December - Empire Broadcast - Christmas Day

1944 Wimbledon Town Hall. *Messiah*. Soloists included Isobel Baillie, Heddle Nash and Henry Cummings. Organist was GD Cunningham.

June - Proms - Handel *Plague Choruses from Israel in Egypt.*
November 23 - *To You, America.* Thanksgiving concert - tribute in music, prose and verse to the United States. LSO - conducted by John Barbirolli.
December - Empire Broadcast - Christmas Day.
1945 January - RAH - Mendelssohn *Elijah* conducted by Charles Proctor - proceeds to Henry Wood National Memorial Fund. This was the first concert promoted by the Alexandra Choir.
February - RAH - Beethoven *Ninth Symphony* - with the National Symphony Orchestra.
May - RAH - Victory Concert.
June - Walton *Belshazzar's Feast,* Elgar *The Music Makers* and last movement of Charles Proctor's *Choral Symphony.* LSO conducted by Charles Proctor.
July - RAH - Good Old London. Tribute to the work of the staff of the London County Council during the war years. This was one of the many concerts and national occasions in which the Choir took an active part during the war years.
September - Thanksgiving Week in the Cockpit, Serpentine Road, Hyde Park, organised by the National Savings, in which several hundred singers took part, with the Brigade of Guards.
RAH - Silver Jubilee of the London Co-operative Society. A programme of national items.
October - RAH - Daily Herald National Brass Band Festival Concert.
November - RAH - American Thanksgiving Day Celebration
December - RAH - Coleridge-Taylor *Hiawatha* - conducted by Charles Proctor
1946 March - RAH - Victory Cavalcade Concert.
March - RAH - music devoted to the works of Vaughan Williams, conducted by Charles Proctor. *A Sea*

Symphony, Benedicite, Job.

May - The Alexandra Choir travelled to Holland to give concerts of British music. Programmes included Walton *Belshazzar's Feast* and Elgar *The Music Makers*. Muriel Brunskill and Henry Cummings were the soloists throughout this tour. The Alexandra Choir was the first Choir to receive an invitation from a foreign country after the cessation of hostilities.

June - RAH - *Salute to Victory* concert. The programme included Elgar *For the Fallen*.

October - RAH - Delius *Sea Drift*, Brahms *Song of Destiny*, Parry *Blest Pair of Sirens*. LSO conducted by Charles Proctor.

October - Central Hall, Westminster. Concert presented by National Savings.

November - Participation with other choral societies in Henry Wood Concert Society *Messiah*, conducted by Malcolm Sargent. Soloists: Isobel Baillie, Mary Jarred, Heddle Nash and Norman Walker.

St Cecilia's Day Festival Concert - conducted by Sir Adrian Boult. On the same day, Charles attended a lunch at the Savoy where the principal speaker was The Rt Hon CR Attlee, and a service at the Church of the Holy Sepulchre.

December - RAH - Elgar *Dream of Gerontius*. LSO - conducted by Charles Proctor. Soloists: Harold Williams, Mary Jarred, Heddle Nash.

1947 Some rehearsals were held by candlelight.

March - RAH - Brahms *A German Requiem*, Borodin *Choral Dances from Prince Igor* and Proctor *Piano Concerto* played by Iris Loveridge. LSO - conducted by Charles Proctor.

April - RAH - Beethoven *Ninth Symphony* conducted by Sir Thomas Beecham.

July - RAH - Press Parade - Light Music

Proms - RAH - Elgar *The Music Makers*, Handel *Plague Choruses from Israel in Egypt.* - conducted by Malcolm Sargent.

September - RAH - Royal Air Force Association Festival of Reunion. Items of National music.

Later in the year, the Alexandra Choir participated in the Henry Wood Concert Society performance of Handel *Israel in Egypt* - conducted by Malcolm Sargent.

October - *Alhambra of the Air* on BBC Radio. Light music programmes

Later in the month, RAH - Trafalgar Day Rally

November - Visit to London by Zang Na Studie Choir from Holland, being the reciprocal visit after the Alexandra Choir's Holland trip in 1946.

Later in the month - RAH - Anglo-Netherlands Festival Concert - conducted by Charles Proctor and Willem Wiesehahn with LSO, Alexandra Choir and Zang Na Studie Choir from Amsterdam.

Also in November - RAH - Beethoven *Ninth Symphony* - conducted by Norman del Mar.

December - RAH - Carol Concert with the strings of the LSO - conducted by Charles Proctor. Soloists: Mary Hamlin and Heddle Nash.

1948 February - RAH - New Era Concert Society. Mozart *C Minor Mass* and Handel *Acis and Galatea*. Philharmonic Orchestra - conducted by Richard Austin.

March - Daily Herald 10,000th issue. Patriotic items - conducted by Charles Proctor. Also LSO conducted by George Weldon.

Later that month - RAH - Coleridge-Taylor *Hiawatha* LSO - conducted by Charles Proctor. Soloists: Joan Cross, William Herbert and Harold Williams.

April - RAH - Coleridge-Taylor *Hiawatha* - conducted by Avril Coleridge-Taylor.

August - Proms - Delius *Appalachia* - conducted by Sir

Malcolm Sargent.

October - Daily Herald Opera Promenade Concert. LSO conducted by Walter Goehr. Soloists: Joan Hammond and Marko Rothmuller.

Also in October, Coleridge-Taylor *Hiawatha* - conducted by Avril Coleridge-Taylor.

October - RAH - Beethoven *Ninth Symphony* conducted by Charles Proctor and *Missa Pro Pace* conducted by Willem Wiesehahn.

November - RAH - Henry Wood Concert Society - *Messiah* - conducted by Sir Malcolm Sargent

December - RAH - Daily Herald Opera Promenade Concert. LSO conducted by Walter Goehr. Soloists: Christina Carroll and Luigi Infantino

Also in December - RAH - Carol Concert. LSO - conducted by Charles Proctor. Soloists: Elsie Morison and Henry Wendon.

1949 February - Daily Herald Opera Promenade Concert. LSO - conducted by Walter Goehr. Soloists: Willa Stewart and Marko Rothmuller.

March - Another Daily Herald Opera Promenade Concert with Joan Hammond and Eugene Conley.

March - RAH - *Messiah*. LSO - conducted by Charles Proctor.

Later in March, Charles Proctor went to Holland and conducted in the Concertgebouw, Amsterdam - Elgar *The Music Makers* and *Sea Pictures* with the Zang Na Studie Choir.

March - RAH - Brahms *A German Requiem*. Philharmonia Orchestra - conducted by Richard Austin: Soloists: Elizabeth Schwarzkopf and Hans Hotter.

April - RAH - Beethoven *Ninth Symphony*. LSO - conducted by Josef Krips.

Later in April, another of the Daily Herald Opera Promenade Concerts with the LSO conducted by

Walter Goehr.

May - Peterborough Cathedral for Peterborough Arts Week. Programme included Vaughan Williams *Benedicite* and Charles Proctor *Veni Creator Spiritus*, which was specially composed for the Peterborough Arts Week.

June - RAH - Elgar Festival. *The Music Makers* - conducted by Sir Adrian Boult. Soloist: Mary Jarred.

October - RAH - Daily Herald Opera Promenade Concert. LSO - conducted by Walter Goehr.

Also in October - RAH - Elgar *The Dream of Gerontius*. LSO - conducted by Charles Proctor. Soloists: Heddle Nash and Muriel Brunskill. Programme also included Charles Proctor *Veni Creator Spiritus*.

November - RAH - Henry Wood Concert Society *Messiah*. Conducted by Sir Malcolm Sargent.

December - Daily Herald Opera Promenade Concert. LSO - conducted by Walter Goehr.

Also on December 10 - Ely Cathedral - the Choir took part in a service of Carols and Christmas Music in the Cathedral The Choir travelled by special train. Soloist: Gordon Clinton.

Later in December - RAH - Carol Concert - conducted by Charles Proctor. Soloists: Robert Easton and Arnold Greir.

1950 February - RAM - Tribute concert to Charles Proctor to acknowledge the tenth birthday of the Choir. Arnold Greir, Muriel Brunskill and Henry Cummings participated.

April - RAH - Tenth Birthday Concert. Wagner *Mastersingers Overture*, Elgar *The Music Makers*, *Serenade for Strings*, Handel *Zadok the Priest*, and Walton *Belshazzar's Feast*.

July - RAH - Proms - Bach Commemoration Concert conducted by Basil Cameron.

November - RAH - Verdi *Requiem* and Proctor *Veni Creator Spiritus*. LSO - conducted by Charles Proctor.

December - RAH - Carol Concert - conducted by Charles Proctor. Soloists: Heddle Nash and Maria Korchinska.

1951 February - RAH - Music by Verdi. London National Orchestra - conducted by Walter Goehr.

Also in February - Sunday Half-Hour, Broadcast from St Jude's Church, North London. St Jude's Choir augmented by members of the Alexandra Choir. Charles Proctor conducted and Harold Darke played the organ.

March - Beethoven *Ninth Symphony*. LSO - conducted by Josef Krips.

April - RAH - Mendelssohn *Elijah*. LSO - conducted by Charles Proctor. Soloists: Ena Mitchell, Freda Townson, William Herbert and Hervey Alan.

May 3 - Opening of the Royal Festival Hall in the presence of His Majesty King George VI and Queen Elizabeth. Dedication by the Archbishop of Canterbury. The Choir participated in the programme of British Music which included Handel *Zadok the Priest*, Parry *Ode at a Solemn Music*, Arne *Rule Britannia*, Vaughan Williams *Serenade to Music*, Elgar *Pomp and Circumstance March No 1*, Purcell *Soul of the World* and the *Hallelujah* and *Amen* choruses from *Messiah*.

June - RFH - Festival of Britain Concert. Dyson *Canterbury Pilgrims* and Elgar *The Music Makers*. Soloists: Jennifer Vyvyan, Muriel Gale, Bradbridge White and Owen Brannigan.

October - RAH - Henry Wood Concert Society *Messiah* - conducted by Sir Malcolm Sargent

November - RAH - Haydn *The Creation*. LSO - conducted by Charles Proctor.

Also in November - RFH - LSO - conducted by Colin

Ross. Programme included Delius *Appalachia*.

December - RFH - Beethoven *Ninth Symphony*. LSO - conducted by Josef Krips. Soloists: Margaret Ritchie, Anne Wood, Richard Lewis and Richard Standen.

Also in December - RAH - Carol Concert - conducted by Charles Proctor.

1952 March - RAH - Bach *B Minor Mass*. LSO - conducted by Charles Proctor. Soloists: Elsie Suddaby, Kathleen Joyce, Richard Lewis, Trefor Anthony.

June - Concert for the Fraternity of the Friends of St Alban's Abbey.

October - RAH - Henry Wood Concert Society *Messiah* - conducted by Sir Malcolm Sargent. Soloists included Kathleen Ferrier.

November - RFH - Musicians' Benevolent Fund St Cecilia Concert in the presence of HM the Queen and HRH the Duke of Edinburgh. LSO - conducted by Sir Malcolm Sargent. Soloists: Elsie Morison, John Cameron, Cyril Smith, Arnold Greir. Programme included the first performance in London of Healey Willan *An Apostrophe to the Heavenly Hosts*, conducted by Charles Proctor, in the presence of the composer.

December - RAH - Carol Concert - conducted by Charles Proctor. Soloists: Robert Easton and Arnold Greir.

1953 April - RAH - Walton *Belshazzar's Feast*, Fauré *Requiem* and Proctor *Veni Creator Spiritus*. LSO - conducted by Charles Proctor. Soloists: Elsie Morison and Dennis Noble.

June - Ely Cathedral. Concert in aid of the Cathedral Restoration Fund. Programme included Proctor *Te Deum* and Healey Willan *An Apostrophe to the Heavenly Hosts*.

Also in June - RAH - Henry Wood Concert Society *Messiah* - conducted by Sir Malcolm Sargent.

November - RAH - Dyson *Canterbury Pilgrims* -

conducted by Charles Proctor. Soloists: Jennifer Vyvyan, William Herbert and Dennis Noble.

December - RAH - Carol Concert - conducted by Charles Proctor. Soloists: Peter Pears, Marie Goossens and Arnold Greir.

1954 May - RFH - Festival Concert for the 150th Anniversary of the Founding of the British and Foreign Bible Society. LSO - conducted by Sir Malcolm Sargent and Charles Proctor.

June - RFH - Beethoven *Ninth Symphony*. LSO - conducted by Josef Krips.

November - RAH - Mendelssohn *Elijah*. LSO - conducted by Charles Proctor. Soloists: Ena Mitchell, Jean Allister, David Galliver, Dennis Noble.

December - RAH - Carol Concert. LSO - conducted by Charles Proctor. Soloist: Hervey Alan.

1955 May - RFH - Beethoven *Ninth Symphony*. LSO - conducted by Anthony Collins. Soloists: Joan Hammond, Norma Procter, William McAlpine, Owen Brannigan.

August - RAH - Proms - Brahms *Song of Destiny* and Dvořák *Te Deum*. LSO - conducted by Basil Cameron. Soloists: Joan Sutherland and Bruce Boyce.

November - RAH - *Messiah*. Henry Wood Concert Society performance. LSO - conducted by Sir Malcolm Sargent Soloists: Elsie Morison, Norma Procter, William Herbert and Trefor Anthony. Choir of 1,000 voices drawn from a number of choirs of which the Alexandra Choir was one.

November - RAH - Elgar *The Dream of Gerontius* and the first concert performance in London of Harold Noble *Mass*. LSO - conducted by Charles Proctor.

December - RAH - in the afternoon, *Messiah*. LSO conducted by Charles Proctor. In the evening, Carol Concert - conducted by Charles Proctor. Soloist:

Robert Easton.

1956 February - Bach *St John Passion* - conducted by Charles Proctor.

April - Central Hall Westminster - Concert of Motets, Folk Songs and Part Songs with Anthony Pini ('cello) - conducted by Charles Proctor.

Also in April - RAH - RAF Anniversary Concert (RAF Benevolent Fund). Conductors: Herman Lindars and Sir John Barbirolli.

November - RAH - Henry Wood Concert Society *Messiah* - conducted by Sir Malcolm Sargent.

June - RFH - Beethoven *Ninth Symphony*. LSO - conducted by Josef Krips.

October - RAH - Honegger *King David* and Fauré *Requiem*. LSO - conducted by Charles Proctor.

December - RAH - in the afternoon, *Messiah*. LSO conducted by Charles Proctor. In the evening, Carol Concert - conducted by Charles Proctor. Soloist: Dennis Noble.

1957 April - RAH - RAF Anniversary Concert. Conductors: Sir John Barbirolli, Eric Coates, Charles Proctor and Wing Commander A E Sims. (Charles Proctor conducted the *Easter Hymn* from *Cavalleria rusticana* and the *Hallelujah Chorus* from *Messiah*.)

May - Central Hall, Westminster - Coleridge-Taylor *Hiawatha*.

Also in May - Central Hall, Westminster. Haydn *The Creation Part 1* and Honegger *King David*. This concert was organised by the British and Foreign Bible Society.

June - RAH - Elgar Centenary Concert. Alexandra Choir and other choirs. Programme included *Enigma Variations*, *Violin Concerto* (soloist Yehudi Menuhin) and *The Music Makers* - conducted by Sir Malcolm Sargent.

October - RAH - Mendelssohn *Hymn of Praise* and Vaughan Williams *Benedicite*. LSO - conducted by

Charles Proctor.

Also in October - concert at Harrow School in aid of the British and Foreign Bible Society.

November - RAH - Henry Wood Concert Society - *Messiah* - conducted by Sir Malcolm Sargent.

December - Hammersmith Town Hall. Carol Concert at the request of Hammersmith Town Council - conducted by Charles Proctor.

Also in December - RAH - Carol Concert - conducted by Charles Proctor. Soloist: Robert Easton.

1958 April - Central Hall, Westminster. Gounod *Faust* - conducted by Charles Proctor.

October - RAH - Julius Harrison *Mass in C* and Dvořák *Te Deum*. LSO - conducted by Charles Proctor.

June - RFH - Beethoven *Ninth Symphony*. LSO - conducted by Josef Krips.

November - RAH - Henry Wood Concert Society - *Messiah* - conducted by Sir Malcolm Sargent.

December - RAH - Carol Concert - conducted by Charles Proctor. Soloist: Robert Easton.

1959 March - Central Hall, Westminster. Mendelssohn *Elijah* - conducted by Charles Proctor.

April - RAH - Vellore Concert. Alexandra Choir and a section of the LPO, with Eileen Joyce. Conducted by Charles Proctor.

June - RFH - International Dairy Congress. Concert conducted by Walter Susskind.

June - RFH - Beethoven *Ninth Symphony*. LSO - conducted by Josef Krips.

September - RAH - Proms - Honegger *King David* - conducted by Sir Malcolm Sargent.

November - RAH - Dyson *Canterbury Pilgrims*. LSO - conducted by Charles Proctor.

Also in November - RAH - Henry Wood Concert Society - *Messiah* - conducted by Sir Malcolm Sargent.

December - RAH - Carol Concert - conducted by Charles Proctor. Soloist: Robert Easton.

1960 March - Central Hall, Westminster. Bach *St John Passion* - conducted by Charles Proctor.

June - RFH - Beethoven *Ninth Symphony*. LSO - conducted by Josef Krips.

November - Central Hall, Westminster. Coleridge-Taylor *Hiawatha* - conducted by Charles Proctor. Soloists: Elizabeth Harwood, William Herbert and John Cameron.

December - RAH - Carol Concert - conducted by Charles Proctor. Soloist: Robert Easton.

1961 April 26 - RAH - Twenty-First Birthday Concert of the Choir. Elgar *The Music Makers* and Walton *Belshazzar's Feast*. LSO - conducted by Charles Proctor. Soloists: Marjorie Thomas and Hervey Alan. Birthday greeting from Sir Arthur Bliss at the front of the programme.

July - RAH - Proms. Walton *Belshazzar's Feast* - conducted by Sir Malcolm Sargent.

November - RAH - Henry Wood Concert Society - *Messiah* - conducted by Sir Malcolm Sargent.

December - RAH - Carol Concert - conducted by Charles Proctor. Soloist: Hervey Alan.

1962 April - Central Hall, Westminster - Bach *St Matthew Passion*.

September - RAH - Proms - Beethoven *Ninth Symphony* - conducted by Sir Malcolm Sargent.

October - Central Hall, Westminster. Vaughan Williams *A Sea Symphony* and Fauré *Requiem* - conducted by Charles Proctor. Soloists: Jennifer Vyvyan and John Carol Case.

December - RAH - Carol Concert - conducted by Charles Proctor. Soloist: Owen Brannigan.

1963 March - Central Hall, Westminster. Honegger *King David* and Kodály *Missa Brevis*.

September - RAH - Proms - Berlioz *Te Deum*, Mozart *Solemn Vespers* and *C Minor Mass* - conducted by Sir Malcolm Sargent.

October - Central Hall, Westminster. *Messiah* - conducted by Charles Proctor.

November - RAH - Henry Wood Concert Society - *Messiah* - conducted by Sir Malcolm Sargent.

December - RAH - Carol Concert - conducted by Charles Proctor. Soloist: Owen Brannigan.

1964 March - Central Hall, Westminster. Bach *B Minor Mass* - conducted by Charles Proctor. Soloists: Eileen Poulter, Barbara Robotham, Robert Tear and John Dethick.

August - RAH - Proms - Vaughan Williams *Dona Nobis Pacem* and Holst *The Planets* - conducted by Sir Malcolm Sargent.

Also in August - RAH - Proms - Mahler *Symphony of a Thousand* - conducted by Charles Groves.

Also in August - RAH - Proms - Elgar *The Dream of Gerontius* conducted by Sir Malcolm Sargent.

October - Central Hall, Westminster. Coleridge-Taylor *Hiawatha* - conducted by Charles Proctor.

November - RAH - Henry Wood Concert Society - *Messiah* - conducted by Sir Malcolm Sargent.

December - RAH - Carol Concert - conducted by Charles Proctor. Soloist: Owen Brannigan.

During 1964, Geoffrey Morgan became organist to the Alexandra Choir.

1965 March - Central Hall, Westminster. Bach *St John Passion* conducted by Charles Proctor.

July - RAH - Proms - Elgar *The Dream of Gerontius* conducted by Sir Malcolm Sargent.

August - RAH - Proms - Brahms *A German Requiem* - conducted by Sir Malcolm Sargent.

October - Central Hall, Westminster - Mendelssohn *Elijah* - conducted by Charles Proctor.

November - RAH - Henry Wood Concert Society - *Messiah* - conducted by Sir Malcolm Sargent.

December - RAH - Carol Concert - conducted by Charles Proctor. Soloist: Owen Brannigan.

1966 March - Central Hall, Westminster - Vaughan Williams *Dona Nobis Pacem* and Brahms *A German Requiem* - conducted by Charles Proctor. Soloists Elizabeth Simon and John Heddle Nash.

April - *Messiah*

Also in April - RAH - Burma Star Association Reunion Celebration - in collaboration with Ralph Reader.

June - Guildford Cathedral - Beethoven *Ninth Symphony*. Surrey Philharmonic Orchestra - conducted by Kathleen Riddick.

July - RAH - Proms - Elgar *The Dream of Gerontius* - conducted by Sir Malcolm Sargent.

August - RAH - Proms - Walton *Belshazzar's Feast* - conducted by Sir Malcolm Sargent.

October - Scala Theatre - performance for the World Day for Animals.

November - Central Hall, Westminster - Verdi *Nabucco* - concert performance - conducted by Charles Proctor.

December - RAH - Henry Wood Concert Society - *Messiah* - conducted by Charles Proctor as Sir Malcolm Sargent was unwell.

Also in December - RAH - Carol Concert - conducted by Charles Proctor. Soloists: John Carol Case and Maria Korchinska.

1967 April - Walthamstow Town Hall - Berlioz *The Damnation of Faust*. Forest Philharmonic Orchestra and Orpington Junior Singers - conducted by Frank Shipway. Soloists: John Shaw, Anna Reynolds and Charles Craig.

May - Duke's Hall, RAM

June - RAH - Burma Star Association Reunion

Celebration in collaboration with Ralph Reader.

July - RAH - Proms - Elgar *The Dream of Gerontius* - conducted by Sir Adrian Boult.

August - RAH - Proms - Walton *Belshazzar's Feast* - conducted by John Pritchard

Also in August - RAH - Proms - Berlioz *Grande Messe des Morts* - conducted by George Hurst.

November - Central Hall, Westminster - Mozart *C Minor Mass* - conducted by Charles Proctor.

Also in November - RFH - Festival of Music and Drama - for the Scout Association. Conducted by Charles Proctor.

December - RAH - Carol Concert - conducted by Charles Proctor. Soloists: John Carol Case and Geoffrey Morgan.

1968 March - Duke's Hall, RAM - Britten *Rejoice in the Lamb* and Rossini *Petite Messe Solennelle* - conducted by Charles Proctor.

June - Bury St Edmund's Cathedral. Organist Harrison Oxley - conducted by Charles Proctor.

August - RAH - Proms - Bliss *Morning Heroes* - conducted by Sir Arthur Bliss.

October - Duke's Hall, RAM - Britten *St Nicholas* - conducted by Charles Proctor.

December - Second Festival of Music and Drama - Scout Association.

Also in December - RAH - Carol Concert - conducted by Charles Proctor. Soloists: Owen Brannigan and Geoffrey Morgan.

1969 March - QEH - Honegger *King David* - conducted by Charles Proctor.

Also in March - Church of the Holy Sepulchre, London - participation in the Henry Wood Centenary Thanksgiving Service.

June - Odeon, Golders Green - Pageant *Pilgrims Progress*

for one week. Music selected, arranged and directed by Charles Proctor. Produced by Ralph Reader.

June - Kensington Festival - Fauré *Requiem*.

August - RAH - Proms - Walton *Belshazzar's Feast* - conducted by Sir Charles Groves.

October - Duke's Hall, RAM - Brahms *Liebeslieder Walzer* and Arnold *John Clare Cantata* - conducted by Charles Proctor. Soloists: Martyn Dyke and Henry Macey.

December - RAH - Carol Concert - conducted by Charles Proctor. Soloists: Owen Brannigan and Geoffrey Morgan.

1970 February - St Jude's, Courtfield Gardens, London - Bruckner *Requiem in D minor* - conducted by Hans-Hubert Schonzeler. First performance in Great Britain.

March - QEH - *Messiah* - conducted by Charles Proctor. Soloists: Janet Price, Patricia Payne, John Duxbury and John Dethick.

May - RAH - Burma Star Association Reunion Celebration in collaboration with Ralph Reader.

June - Guildford Cathedral - Beethoven *Ninth Symphony*. Surrey Philharmonic Orchestra.

October - Beethoven *Ninth Symphony*. East Surrey Symphony Orchestra

Also in October - Duke's Hall, RAM. Beethoven Bicentenary Concert. *Mass in C, Choral Fantasia* and Proctor arrangement of the Slow Movement of the *String Quartet op 135* - conducted by Charles Proctor. Soloists: Barbara Yates, Sylvia Swan, John Steel, Colin Wheatley and Malcolm Sykes

November - Central Hall, Westminster - Westminster Festival of Music - with Kneller Hall Band and Trumpeters.

Recording of the Bruckner *Requiem in D Minor* for Unicorn Records. LPO conducted by Hans-Hubert Schonzeler.

December - RAH - Carol Concert - conducted by Charles Proctor. Soloists: Owen Brannigan and Geoffrey Morgan.

1971 March - QEH - Handel Concert. *Passion of Christ, Organ Concerto in B flat* and *7th Chandos Anthem* - conducted by Charles Proctor. Soloists: Helen Greener, Wynford Evans, Alastair Thompson, Peter Lehmann Bedford and Geoffrey Morgan.

May - Alexandra Palace - participation in *Messiah* performance with the NPO conducted by Yehudi Menuhin.

June - RFH - Petro Petridis *St Paul*. RPO - conducted by the composer. First English performance.

October - QEH - Bruckner *Requiem in D minor* and Bach *Cantata no 206* - conducted by Charles Proctor.

December - RAH - Carol Concert - conducted by Charles Proctor. Soloists: Owen Brannigan and Geoffrey Morgan.

1972 March - RAH - Entente Cordiale. RPO Silver Jubilee Season. In the presence of the Prime Minister and the French Ambassador. Conductors - Charles Groves and Claude Monteux.

May - Southwark Cathedral - Mendelssohn *Elijah* - conducted by Charles Proctor.

October - Fairfield Hall, Croydon - Coleridge-Taylor *Hiawatha* - conducted by Charles Proctor. Soloists: Marion Studholme, Wynford Evans and Robert Bateman. TC Fairbairn and Stiles Allen were in the audience.

November - Central Hall, Westminster - Westminster Festival of Music - with Kneller Hall Band and Trumpeters.

December - RAH - Carol Concert - conducted by Charles Proctor. Soloists: Ian Wallace and Geoffrey Morgan.

1973 January - RAH - participation with the Wembley Philharmonic Choir and others in *Messiah* - conducted by Rae Jenkins. Concert in aid of the Sir Malcolm Sargent Cancer Fund for Children.

March - QEH - Rossini *Petite Messe Solennelle* and items by Britten - conducted by Charles Proctor. Soloists: Valerie Hill, Sybil Michelow, Paul Taylor, Ian Caddy, Graham Johnson, Richard Markham, Geoffrey Morgan.

April - Southwark Cathedral - Bach *St John Passion* - the first performance of what was to become an annual event. Conducted by Charles Proctor. Soloists: Susan Campbell, Helen Attfield, Neil Jenkins, Brian Rayner Cook, Christopher Weaver, Geoffrey Morgan.

June - Bury St Edmund's Cathedral - Proctor *Missa Brevis* and Fauré *Requiem* - conducted by Charles Proctor.

October - RCM - Brahms *A German Requiem* and Parry *Blest Pair of Sirens* - conducted by Charles Proctor. Soloists: Sally Le Sage, Peter Knapp.

December - Wembley Town Hall - Beethoven *Ninth Symphony*. Brent Symphony Orchestra - conducted by Harry Legge.

Also in December - RAH - Carol Concert - conducted by Charles Proctor. Soloists: Ian Wallace and Geoffrey Morgan.

1974 January - participation with the Wembley Philharmonic Choir and others in *Messiah* - conducted by Rae Jenkins. Concert in aid of the Sir Malcolm Sargent Cancer Fund for Children.

March - Southwark Cathedral - Annual Bach Passion performance - *St John Passion* - conducted by Charles Proctor. Soloists: Sandra Wilkes, Janet Edmunds, Neil Mackie, Brian Rayner Cook.

Also in March - RAH - Verdi *Requiem*. Participation with other choirs in a concert promoted by the Ernest Read Music Association - conducted by Terence

Lovett.

April - QEH - Vivaldi *Gloria* and Haydn *Nelson Mass* - conducted by Charles Proctor. Soloists: Anne Hodges, Margaret Duckworth, John Kingsley-Smith, Antony Ransome.

October - Grosvenor Square, London. Participation in broadcast of Charles Ives Centenary Celebrations with the Band of the Life Guards - outside the American Embassy. Conductors: Charles Proctor and Captain A Richards of the Life Guards.

November - St John's, Smith Square, London - Palestrina *Missa Brevis* and Honegger *King David* - conducted by Charles Proctor. Soloists: Sandra Wilkes, Rosemary Greenhalgh, Charles Corp, John Mackey, Helen Hurden.

Also in November - Central Hall, Westminster - Westminster Festival of Music - with Kneller Hall Band and Trumpeters - conducted by Lieutenant-Colonel T le M Sharpe.

December - Wembley Town Hall - Brahms *A German Requiem*. Brent Symphony Orchestra - conducted by Harry Legge.

Also in December - RAH - Carol Concert - conducted by Charles Proctor. Soloists: David Dunn (harp), Bernard Brown and Howard Hawkes (trumpets) and Geoffrey Morgan.

1975 January - RAH - participation with the Wembley Philharmonic Choir and others in *Messiah* - conducted by Rae Jenkins. Concert in aid of the Sir Malcolm Sargent Cancer Fund for Children.

March - Southwark Cathedral - Annual Bach Passion performance - *St John Passion* - conducted by Charles Proctor.

May - QEH - Dvořák *Mass in D* and Bruckner *Requiem in D minor* - conducted by Charles Proctor. Soloists:

Barbara Yates, Sylvia Swan, John Steel and Colin Wheatley.

July - Ely Cathedral - Kodály *Missa Brevis*, Finzi *Magnificat* and Proctor *Te Deum* - conducted by Charles Proctor. Concert given for the Friends of Ely Cathedral.

Also in July, this concert was repeated in the Church of the Holy Sepulchre in London.

October - St John's, Smith Square, London - Beethoven *Mass in C* - conducted by Charles Proctor. Soloists: Mary Clarkson, Pamela Reed, Keith Lewis and Arnold Dvorkin.

December - RAH - Carol Concert - conducted by Charles Proctor. Soloists: Bernard Brown and Howard Hawkes (trumpets) and Geoffrey Morgan.

1976 January - RAH - participation with the Wembley Philharmonic Choir and others in *Messiah* - conducted by Rae Jenkins. Concert in aid of the Sir Malcolm Sargent Cancer Fund for Children.

April - Southwark Cathedral - Annual Bach Passion performance - *St John Passion* - conducted by Charles Proctor.

May - QEH - *Messiah* - conducted by Charles Proctor. Soloists: Sandra Wilkes, Rosemary Greenhalgh, Neil Jenkins, Antony Ransome.

July - Arundel Cathedral, Sussex. Concert conducted by Charles Proctor. Robert Hill (organ).

December - St John's Church, West Meon, Hampshire - Programme of Christmas Music - conducted by Robert Hill as Charles Proctor was indisposed.

December - RAH - Carol Concert - conducted by Charles Proctor. Soloists: David Cutler and Tony Waller (trumpets), Roger Ward (harpsichord) and Geoffrey Morgan.

1977 March - Southwark Cathedral - Annual Bach Passion performance - *St Matthew Passion* - conducted by

Charles Proctor.

May - QEH - Mozart *Requiem* and Vivaldi *Gloria* - conducted by Charles Proctor. Soloists: Hilary Thomas, Eirian James, Gareth Roberts, Mateo di Monti.

October - St John's, Smith Square - Mendelssohn *Elijah* - conducted by Charles Proctor. Soloists: Elizabeth Tippett, Iona Jones, Jeffrey Cresswell, Brian Kemp.

December - RAH - Carol Concert - conducted by Charles Proctor. Soloist: Geoffrey Morgan.

1978 March - Southwark Cathedral - Annual Bach Passion performance - *St Matthew Passion* - conducted by Robert Hill as Charles Proctor was indisposed. Soloists: Sandra Wilkes, Elisabeth Holden, John Kingsley-Smith, Michael Lewis.

May - Lambeth Methodist Mission, London - Concert of miscellaneous choral items including Brahms *Liebeslieder Waltzer*.

June - Queen Elizabeth Hall - Haydn *The Creation* - conducted by Charles Proctor

Also in June - Guildford Cathedral - Programme included Dvořák *Mass in D* and Proctor *Te Deum* - conducted by Charles Proctor.

November - St John's, Smith Square, London - Proctor *Missa Brevis*, Janáček *Suite for Strings* and Cherubini *Requiem in C minor* - conducted by Charles Proctor.

December - RAH - Final Carol Concert - conducted by Charles Proctor. Soloists: Molly Townson (mezzo-soprano), Mary Densem (piano) and Geoffrey Morgan.

(This list is not exhaustive.)

APPENDIX B
LIST OF WORKS BY CHARLES PROCTOR

(See also the list of works held in Trinity College of Music Library)

Choral

There is Sweet Music - Choric Song	Lengnick	1945
Missa Brevis in E. (BCP Text)	Lengnick	1950
Te Deum Laudamus (Composed for the Woodhouse School Commemoration Service)	Lengnick	1951
A Song of Praise (Composed for the Orange Hill Girls' Grammar School)	MS	1959
The Winchelsea Communion Service Series III	Lengnick	1977
Rye Parish Communion - Series II	MS	1977?
Missa Sancti Francisci (Latin Text)	MS	
Holy Communion Service ASB (Rite A)	MS	
A New Parish Mass	Oecumuse	1977
Anthem: *The Souls of the Righteous:* In Memoriam	Oecumuse	
Anthem: *O Holy Spirit:* Wedding Anthem	Oecumuse	1977
Anthem: *A Prayer of St Augustine*	Oecumuse	
A New Parish Mass	Oecumuse	1977
Five Amens	Oecumuse	1977
Magnificat and Nunc Dimittis	Oecumuse	1978
Carol: *Gabriel's Message*	Oecumuse	1978
Benedicite (Shortened form)	Oecumuse	1978
Missa in Nomine Jesu Christe	MS	1980

Anthem: *Go on your way*	Oecumuse	1980
Anthem: *My Precious Lord* (The Fugitive)	Oecumuse	1980
Anthem of Dedication	Oecumuse	1980
Carol: *Sweet Mary*	Oecumuse	1981
The Angelus	Oecumuse	1981
Anthem: *Prayer of St Francis*	Oecumuse	1983
Anthem: *Prayer of Alcuin*	Oecumuse	1984
Six 17th Century Chants (arr. Proctor) from Gibbons and Lawes	Oecumuse	
'Twas God the word that spake it	MS	1988
Motet: *Diligam te, Domine* - Psalm 18	MS	1991
Love Incarnate	MS	1991
Shop Early!	MS	1991
Mon Petit Jesu	MS	1992
Pax Vobiscum	Oecumuse	1993
Music	MS	1993
Hymne to God	MS	1996
The Young Prince	MS	1996

Chorus, Orchestra and Soloists

Cantata *A Song of England*	MS	1933
Motet *Trumpet of God*	MS	
Choral Symphony (Words by Walt Whitman)	MS	

Instrumental

Sonata in A minor for Violin and Piano	Lengnick	1945
Sonata in E minor for 'Cello and Piano	Lengnick	
Sonatina No 1 in A minor for Piano	Lengnick	1945
Alla Gavotta in B minor for Piano	Lengnick	1946
Five by Ten: Ten Pieces for Piano	Lengnick	1952

Humoresque for Clarinet and Piano (Jack Brymer Clarinet Series)	Weinberger	
Sonatina No 2 in A for Piano	MS	1982
Winter Gavotte and Carol for Recorder and Regal	MS	
Triptych for Oboe/Clarinet, 'Cello and Piano	Typeset	1985
Epicedion for 'Cello and Piano	Typeset	1998

Orchestra

Piano Concerto in F minor	Lengnick	
Elegia (from Organ Sonata No 1) for Full Orchestra and extra Brass	Lengnick	
Alla Gavotta for Full Orchestra	Lengnick	
Four Various Songs for High Voice and Strings	Lengnick	
Three Children's Songs for High Voice and Strings	Lengnick	
Motet for Chorus and Orchestra *Veni Creator Spiritus* (Composed for the Peterborough Festival Arts Week)	Lengnick	1949
Gabriel's Message for High Voice and Strings and Harpsichord	MS	
St Joseph's Carol for Choir and Orchestra (Strings, percussion and organ)	MS	
Canzona for Organ and Strings	MS	

Organ

Organ Sonata No 1 in D Minor	Lengnick
Organ Sonata No 2 in F sharp Minor	Lengnick
Organ Sonata No 3 in C	Lengnick

Canzona, Chorale and Passacaglia	Lengnick	
Three Intradas:	Lengnick	
The Litany of St Thomas at Winchelsea		
Plainsong Prelude of St George at Brede. *Adoro te*		
Carillon Prelude *Corde natus exparentis*		
Trumpet Prelude (A)	MS	
Chorale Prelude *Es ist Ein*		
Ros' Entsprungen	Oecumuse	
A Christmas Piece for		
St Mary's Church, Rye	MS	
A Wedding March	MS	
Chaconne	MS	1974
Chaconne	Weinberger	1975
Rouen Carillon	Oecumuse	1978
Two Rouen Interludes	Oecumuse	1978
The Lord Warden's Rondo: Celebrating		
the Visit of HM The Queen Mother,		
Lord Warden of the Cinque Ports,		
to Rye in 1980	Oecumuse	1981
Chaconne Solennelle	MS	1981
Célébration	Oecumuse	1982
Eight Interludes on Rouen Melodies	Oecumuse	1983
A Dedication Peal		
In Memoriam Canon John		
Williams, Vicar of Rye 1965 - 1981	Oecumuse	1983
Duo Concertante for 'Cello and Organ	Typeset	1985
Duo Concertante No 1 for		
Piano and Organ	MS	
Passacaglia on a given theme	Oecumuse	1987
Resurgam	Oecumuse	1988
Commemoration Passacaglia	Oecumuse	1988
(To mark the Church and Town Celebrations		
for the 700th year of the Foundation of Winchelsea)		
Ten Occasional Pieces		
(including *Marche Joyeuse*)	Oecumuse	1991

Jubilation	MS	1991
Seven Chorale Preludes	Oecumuse	1992
Partita on *The Seven Good Joys of Mary*	MS	1992
Duo Concertante No 2		
for Piano and Organ	Oecumuse	1994
Chorale Prelude *Gelobt sei Gott*	MS	1994
Postlude on *Gelobt sei Gott*	MS	1994
Winchelsea Carillon	MS	1994
Prelude and Postlude on		
Aberdeen (Anniversary of		
HM Queen's Accession)	MS	1985
Prelude on *Heiliger Geist*	MS	1995
Prelude on *Ave Maris Stella*		
for the Feast of the Annunciation	MS	1995
Postlude for the Feast of the		
Annunciation	MS	1995
Chorale Prelude on *Solemnis Haec*		
Festivitas - Angers Church Melody	MS	1995
Postlude on Easter Hymn	MS	1995
Chorale Postlude on *Lyra Davidica* Melody	MS	1995
Postlude on *Llanfair*	MS	1995
Prelude on *Veni Creator*	MS	1995
Postlude *Adeste Sancta Trinitas*	MS	1995
Postlude on *Wachet Auf*	MS	1995
Postlude on *Lucis Creator*	MS	1996
Prelude and Postlude on *Tantum Ergo*	MS	1995
Prelude on *Albano*	MS	1996
Postlude on *Plaistow*	MS	1996
Prelude on *Tunbridge*	MS	1996
Ceremonial Postlude	MS	1996

Vocal

Three Children's Songs:
  The Children's Carol
  Little Lamb
  Come, Live with me
	Lengnick	1945

Four Various Songs
  King David
  Vocalise
  Litany
  The Earth's Holiday
	Lengnick	1945

Five Mystic Songs
  Christ, my Beloved
  Our Lady's Lullaby
  Love bade me welcome
  That he whom the Sun serves
  Lord, Thou art mine and I am Thine
	Lengnick	1948

Quatre Vocalises *(Le printemps, L'été, L'automne, L'hiver)*	Oecumuse	1978
All Lovely Things	MS	1989
He Rode Like any King	Oecumuse	
Orpheus with his Lute	Oecumuse	

Arrangements

Bach - Thirty-six Fugues from the '48' for Piano Duet	Lengnick	

Bach - Chaconne from
  Violin Sonata No 4 for Full Orchestra
  (On hire)
	British & Continental	

Couperin - *Chaconne* for Organ	Lengnick	
Purcell - *Trumpet Gavotte and March* for Organ	Oecumuse	
Handel - *Suite in B flat*	Oecumuse	1993

Handel - *The Musick for the Royal Fireworks*
for Organ   Oecumuse   1985
Mozart - Wedding March from
The Marriage of Figaro for Organ   Oecumuse   1984
Purcell - *Dido's Lament* for Organ   Oecumuse   1985
Beethoven - *Three Equali* for Trombones
arranged for Organ   Oecumuse   1986
MacDowell - *AD 1620 (Sea Pictures No 3)*
for Organ   Oecumuse   1987
MacDowell - *Starlight (Sea Pictures No 1)*
for Organ   Oecumuse   1988
In modo d'una Marcia
(Transcription of the Slow Movement
of the Schumann *Piano Quintet* op.44.)   Oecumuse   1991
National Anthem   MS
Christmas Pudding Song   MS

Author

Music - in the *Reason Why* Series   Jenkins   1950
To be a Professional Musician   Methuen   1951
Harmonization at the Keyboard   Jenkins   1961
The Class Music Teacher   Jenkins   1965

Editor

Everybody's Carols   Lengnick
The Herbert Jenkins Series on Musical Subjects including:
   The Elements of Orchestration by Dr Gordon Jacob
   A First Harmony Book by Dr Reginald Hunt
   Music and the European Mind by Dr Wilfred Dunwell
   Music at your fingertips by Ruth Slenczynska
   The Organ by Herbert Norman
   The Recorder and its Music by Edgar Hunt

Jane Spurr

Film Music

The Prince of Peace	Gaumont-British
Portrait of Palestine	Anglo-Scottish

All enquiries regarding Charles Proctor's works published by Oecumuse should be directed to: The Author, c/o UPSO Ltd, 5 Stirling Road, Castleham Business Park. TN38 9NW

WORKS OF CHARLES PROCTOR IN TRINITY COLLEGE OF MUSIC LIBRARY

(Some works appear in the previous list but for the sake of completeness, the whole collection in the Trinity College of Music Library is listed complete.)

Choral

Agnus Dei
Benedicite
Benedicite - shortened form
Breathe on me, breath of God
Christmas Pudding Song
Corpus Christi Introit
Diligam te Domine
Five chants
Gabriel's Message
Holy Communion Service (Rite A)
Love Incarnate
Magnificat and Nunc Dimittis
Missa Brevis
Missa di Pappa
Missa in Nomine Jesu
Missa Sancti Francisci
Pax Vobiscum
Prayer of Alcuin
Prayer of St Augustine
Rejoice, O land
Responses (Eucharist)
Rye Parish Communion
Saints of Sussex

Shop early - carol
St Joseph's Carol
Sweet Mary - carol
The Fugitive (My precious Lord)
The Lord is my Shepherd
The Lord's Prayer
The Winchelsea Mass - Series III
The Winchester grace
Three chants (after Gibbons)
Tuba Dei

Chorus, Orchestra and Soloists

Choral Symphony

Instrumental

Cadenza for Mozart Concerto in C, K467	Piano
Canzona and Choral	Strings and organ
Chaconne, Sicilienne and Rigourdon	Recorder and piano or harpsichord
Duo concertante	'Cello and piano
Duo concertante	'Cello and organ
Duo concertante No.2.	Piano and organ
Epicedion	'Cello and piano or organ
Epicedion	B flat clarinet and piano
Epicedion	Solo 'cello
Humoresque	Clarinet in A
March Hares (Giddy Spring Waltz)	Recorder and organ
My Ladye Millais' Note Booke	Keyboard
Opusculum	Piano
Sonata da camera	Two pianos
Sonatina	Piano

Suite for 2 pianos, 12 hands	Two pianos
Triptych	Oboe/B flat clarinet, 'cello and piano
Winter Gavotte and Carol	Recorder and regal

Orchestra

Elegia

Organ

Célébration
Chaconne
Chaconne solennelle
Choral Partita on *O filii et filae*
Choral Partita on *Solothurn*
Choral Prelude on *Conditor alme siderum*
Choral Prelude on *O Haupt voll Blut und Wunden*
Choral Prelude on *O quanta qualia*
Choral Prelude on *Pange Lingua*
Choral Prelude on *Solothurn*
Choral Prelude on *Solothurn* (revised version)
Choral Prelude on the Office Hymn for Advent
Choral Prelude on *Verbum supernum prodiens*
Coelites plaudant
Commemoration Passacaglia
Corona
Dedication Peal
Fêtes de jour (Ten occasional pieces)
Intrada: Threnody
Introitus: Winchelsea 1288-1988 AD
Jubilation (revised version)
Lord Warden's Rondo (organ or piano)
Marche Joyeuse
Missa organum

Partita
Partita on *The Seven Joys of Mary*
Passacaglia on a given theme
Passacaglia: Winchelsea 700
Piece for a ceremonial occasion
Postlude for the Feast of the Annunciation
Postlude on *Es ist ein Ros' entsprungen*
Prelude for the Feast of the Annunciation
Resurgam: 82 interpretations on a ground bass
Rouen carillon
Seven choral preludes
Short voluntary
Sinfonia
Trumpet Prelude
Veni Creator Spiritus
Wedding march

Vocal

Untitled "Afoot and light hearted..."
Vocalise

Arrangements

Bach - 15 studies for left hand alone (incomplete)	Organ
Bach - *Wachet Auf*	SATB, strings and organ
Beethoven - Three Equali	Organ
Handel - Suite in B flat	Organ
Handel - Musick for the Royal Fireworks	Organ
MacDowell - AD MDCXX	Organ
Mozart - Wedding March from *The Marriage of Figaro*	Organ
Purcell - Dido's Lament	Organ

A Song of Farewell

Purcell - Trumpet gavotte   Organ
Silent Night   Strings
Zion's Children   Military Band